EXPLORATIONS IN CATHOLIC THEOLOGY

PAPERS FROM
THE CATHOLIC THEOLOGICAL ASSOCIATION

with a Foreword by Cardinal Basil Hume

Edited by

Geoffrey Turner & John Sullivan

LINDISFARNE
BOOKS

First published 1999 by
Lindisfarne Books
7/8 Lower Abbey Street
Dublin 1

Available in the UK from:
Veritas Company (UK) Ltd
Lower Avenue
Leamington Spa
Warwickshire CV31 3NP

Lindisfarne is an imprint of Veritas Publications

ISBN 1 85390 498 8

British Library Cataloguing
in Publication Data.
A catalogue record for
this book is available
from the British Library.

Cover design by Bill Bolger
Cover illustration is a detail from the Lindisfarne Gospels.
Reproduced by kind permission of the British Library.
Printed in the Republic of Ireland by *The Leinster Leader*,
Naas, Co. Kildare.

CONTENTS

FOREWORD

I warmly welcome the publication of this selection of papers from the Conferences of the Catholic Theological Association of Great Britain. It shows the vitality of Catholic theological reflection in this country and the growing contribution which Catholic theologians are making to the field of higher education and to the life of the Church in Britain.

The ancient phrase *lex orandi lex credendi* (the rule of prayer is the rule of belief) points to the experience of prayer as the chief source of our understanding of God. We need, as von Balthasar said, 'kneeling theologians' whose life of faith flows into what they teach and write. The words used by theologians must be close to God's Word, Jesus Christ our Lord. In that way, theology can be a service to the Church by enabling it to recognise and grasp the divine mystery at the heart of its life.

If theology really springs from the experience of faith and prayer, then it will contribute to the Church's mission of enabling the Gospel to become a living voice in British culture and life. I commend this volume of essays to Christians of all churches and to all those who are interested in how Catholic theologians in this country are contributing to our common Christian life, faith and understanding.

CARDINAL BASIL HUME OSB

PREFACE

We are the Catholic Theological Association of Great Britain. These three terms qualify one another. I for one would not be much interested in an association of people who studied theology with a membership arbitrarily or for convenience limited to Roman Catholics resident in Great Britain. If this were the intention, it would have been pointless to found our Association, as there already existed other societies in Britain for the study of theology, which Catholics are free to join. Our Association only has its justification if we understand it as a society of those interested in *theology* pursued within the *Catholic* tradition in accordance with the culture and needs of *Britain*. Let me give my personal understanding of each of these factors separately.

First, our pursuit is *theology*. By this I mean that our concern should not stop at the precise exegesis of texts or the accurate tracing of the development of events or ideas. What we are interested in is the revealed truth about God and his relationship with mankind. Unless scripture scholars go beyond literary criticism to consider the truth contained in the sacred books they are studying, unless church historians go on to consider the working of the Holy Spirit underneath the vagaries of human behaviour, they may be producing valuable scholarly work, they may be providing the material for theology, but they are not engaged in theology itself.

Unlike pure exegesis or pure history, theology requires commitment. The non-believer can point out logical flaws, gaps and unproved assumptions in a theological exposition, but he has no competence to pronounce on its truth, any more than a congenitally blind man is competent to pronounce on the harmony of a colour scheme. Indeed, one of my colleagues at Campion Hall recently reminded me that there is a strong patristic tradition that only a good person can be a theologian;

virtue and asceticism are required for the contemplation of divine truth. If so, orthopraxis is not only the expression of orthodoxy, but is the precondition for any degree of orthodoxy beyond that of a parrot mimicking without understanding the sounds which others have made.

Secondly, the theology with which our Association is concerned should be distinctively *Catholic*, in the sense that, while learning from the insights of Anglican, Orthodox and Protestant writing, it should be an authentic expression of the Catholic tradition. We should be no less dedicated to 'thinking within the Church' than Saint Ignatius Loyola when he was writing the *Spiritual Exercises*. I do not mean by this that our theology should take the scholastic form of the blind acceptance and interpretation of 'the documents of the magisterium' in what is sometimes disparagingly referred to as 'Denzinger theology'. What I mean is that to feel free to theologise outside any church tradition or to indulge in an individual eclecticism is necessarily to produce bad theology. As Newman and Barth taught us, our religion is a revealed religion and our dogmatics must be church dogmatics. The best theologians of this century – such as Barth, de Lubac, Congar, Rahner, von Balthasar – have each written from the hearts of their traditions. The Catholic theologian ought to love his Church, even when he feels obliged to criticise it.

Thirdly, our theology should be *British*. What should be the qualities of British theology in the last years of the second millennium?

A British theology means first of all a theology written in Britain, and not a translation from French or German or Dutch, or an original written in the USA. This is first of all a matter of *language*. If our theology is to serve a pastoral as well as an academic purpose, if it is to resonate to the best human values, if it is to make the truth attractive as well as clear, it must be written in elegant, unpretentious, jargon-free English. Style is not only the man – or the woman – it is also the theologian.

Style, like the medium, is part of the message. But it is not only a question of language. To correspond to the worthiest elements in a culture, theology must be allusive, finding its source, vocabulary and concepts not only in scripture, the magisterium and the classical church writers, but in secular literature and art. A British theology will be British especially in its inspiration, its allusions and its illustrations.

Again, our theology must be British in its *pastoral implications*; it must bear a relevance to the social situation of its British writers and readers, just as the Latin American liberation theologians insisted that theirs was a theology for Latin America, which would not apply without modification to the situation in other continents. Each region must produce its own social theology. A British theology will be a *British* theology of liberation, relevant to the search for freedom at every level of British society. It will bring good news to the poor, not only the economically poor – the unemployed, the pensioner, the sick waiting for an operation on an underfunded National Health Service – but also to the spiritually poor – the unhappily married or deserted spouse, the young who cannot commit themselves to marriage, the divorced or lapsed Catholic, the parents who cannot cope with their children, the drugs and AIDS sufferers, the alcoholic and the workaholic, the bored, the brutish. It will also bring the good news of liberation to the rich, the materialistic and the spiritually dead rich of the consumer boom.

The theology that I am recommending will be British in *method*. One can, in a rough way, though with some danger of caricature, point to national methods of theology. One recognises a German method which is abstract and philosophical, and delights in the formulation of problems. There is a French method which allows beautiful, abstract, general theories to grow by induction from a sampling of historical sources. What should be the British method?

The first characteristic of British theological method, I suggest, is that it will have an empirical bent; it will be anxious to bring abstractions down to earth, to show how theological principles will impinge on experience, to apply theory to practice. In what one of our members has called 'theology after Wittgenstein', it will not only ask, 'What does this statement mean?'; it will also ask the question, 'What is this theological statement *doing*?' For example, if an explanation of the Trinity is not saying something about life, it may be *doing* something else very dangerous, namely giving the impression that the doctrine is not relevant to living – which is what, I take it, we find fault with when we criticise a form of theology as 'scholastic', or what a Labour politician meant when, believing that clause 4 of the party constitution was out of touch with contemporary needs, he described it as 'theology'.

The second characteristic of British theological method, I believe, is that it is historical, sharing the French method of allowing theology to emerge from the writings of the past (or perhaps of the present). It will, of course, set itself rigorous standards of historical accuracy and contextualisation, resisting the temptation of eclectic serendipity, which would use historical sources primarily as a quarry for apt quotations.

The obvious example of the kind of British theology I have been describing is John Henry Newman, whose style is a model of elegance, whose philosophy is empirical rather than abstract, and whose method was to allow the truth to grow out of the close study of history.

EDWARD YARNOLD

ACKNOWLEDGEMENTS

The chapters by Timothy Radcliffe, Janet Martin Soskice, Nicholas Lash, Peter Phillips, Eamon Duffy and Bruce Harbert have already appeared in *New Blackfriars*.

The chapters by Herbert McCabe, Geoffrey Turner, John McDade, Sarah Jane Boss, Gavin D'Costa, Michael Barnes and Jack Mahoney have already appeared in *The Month*.

We are grateful to the editors for permission to reprint them.

INTRODUCTION

The Catholic Theological Association of Great Britain was founded in 1984 as a forum for Catholic theologians in the ecclesiastical provinces of England and Scotland. Since 1985 we have met every year in conference at Trinity and All Saints College in Leeds, appropriately situated midway between Edinburgh and London. These conferences have all been concerned with topics of perennial and also contemporary relevance. We began in 1985 with 'The Christian Understanding of God' and continued through themes such as Christology, Power, Sacrament and Knowing the Other down to 'The Responsibilities of Theology', our most recent topic and one of some concern to theologians in the Roman Catholic Church as we move into the third millennium of Christian history.

The emergence of the Association in the 1980s along with a vastly increased participation of Catholics in the work of theology departments in British universities, was a state of affairs which would have gratified John Coulson, the editor of the symposium *Theology and the University* (London: 1964) and a member of the Association until his death in 1993. Yet it is by the same token a phenomenon scarcely comprehensible to theologians in Rome and even in the rest of Europe where, though theologians abound, faculties are narrowly denominational. Since the Association was founded members have held chairs in the Universities of Birmingham, Bradford (Peace Studies), Bristol, Cambridge, Edinburgh, Leeds, London, St Andrews (Philosophy) and Southampton. Another sign of the times has been the ever-increasing number of women theologians belonging to the Association, two of whom have contributed papers to this collection.

The papers printed here were all read at conferences and, while papers are sometimes invited from those who are not members or not Catholics, all those selected for publication here are by members of the Association: Roman Catholics; lay men and women, members of religious orders or diocesan clergy teaching in seminaries. The papers all in various ways reveal traces of their origins: some are presented as they were read at the conference without footnotes, others are lightly or heavily footnoted for publication. However, no attempt has been made to update them, except for the excision of a very small number of specific time references.

The anthology opens with a preface by EDWARD YARNOLD which combines ideas he expressed in two Presidential addresses in 1989 and 1990 on the need for us to develop a distinctively British and Catholic Theology. These ideas are still pertinent after ten years and appropriately introduce the longer papers which follow.

We begin with christology. TIMOTHY RADCLIFFE develops an exposition of the concept of priesthood in the Letter to the Hebrews, which is by no means the conventional exegesis that we get in commentaries on Hebrews. Here we find an attempt to reconcile the lay theology of the Gospels with the priestly language of Hebrews to see how the Letter might influence our own forms of church ministry. The author concludes that 'any form of ministry that looks to Hebrews for justification must be seen to speak a word that gathers people into God's sabbath rest, that brings in those who feel themselves to be unclean, impure, weak and suffering, overthrowing the distinction between lay and priest'.

After looking at the significance of Jesus for the politics of his own time, particularly in the light of the circumstances of his death, executed by the state authorities, HERBERT MCCABE considers how this might influence the self-understanding of the Church in its relation to the state in our time. He outlines four possible models for the Church in the world: as an *alternative* to political society, as a *model* for society, as *social cement* and, finally and more plausibly, as a *challenge* to society. Using Marx but looking beyond him to Aquinas, the author reflects on a theology of the eschaton in which the Church ('the sacrament of the divine life in humankind') will no longer exist; a time when there will be 'no longer a church but just human beings in and through whose human lives God will be manifested'.

Speaking from the experience of a death in his own family, NICHOLAS PETER HARVEY argues that any christology must have the death of Christ at its centre, 'the first properly human death'. He considers that Jesus approached his death as something to be desired, an attitude which left his disciples in disarray. It is by focusing on his death in obedience to God that we avoid a specious christology based on Jesus as moral teacher and exemplar, Jesus the prophet and social liberator or simply 'a blandly resurrected Jesus'.

Moving on to the figure of Mary, SARAH JANE BOSS wonders what has gone wrong with mariology. She reckons that all was well until the sixteenth century when a turning point was reached with Francisco Suarez, with mariology becoming a discipline in its own right divorced from christology and ecclesiology. Since then we have had maximalists who want to draw her close to the Godhead by emphasising the role of Mary in redemption, and minimalists who want to identify her as one of the Church of believers, herself redeemed by God. The more integrated vision advocated here rejects both these routes and draws the figure of Mary back into christology.

JOHN MCDADE responds to the emergence of a quasi-religion that he calls 'green faith' which expresses a serious concern for the environment, for the natural order and the achievement of authentic personhood; what Christian theology calls creation and salvation. He seeks to renew our understanding of God by rediscovering the Thomistic sense of God as an 'energy' through which the world has its being and its autonomy, and the interaction of God with creation that we find in Eastern Orthodox theology, particularly in Maximus the Confessor. He also considers the phenomenon of death: our

death as well as the death of Christ, a death which leads to the
renewal of creation.

   Beginning with an interest in the work of Emmanuel Levinas
on 'the Other', JANET MARTIN SOSKICE moves to a
consideration of women as 'other' and to the place of sexual and
procreative metaphors in the history of philosophy and recent
trinitarian theology. The author distinguishes the God of the
philosophers, which has been the subject of much secular
criticism, from the God of Christianity which is a Trinity of
persons. The gendered language of trinitarian theology does not
show what it is like to be a man or a woman, 'the doctrine tells
us nothing of sexual difference'. It does, however, 'let us glimpse
what it is, most truly, to be. 'To be' most fully is 'to-be-related'
in difference'.

   In pursuing the theme of the Other, GAVIN D'COSTA looks
at non-Christian religions and whether Christ might be
discovered there. In opposition to other critics, he outlines what
he calls 'an open form of eschatological trinitarian inclusivism'
which allows us to explore the question of God in other
religions without pre-defining the character of those religions or
what we mean by 'God'. He says that the purpose of his paper
is to argue for a theology of religions using a trinitarian logic of
relationship, freedom, love and service.

   MICHAEL BARNES' interest in inter-faith dialogue also leads
to a discussion of how we can remain faithful to our Christian
identity, how we can promote evangelisation and yet learn from
other religions in partnership.

   Continuing the theme of evangelisation and how people
might come to the gospel, GEOFFREY TURNER wonders why
there is such a gulf between the reading which takes place in
Bible study groups and the interpretations of the Bible
produced in academic tutorials. He attributes this to the
habitual use of critical-historical method in academic work
which in other groups is seen implicitly as a threat to faith. He
focuses on Lessing's 'ugly ditch' which has opened up between

history and faith and looks for a way of bridging the ditch through the concept of 'understanding'. Building a bridge of some sort is seen to be essential for moving between critical investigation and the faith we share in the Church.

NICHOLAS LASH brings us to the practice of theology itself in a ministry of the word in the Church, in which the theologian must be a philologist, one who cares for the word. His agenda in what was Mrs Thatcher's Britain is what might be 'the cultural and political responsibilities of a community which seriously supposed its identity to be that of a ministry of the word, and…the plight of preaching and adult catechesis in contemporary British Catholicism.' He describes the Church as an academy of word-care; we care for the word in the Church in order that we may correct how words are used in society and out of this comes a ministry to teach, even if it is inadequately fulfilled at the present time.

JACK MAHONEY offers an important exercise in ecclesiology. He looks at the idea of subsidiarity as it developed in the Church before it acquired a wider use in the politics of the European community. He outlines its ecumenical implications, particularly for conversations between the Catholic Church and the Church of England. Looking for a leading light to help him negotiate the ecumenical complexities of the time and particularly the relations between the English Catholic Church and the Church of England, he comes to the conclusion that subsidiarity will not do the job, being too much like a derogation from centralised imperial control. He invokes instead a more horizontal principle of non-absorption such as might serve as a model for a unified church with self-governing local churches who preserve their own traditions.

From ministry to sacraments. PETER PHILLIPS moves from a discussion of George Steiner's book *Real Presences* to the real presence in the eucharist. He explores the idea of sacrament and what we encounter in the sacrament of the eucharist through the idea of 'substance', i.e. what something really is. In the

sacraments God transforms substances and presents himself
through what God is not, rather as a poet speaks of realities that
are made present in the words.

EAMON DUFFY uses his research into the period immediately
before the Reformation to examine how lay people related to
the sacramental practice of the Church and how they extended
officially approved rituals with spontaneous practices of their
own. He wishes to challenge the view of Josef Jungmann and
others – a view that fed into the Vatican II document
Sacrosanctum Concilium – that medieval liturgical practice is a
story of decline from full participation of the faithful in the
early period to a 'subjective and uncomprehending pietism' in
the period before the Reformation. He claims to show evidence
of the creativity on the part of lay people in the development of
new local 'sacramental' rituals.

Before becoming a teacher of theology, BRUCE HARBERT
taught English in Oxford and he uses his linguistic skills here to
examine the adequacy of recent translations of liturgical
language. He finds there an often impoverished language which
has lost important perspectives of understanding. Through
particular examples he considers how we might regain subtleties
and nuances of meaning in modern English translations.

This a wide-ranging collection of papers, though the reader
will no doubt be aware of a recurring preoccupation with
themes such as the Trinity, Christ, the Church and the Other.
We commend them both to members of the Catholic
Theological Association and to the general reader, with a degree
of satisfaction in the past and continuing progress of an
Association unique in being, as Edward Yarnold points out, at
once British, Catholic and theological. It is also, we should add
with equal satisfaction, a convivial Association of friends who
worship and laugh together.

CHAPTER ONE

Christ in Hebrews: Cultic Irony

TIMOTHY RADCLIFFE

How can the Letter to the Hebrews apply priestly, cultic language to Christ while the gospels always present him as a layman? In them he is shown ignoring the rules of cultic purity, touching lepers and corpses, declaring all food clean and cleansing the Temple. The priests are primarily to blame for his death. I am not concerned here with what the historical Jesus actually thought about purity or the cult, but with a clash of theologies. Is Hebrews a retreat from the lay spirituality of the gospels? Having killed Jesus, do the clerics subvert his gospel? One can only answer that question by looking at the function of the cult in the Jewish tradition and at what Hebrews does with the language of liturgy. Why was the image of a celestial cult, shared with 'innumerable angels in festal gathering' (12:22) quite so attractive? Would not an eternal banquet be a more obviously appealing image of heavenly bliss than a never-ending service?

It is an intriguing fact that in the first century many Jewish and Christian groups could imagine nothing more exciting than sharing with the angels in the celestial liturgy. Perhaps the most remarkable parallel to the Letter to the Hebrews is 'The Songs of the Sabbath Sacrifice', the Sabbath Shirot, found at Qumran. According to Carol Newsom this cycle of thirteen songs, describing the angelic liturgy, was supposed to give the singers a mystical experience of being transported to heaven to worship with the angels. Having withdrawn from the defiled Jerusalem cult, this priestly community had to find a substitute, a legitimation for their identity as priests:

> The hypnotic quality of the language and the vividness of the description of the celestial temple cause even the modern reader of these fragments to feel the power of the language to create a sense of the presence of the heavenly temple. The carefully developed and sophisticated form of the cycle of the Shirot further reflects the intention to produce and guide a particular form of experience... To the extent that the worshipper experienced himself as present in the heavenly temple through the recitation of the Sabbath Shirot, his status as a faithful and legitimate priest would have been convincingly confirmed in spite of the persistent contradiction of his claims in the world.[1]

The Essenes were not the only people fascinated by ascent to the presence of God. Just before the Temple was destroyed in AD 70, Johanan ben Zakkai, the founder of rabbinic Judaism, had himself carried out of Jerusalem in a coffin so as to escape the siege. And he and his disciples sought to recapture Ezekiel's experiences after the destruction of the first Temple by meditating on the prophet's descriptions of the throne or chariot of God. This time one drew near to God and shared in the vision of the angels not by singing songs but by meditating on the Torah. When Rabbi Eleazar ben Arak expounded Ezekiel to Johanan ben Zakkai, 'Fire came down from heaven and encompassed all the trees that were in the field. All of them began a song. What was the song that they sang? Praise the Lord from the earth, dragons and deeps, fruitful trees and cedars, praise the Lord. And an angel answered from the fire "This

---

1. Carol Newsom, *Songs of the Sabbath Sacrifice: A Critical Edition*, Harvard Semitic Studies 27 (Atlanta: 1985), p. 72.

indeed is the story of the chariot"'.[2] And the Christians were
obviously fascinated by the search for an experience of the
celestial liturgy. Think of the vision of the throne of God
surrounded by the angels and the elders, in the Book of
Revelation, once again deeply influenced by Ezekiel, or of Paul
caught up into Paradise, hearing 'things that cannot be told,
which man may not utter' (2 Cor. 12:4). So then, three groups
of people, Essene, rabbinic and Christian, all of whom were
unable to take part in the Temple liturgy in Jerusalem, either
because they had excluded themselves or because the Temple
had been destroyed, all seek to compensate for this deprivation
by some experience of the angelic liturgy, an ascent to the
presence of God.

Faced with his discouraged Christians, with drooping hands
and weak knees (12:12), Hebrews makes the bold move of
refusing to offer any alternative experience of the celestial
liturgy. Shut off from the daily drama of the Temple ritual, its
author attempts to make sense of the absence of this cultic
experience. It is an attempt to make theological sense of tedium.
Instead of some experiential participation, we only have hope.
'We have this as a sure and steadfast anchor of the soul, a hope
that enters into the inner shrine behind the curtain, where Jesus
has gone as a forerunner on our behalf, having become high
priest for ever after the order of Melchizedek' (6:19). And the
basis of that hope was a new theology of creation that
transformed the meaning of cultic language. Let me explain. All
these groups which could no longer take part in the liturgy of
the Temple went on using cultic, priestly language. And this was
not mere nostalgia, as a traditional Catholic might hanker for
the Tridentine rite of the good old days. Cultic language went
on being used because it was the given, traditional way of
talking about God's relationship with his creation. It was the

2. On the chariot mysticism of these early rabbis, see Christopher Rowland,
The Open Heaven: A Study of Apocalyptic in Judaism and Early Christianity
(London: 1982), esp. pp. 269-348.

traditional metaphor for God's creativity. The liturgy was not
just the specialised activity of a few hereditary families
butchering sheep and goats, but a metaphor for God's making
and sustaining of the cosmos. So even when the cult finally
ceased in Jerusalem, one still had to go on talking about God,
the creator of heaven and earth. But what was now the ground
of such a discourse? Some people took the route of an
alternative access to the angelic liturgy; Hebrews transformed
what it meant to talk of God as creator, and so subverted the
meaning of cultic language. Hebrews is faithful to the proper
reference of sacrificial and priestly language but it transforms its
meaning by seeing God's creative act as being not, most
typically, the great conquest of chaos in Genesis 1, but the death
and resurrection of Christ.

According to the Priestly Writer, God's creativity was above
all disclosed in the great cosmic separations of the beginning: of
light and darkness, day and night, the waters above and the
waters below. One acknowledged the holiness of God by
recognising and celebrating these fundamental cosmic
separations. Indeed, Israel had been separated from the other
nations for just that purpose, to be a holy people whose law and
cult articulated the basic structures of creation:

> I am the Lord your God who have separated you from the
> peoples. You shall therefore make a distinction between
> the clean beast and the unclean, and between the unclean
> bird and the clean; and you shall not make yourself
> abominable by beast or bird or anything with which the
> ground teems, which I have set apart for you to hold
> unclean. You shall be holy to me; for I the Lord am holy
> and have separated you from the peoples that you should
> be mine. (Lev. 20:24-26)[3]

---

3. Cf. e.g. Bruce Malina, *The New Testament World* (London: 1981), pp. 122-152.

So the rules of purity are ordered towards a Temple liturgy that mirrors the order of the cosmos. Blenkinsopp has shown that when the Priestly Writer describes Moses constructing the tabernacle in the wilderness, he is deliberately echoing Genesis 1.[4] This is the goal of creation, a tent in the wilderness. After hovering over the face of the water in the beginning, the Spirit of God makes its first reappearance when it is given to Bezazel to help him to make a sanctuary. And it is interesting that this tradition of a connection between the creating of the universe and the building of the sanctuary persists for almost a thousand years. It can be found in the Babylonian Talmud:

> Rabbi Judah said Bezazel knew how to combine the letters by which the heavens and the earth were created. It is written here, 'And he hath filled him (Bezazel) with the spirit of God, in wisdom and understanding and in knowledge,' and it is written elsewhere, 'The Lord by wisdom created the earth, by understanding he established the heavens,' and it is also written, 'By his knowledge the depths were broken up'. (B. Berakoth 55a).

Josephus, a near contemporary of Jesus, thought of the Temple as a microcosm, a sort of cosmic plan; the patterns of the courts and the boundaries, the ornaments of the Holy Place, gave you a picture of the heavens and the earth. He called it 'an imitation of the nature of the totality'.[5] Philo put it the other way round: the universe was a gigantic Temple: 'The Highest in the truest sense, the holy Temple of God, as we must believe, is the whole universe, having for its sanctuary the most sacred part of all existence, even heaven, for its votive ornaments the stars, for its priests the angels who are servitors to his powers.'[6] So

---

4. Joseph Blenkinsopp, *Prophecy and Canon: A Contribution to the Study of Jewish Origins* (Notre Dame and London: 1977), pp. 54-79.
5. *Jewish Antiquities* III, 123.
6. *De Spec. Leg.* I.66.

then, the yearning to take part in the angelic cult is not a mysterious desire for an eternal benediction; it is a longing to take part in the liturgy whereby the world is sustained, the cult that makes day and night alternate, the dew descend at the right time, the rivers flow in the right direction, and men and women obey the Torah, which was on the knees of God when He made the world.[7] So the language of the liturgy is the language of creation. Sacrifice was given for the healing of the world, for the purity regulations, to quote Mary Douglas, 'set up the great inclusive categories in which the whole universe is hierarchised and structured'.[8]

So when Hebrews applies the language of priesthood and sacrifice to Christ, it is not the case that the author is using ordinary language metaphorically, as when he talks about being a Christian in terms of gardening or athletics. The language of the cult is always metaphorical, as anthropologists have long recognised. Luc de Heusch, in his recent book, *Sacrifice in Africa*, defines sacrifice as 'a symbolic labour on living matter'.[9] When the Nuer offer a wild cucumber to the gods in place of a wild ox, it is not that they expect to fool the gods; they recognise that it will work metaphorically. It is through these sorts of symbolic acts that, for example, the Dogan people 'maintain the world in working order'.[10] The novelty of Hebrews is in locating God's supreme creative act, not in the setting up of the cosmic distinctions of Genesis 1, but the death and resurrection of Jesus.

This interpretation of the purpose of the Hebrews is confirmed by a glance at the opening verses of the Letter. Here they are in the RSV translation:

---

7. Cf. *Bereshith R.* I:I, and *The Testament of Adam*.
8. J. Neusner, *The Idea of Purity in Ancient Judaism* (Brill: 1973). The reply to Neusner by Mary Douglas, p. 139.
9. Luc de Heusch, *Sacrifice in Africa: A Structuralist Approach* (Manchester: 1985), p. 50.
10. Ibid., p. 200.

> In many and various ways God spoke of old to our fathers
> by the prophets; but in these last days he has spoken to us
> by a Son, whom he appointed the heir of all things,
> through whom also he created the world.

This is usually read as showing that Hebrews has not only a rich
sense of the humanity of Christ, but also a clear theology of his
pre-existence. As well as suffering for us on the cross he also
created everything in the beginning. This is to fail to sense the
author's dynamic understanding of creation. The letter starts,
like Genesis, with God speaking in creative words; these only
come to full articulation in Christ. He is the heir, the one whom
God had in mind from the beginning. The Greek says that he
created *tous aionas*, 'the ages'. Through the Son God created a
whole sequence of ages through which he brings the world to
completion. This is suggested by 11:3; the Anchor Bible
translation is best: 'By faith we consider the ages to have been
put in order by the word of God so that what is seen has not
come into existence from things that are visible.' This has
nothing to do with an instantaneous *creatio ex nihilo* at the
beginning. The whole history of Israel is the matrix of God's
creative act; it shapes the world that he intends. This is the
perspective that lies behind the next couple of verses of the
opening chapter:

> He reflects the glory and bears the very stamp of his
> nature, upholding the universe by his word of power.
> When he had made purification for sins, he sat at the
> right hand of the Majesty on high, having become as
> much superior to the angels as the name he has obtained
> is more excellent than theirs.

At first glance one might make the mistake of thinking that
the author is changing from talking about Jesus in terms of his
divinity and sharing in the Father's creative act, to Jesus as high

priest. This is not the case. He is upholding (*pheron*) the universe by his power. This does not simply mean that he is keeping things in existence. It is, once again, a dynamic word; he is carrying the universe, bearing it along, towards completion. And he does that precisely by 'making purification for sins', because it is sacrifice that puts the world to rights and repairs the cosmos. It is through the sacrificial system that we share in God's making and remaking of the world. And the final goal of this dynamic is to sit at God's right hand, to enter His rest in the final Sabbath. A similar conjunction of themes can be found in the contemporary apocalyptic document, 2 Baruch: 'And it shall come to pass when he (The Messiah) has brought low everything that is in the world, and has sat down in peace for the age on the throne of his kingdom, that joy shall be revealed, and rest shall appear' (73:1).

Unfortunately we do not have the space here to follow through the successive transformations of the doctrine of creation, but one might say that it evolved through attempts to make sense of ever more radical experiences of failure. It was the failure of the Exile, the collapse of the State, that pushed Israel beyond a perception of the cosmic order as disclosed in the annual cycle of the seasons to the great creative event of the beginning which we find in P. Similarly it was the doctrine of the resurrection, born of the suffering of martyrs, that brought both Judaism and Christianity to a doctrine of *creatio ex nihilo*.[11] And both the rabbis and the Christian theologians noticed that that seventh day of creation was never said to end. It became a symbol of a completion, the entering of God's rest, to which we are all travelling, symbolised by the entry into God's presence on the Day of Atonement. That was when the ram's horn was blown and sabbatical years began. All this lies behind the image of Jesus making sacrifice for the purification of sins and taking his seat at the right hand of God.

---

11. Cf. Jonathan Goldstein, 'The Origins of the Doctrine of *Creatio ex Nihilo*' in *The Journal of Jewish Studies*, vol. 35, (1985), pp. 127-135.

Hebrews takes a more radical step than this. It subverts the OT conception of what it means for God to be creative. In Genesis 1, as I have suggested, the cosmic separations ground the social separations of Jew/Gentile, male/female, lay/priestly. As is said in a prayer from the time of Jesus: 'Blessed is he who distinguishes between holy and profane, between light and darkness, between Israel and Gentiles, between the seventh day and the six working days, between water above and water below, between priest and levite and Israelite'. But the author of Hebrews turns this principle on its head and bases the priesthood of Christ on his solidarity, closeness, to others. The OT priest was such by virtue of his separation from others; Jesus is the great high priest by virtue of his solidarity with us:

> Since therefore the children share in flesh and blood, he himself likewise partook of the same nature, that through death he might destroy him who has the power of death, that is, the devil, and deliver all those who through fear of death were subject to lifelong bondage... Therefore he had to be made like his brethren in every respect, so that he might become a merciful and faithful high priest in the service of God, to make expiation for the sins of the people (2:14f, 17).

And what underpins this new theology of solidarity is a more fundamental innovation, which is a transformation of God's relationship to suffering and death. God had been perceived as the source of all life and holiness precisely in his separation from death. The purity regulations aim at creating the maximum distance between the corpse and the Holy of Holies. The corpse was the ultimately impure object, 'the father of the fathers of impurity'.[12] It radiates impurity as God radiates holiness. The High Priest was not allowed to mourn even his closest relatives,

---

12. Cf. Mary Douglas, *Purity and Danger: An Analysis of the Concepts of Pollution and Taboo* (London: 1966).

follow behind their coffins or touch their corpses, lest he be
unable to enter into the Holy of Holies on the Day of
Atonement.[13] He must be physically perfect, free from
deformity, hence the cunning move of Antigonus in biting off
the ears of his predecessor, Hyrcanus, so as to disqualify him for
ever from the high priesthood. But in Christ God's creative act
happened in a grasping of the ultimate impurity and its
transformation so that 'through death he might destroy him
who has the power of death'. So his use of cultic language is
ultimately ironic. For us the most holy object is the 'father of
the fathers of impurity', a corpse. The focal point of our cultic
space, that around which the community gathers, is not, as in
the Temple, that which is farthest from death, but that which is
closest, the cross. So our use of cultic language is a subversion,
made possible by a new theology of creation; God the creator is
the one who raises from the dead.

One can spot this irony in, for example, Hebrews' use of the
word *teleioun*, which primarily means 'to perfect'. Christ is
perfected through suffering, as in 2:10. 'For it was fitting that
he, for whom and by whom all things exist, in bringing many
sons to glory, should make the pioneer of their salvation perfect
through suffering.' The obvious context is that of God as
creator; He is described as the one 'for whom and by whom all
things exist', and He brings Jesus to perfection, fullness of
being. It is, of course, a paradox that God is creative through
suffering and death, and it is that which grounds the irony that
teleioun is a word with cultic resonances. Albert Vanhoye has
shown that in the LXX it is frequently used for the consecration
of a priest. The Hebrew expression for consecration, 'to fill the
hands', becomes in the LXX 'to perfect the hands', and so
priestly ordination is described as *teleiosis*, 'the act of making
perfect'.[14] So for Hebrews that which consecrates Christ is his

---

13. J. Jeremias, *Jerusalem in the Time of Jesus* (London: 1967), pp. 147-159.
14. Albert Vanhoye, *Old Testament Priests and the New Priest*, (Leominster: 1986), pp. 130-133.

entry into the realm of death; he is ordained by immersion in the impure.

Several important consequences follow for our use of cultic language. It will have to acquire a new grammar.[15] The OT language of creation and cult was essentially binary; it was founded on oppositions such as day/night; male/female; priest/lay. But if God's holiness is disclosed in laying hold of its opposite, then our use of this language will be transformed. This is what lies behind 13:11-13:

> For the bodies of those animals whose blood is brought into the sanctuary by the high priest as a sacrifice for sins are burned outside the camp. So Jesus also suffered outside the gate in order to sanctify the people through his own blood. Therefore let us go forth to him outside the camp, and bear the abuse he endured.

Exegetes have been puzzled by how the death of Jesus could be compared with the dumping of these corpses outside the camp. His death was sacrificial, but in their case it was just a matter of disposing of impure objects. Clearly the author of Hebrews had not read his rubrics! But I would propose that this suggests the new grammar of the word 'holy'. That which makes holy, our *sacra-ficium*, is precisely this corpse outside the city gates, and so we too sanctify the world by going out. The impure is that which is to be grasped and transformed. There is a similar paradox in Rev. 5:6, in which the seer sees before the throne of God 'a lamb standing as though slain'. Vanhoye has shown that although the context is cultic, sacrificial, the words used are not. Neither the Greek words for 'lamb' or 'slain' come from the priestly vocabulary. It is as though one were to say 'I saw this woolly ruminant butchered upon the altar'. Or, as

---

15. L. Wittgenstein, 'Grammar tells us what kind of an object anything is (Theology as Grammar)' in *Philosophical Investigations* 373, eds. G. E. M. Anscombe and R. Rhees, trans. G. E. M. Anscombe (Oxford: 1953).

Vanhoye puts it, more elegantly, 'John has inserted a non-ritualistic expression (*arnion esphagmenon*) into a sacrificial structure. In this way he has described the Christian paradox: a death which had nothing to do with ritual – the death of Jesus, a penal execution of an unjust sentence – has been transformed into a perfect sacrifice and so has become the decisive event of human history.'[16] This means that there can be no ultimate contradiction between the gospels' presentation of Jesus as a layman, ignoring the rules of purity, in conflict with the priesthood, and Hebrews' theology of Christ as high priest, for the latter is a theology that seeks to transcend the binary opposition of lay and priestly. Is it a coincidence that the typical New Testament word for 'community' is *koinonia*? In the LXX words from this family are usually used in a negative sense, the community of sinners.[17] *Koinos* means 'common', and by the time of Jesus had come to mean 'impure', as when the Pharisees accuse Jesus of eating with 'common' hands, in Mark 7. The holy is that which is withdrawn from the common. But our *koinonia* is founded on the consecration of the common.

It also follows that it would make no sense to speak of Christ as if he was the sole priest, in some exclusive sense. The Old Testament priest or levite was such in virtue of the fact that some other people were not. But Christ's priesthood, being derived from his solidarity with us, communicates itself. It is no longer the case, as on the day of Atonement, that the high priest detaches himself from the Gentiles, from the women, from the male Israelites and finally from the priests when he enters the Holy of Holies alone. It is his solitude which defines his role. Christ's high-priesthood means that we all flock in: 'Therefore, brethren, since we have the confidence to enter the sanctuary by the blood of Jesus, by the new and living way which has opened for us through the curtain, that is his flesh...' (10:19f). And

---

16. Vanhoye, *Old Testament Priests and the New Priest*, p. 282.
17. cf. '*koinos*', F. Hauck in *Theological Dictionary of the New Testament*, vol. 3, ed. G. Kittel (Michigan: 1965), pp. 800-803.

that is why *teleioun*, to perfect or consecrate, is eventually applied to all of us. His consecration is ours too. So the priesthood of Christ and of the people is, in a sense, one and the same thing.

The people to whom this document is addressed are discouraged. They have weak knees and drooping hands. Although they have been baptised they find themselves suffering, members of an impure and imperfect world. There is not even the consolation of that dramatic metaphor of recreation, the cult of the Temple. The author resists the temptation to offer an alternative experience, a moment of mystical ascent, through liturgy or meditation on the scriptures. Rather he claims the experience of tedium, the discouragement and the suffering, as the place in which God's act of recreation now takes place. That is why we may have hope. So it is not the case that Christ is merely metaphorically a priest; we all know that he was really a layman. It is rather the case that the old cult was merely metaphorically recreative. In the old cult 'gifts and sacrifices are offered which cannot perfect the *suneidesin* (not 'conscience' so much as 'deepest being') of the worshipper'. It is as if this cultic language had been awaiting its proper application, the act of real transformation to which it pointed but was unable to achieve. Hebrews twice uses the cultic word for 'to dedicate', *engkainidzo*, literally 'to make new'. The Feast of the Dedication was *Ta Engkainia*, The Making New. One might suggest that Christ's death and resurrection disclosed a novelty, a newness, that the old cult merely hinted at. Cultic, priestly language comes into its own for the first time. Luke's gospel begins with Zechariah struck dumb in the Temple, the people awaiting a blessing that is not given. It concludes with Jesus being taken up into heaven and performing the priestly gesture of blessing the disciples, who return to the Temple, praising God. The Resurrection allows the Temple liturgy to find completion, to attain its goal.

What are the consequences for our own theology of the ministry? What place can we offer to cultic figures? Wittgenstein said that 'man is a ceremonious animal'.[18] And Fergus Kerr has commented that we need 'a theology for ceremonious animals, so as to speak, rather than for celebrating solipsists; a theology that starts from the deep sinister thing in human nature, rather than from a hypothesis about a deity.'[19] Whatever our theology of the priesthood may be, we will need to find ceremonious ways of articulating our faith, of expressing it by ritual, gesture and cult. It is a theology that will have to be enacted. The question we must ask is this: what theology of creation is implicit in our rituals? Is it a levitical theology of creation as separation, of sustaining and articulating binary oppositions, of holding chaos at bay and removing oneself from infection by the impure? Or do our rituals embody the theology of recreation which we find in Hebrews, in which 'the deep and sinister thing in human nature', the impure, the blemished the chaotic, is grasped and transformed? Our rituals should enact the paradox of gathering a holy assembly around the image of a corpse. The central actions and words of the Eucharist do just that, the remembrance of a man who takes upon himself his death in the hope that the Father will make something new out of it. The gestures of the Last Supper express belief in God's power to create out of nothing. Here are the roots of a doctrine of *creatio ex nihilo*. But maybe this gesture, which is 'holy' in a paradoxical, ironic sense, is often contradicted by rituals which suggest a more levitical theology of the priesthood.

Hebrews does not say anything about a special group of ordained priests within the community. This does not mean that there should not be such a group; just that we must test its constitution and function against Hebrews' theology of holiness. Christ is, of course, *the* high priest, but we have seen

---

18. *Remarks on Frazer's Golden Bough,* ed. Rush Rhees, trans. A. C. Miles and R. Rhees (Retford: 1979), p. 7.
19. Fergus Kerr OP, *Theology after Wittgenstein* (Oxford: 1986), p. 163.

that his priesthood is, like the Good, *diffusivum sui*; it communicates itself. It follows that any particular ministry in the Church can only be justified insofar as it nourishes and realises the priesthood of the whole community. Something has gone wrong if, for example, the presbyterate has the effect of concealing or qualifying the priesthood of the whole body of Christ. What is theologically primary is the priesthood of the people; because of the complex, social nature of human beings, this needs a body like the presbyterate to be effective. Certainly Hebrews offers no support for the idea of an exclusively male presbyterate. This may be justified on other grounds, but the male/female polarity appears to be one of those binary oppositions so beloved of levitical theology. It is one of those fundamental polarities which were articulated by the ritual of the Temple, whereas in Hebrews the holiness of God is disclosed in God's grasping and transforming the other. Hebrews is certainly antipatriarchal. Melchizedek is the man without genealogy, without father or mother, who belongs to no lineage of male descent. His priesthood is placed in opposition to that of 'dying men' (7:8), who are priests in virtue of being sons and grandsons. It is Abraham, explicitly identified as 'patriarch', the source of fatherhood, who offers tithes to the one without children. (Now, if one were really desperate, one might use this as a rather feeble argument for an unmarried priesthood, but not for an exclusively male one!)

Hebrews does suggest one fruitful line for a theology of priesthood. Its author writes, 'Remember your leaders, those who spoke to you the word of God' (13:7). There are some people within the community, leaders, who have the task of speaking the word, and this speaking of the word of God is clearly, for him, a priestly work. The letter starts with God speaking the word: 'In many and various ways God spoke of old to our fathers by the prophets, but in these last days he has spoken to us by a Son ...' (1: 1). It is through the speaking of a word that God brings the world into existence, and the final

form of that creative word is Jesus' priestly act of dying and
rising, of making the sacrifice that completes creation. If the
cult is seen as symbolic of God's creative activity, then our cult
must involve speaking a creative word that makes and remakes
our world. And this is precisely what Hebrews itself does. It is a
recreative word that lifts the drooping arms and strengthens the
weak knees. It is a word of exhortation (13:22), that mediates
the word that is Christ. It communicates Christ's solidarity with
us in our weakness. It is a consecrating, perfecting word, that
grasps these discouraged people in their alienation, and claims
their experience for the sacred. So the letter itself is a sort of
reaching out, an extension of Christ's drawing close. In fact the
author even seems to identify his words with those of Christ at
one point: 'See that you do not refuse him who is speaking.'
(One assumes this to be the author.) 'For if they did not escape
when they refused him who warned them from earth, much less
shall we escape if we reject him who warns from heaven'
(12:25). To conclude, any form of ministry that looks to
Hebrews for justification must be seen to speak a word that
gathers people into God's sabbath rest, that brings in those who
feel themselves to be unclean, impure, weak and suffering,
overthrowing the distinction between lay and priest.

CHAPTER TWO

Christ and Politics

HERBERT MCCABE

In the first part of this article I shall say briefly why I think that, if we are to take 'politics' in the ordinary modern sense, political interpretations of the Gospels are mistaken. I do not think that Jesus sought political power in order to change society or that either he or his followers were concerned with the political independence of the section of the Roman empire where they lived. In the second part I want to talk of the relevance the gospel has, nevertheless, to the things that do concern politicians in the modern sense. I take it that every christology implies an ecclesiology; so that section will be a discussion of what, in view of what we have to say about Jesus, is the relationship of the body of Christ to the body politic.

Let us begin with Simon. I do not think that the Apostle whom Luke, both in his Gospel and in Acts, called 'Simon the zealot' could have been a zealot in the restricted and technical sense that the word acquired only some years after the crucifixion of Jesus. Simon was, perhaps, or had been, one zealous for the exact observance of the Law and disapproving of other Jews who might have been more free and easy. Maybe he belonged, or had belonged, to a Jewish sect rather like some extreme right-wing, super-orthodox groups in modern Israel. (Or perhaps he just had a nickname somehow related to this.) Much later 'zealot' also came to mean one of an organised group engaged not in the defence of the Law against back-sliding Jews but in subverting by violence the Roman colonial rule.

When I say that I think these things you must not suppose
that I claim any personal expertise or authority in these matters.
I am merely indicating that I have been convinced by E. P.
Sanders in *Jesus and Judaism*, and, especially, by the arguments
of Raymond Brown in his recent book, *The Death of the
Messiah*.

Brown points out that the Roman direct rule of its province
in Palestine by Prefects or Procurators falls into two periods
separated by the short reign of Herod Agrippa I, between 41
and 46 CE. He argues that Roman rule and Jewish attitudes to
it were very different in the two periods; and, of course, the
ministry of Jesus belonged exclusively to the first. Much
misguided reading of the Gospels, from Kautsky to Brandon
and Winter, for whom Jesus was a political activist against
colonial rule, arises, he suggests, from treating this first period
(when there were Prefects, for example Pontius Pilate, only of
Judaea) as exactly like the second, when direct rule extended
north into Galilee.

> Too often the final years before the Revolt with their
> seething discontent and Zealot terrorism have been
> thought characteristic of the earlier period in which Jesus
> lived. This has facilitated the creation of the myth that
> Jesus was a political revolutionary.[1]

I have, for some years, argued that Liberation Theology is
not helped but hindered by a mistaken 'process theology' of
God – produced largely by bourgeois academics in Europe and
the USA. It is now, I suppose, time to argue that it is not helped
either but hindered by misreading the accounts of Jesus in the
New Testament.

Brown also notes the particularly savage in-fighting during
the century before Christ amongst various Jewish factions and
contenders for power – a bloody history of massacres and

1. R. E. Brown, *The Death of the Messiah*, p. 677.

crucifixions. The last of the successors of Herod the Great, Archelaus,

> was such a bad ruler that, at the request of his Jewish subjects, the Emperor removed him and appointed... the first prefect of Judaea... after such a baneful history [of Jewish rule] the Roman prefecture represented a more sane and orderly administration, even if foreign rulers are rarely liked.[2]

We are, I think, entitled to add a pinch of salt to that 'request'; I can think of no successful takeover of a country by a foreign power which did not subsequently turn out to have been 'requested'. Nevertheless, Brown's main point stands.

It is, indeed, hard to imagine anyone actually liking Pontius Pilate but he was not notably bloodthirsty, either by the standards of the earlier warring Hasmoneans and Herodians or of the later corrupt and repressive Roman colonial rulers. Indeed the whole reign of the (personally detestable) Emperor Tiberius (14-37 CE), which covered the whole public ministry of Jesus, was generally recognised as remarkably peaceful (*sub Tiberio quies*, as Tacitus put it) or, as we say in the praeconium with which (at least in the Dominican rite) we introduce the liturgy of Christmas: 'In the sixth age of the world, when the whole world was at peace: Jesus Christ, eternal Son of the eternal Father, was born in Bethlehem in Juda of the Virgin Mary'.

Finally, a Spanish scholar, pleasantly and ironically called Guevara, is quoted by Raymond Brown, in what he describes as 'his most detailed study of the political context in Judaea' as saying 'The response of the sources is very clear: the epoch of the public life of Jesus was a peaceful epoch'.[3]

However, during this peaceful epoch Jesus was undoubtedly crucified. Moreover, every gospel indicates that the charge laid

---

2. Ibid., p. 678.
3. Ibid., p. 679.

against him before Pilate was that he claimed to be 'King of the Jews'. (And this despite the fact that before his trial nobody in the Gospels ever calls him King of the Jews except a legendary Magus at the beginning of Matthew.) There is surely at least a whiff of politics about all this.

A plausible explanation, however, is that the work of Jesus, although not political, and his teaching, although also not political, had a *de facto* political effect. He was a troublemaker in an unstable society. As E. P. Sanders says, speaking of Jesus' announcement of the end of the temple and, even more, his symbolic attack on the place itself, this

> would have been offensive to most Jews. The gesture, even if it did not raise much tumult, could readily have led the Romans to think that Jesus was a threat to public order. In particular the physical demonstration against the temple by one who had a notable following looms as so obvious an occasion for the execution that we need look no further.[4]

and again:

> We can understand [the execution of Jesus] simply by knowing that he spoke of a kingdom and stirred the hopes of the people. His miracles also produced excitement, and excitement carries its own dangers... a man who spoke of a kingdom, spoke against the temple and had a following was one marked for execution; but no one need have regarded him as a military leader... the Romans regarded him as dangerous at one level but not at another; dangerous as one who excited the hopes and dreams of the Jews, but not as an actual leader of an insurgent group.[5]

---

4. E. P. Sanders, *Jesus and Judaism* (London: 1985), p. 302.
5. Ibid., p. 295.

There was no insurgent group: none of Jesus' followers was arrested or harassed by the Roman authorities after the crucifixion.

It has to be said, though, that Jesus himself is presented in the Gospels as somewhat ambiguous (or at least sesquiguous) on the question of his role. The early churches knew of two interrogations of Jesus after his arrest, one by his fellow Jews and one by the Roman authorities, and they give us fascinating (but in historical detail not very credible) dramatic accounts of how they imagined these interrogations took place. As they present it, both interrogations really centred on the question: in what sense is Jesus the *Christos*, the name which after the resurrection, and only after the resurrection, became the commonest title of Jesus. The questioning seems, at first sight, quite different on the two occasions.

In the first, it is what we would call religious but in the second, political. The Jewish interrogators are presented as concerned about whether Messianic (Christological) claims about Jesus involve a claim to be in some specially deep (and putatively blasphemous) sense 'son of the Blessed', that is divine, a demi-god. In the Roman interrogation Pilate is concerned about whether the claim is, in the ordinary sense, political: is it a claim to independent kingship. 'Are you the king of the Jews?' In almost every case Jesus replies to this *sy legeis* which has hitherto been rendered in English as 'Thou hast said it' or, as in Brown: 'You say'. We are now, happily, able to be more accurate: since *The House of Cards*, we know that what Jesus said was 'You might say that: I couldn't possibly comment'.

There is, of course, no doubt at all that Jesus announced the coming of 'the Kingdom', the kingdom of heaven, the kingdom of God or 'your kingdom', as, for example, when the wife of Zebedee came up to him with her sons and said to him 'Command that these two sons of mine may sit one at your right hand and one at your left, in your kingdom' (Mt 20:20).

Jesus replies that that sort of thing is really not his business. His business is to 'drink the cup', to suffer and die: it is the business of his Father to decide what will happen next: the resurrection and glorification of Jesus, the sending of the Spirit and the acknowledgement of Jesus as the Christ (which is what the Church is about).

In the Gospel of John, as a matter of literary device, all interlocutors of Jesus have at least one thing in common: they have to misunderstand him – so that he can develop what he has said at a deeper level. Usually this takes the form of a crassly literal misunderstanding of what Jesus has said: Nicodemus: 'Can a man enter again into his mother's womb'. The woman at the well: 'give me some of that water, that I may not thirst, nor come here to draw' (though I think she is joking). So also with the people after the feeding of the five thousand. But in the synoptics, too, the people regularly miss the point of what Jesus is doing or saying.

At the demonstration on Palm Sunday, Mark reports the crowd as shouting 'Blessed is the kingdom of our father David that is coming. Hosanna in the highest'. Luke says they shouted 'Blessed is the king who comes in the name of the Lord'; John has 'Blessed is he who comes in the name of the Lord, even the king of Israel' but adds, 'His disciples did not understand this at first, but when Jesus was glorified, then they remembered'.

So the misunderstanding involved in Jesus' condemnation on a political charge is a sort of culmination of a series of inevitable misunderstandings throughout his ministry. I think this is part of the positive teaching of the evangelists: Jesus is not so much 'the man for others', as 'the man to be misunderstood by others'. His identity, what his place is in the story, his part in the play, cannot be captured in any human categories (including the human category of 'the gods'). Jesus is a mystery. In fact, as John came to see and, at Chalcedon, the Church eventually came to define, Jesus is the Word in which the ultimate mystery, God, speaks himself.

For John, I think, Jesus has no definable place in the story because he is also, in some way, author of the story. That is why Flann O'Brien's *At Swim Two Birds*, in which an author comes under criticism and attack by his fictional characters, is essential reading for any Christologist.

As is well-recognised, there is a clear implication in, I think, all the Passion narratives that the misunderstanding by Pilate is not accidental but manipulated by the chief priests. Their real case against Jesus, it is suggested, has to do with his claims to forgive sinners without the proper religious rituals of repentance, to be closer to God than is the temple, and so on; but, since they wanted him executed, while religious squabbles in the local alien cult would cut no ice with Pilate, they put the thing in political terms. In a tantalisingly short paragraph, E. P. Sanders notes that Schweitzer, in his *Quest of the Historical Jesus*, had already suggested that:

> *what* Judas betrayed (a point on which the Gospels are unhelpful) was that Jesus and his small band thought of him as 'king'... Judas conveyed Jesus's pretension to the chief priests... It was the final weapon they needed: a specific charge to present to Pilate, more certain to have fatal effect than the general charge of 'troublemaker'.[6]

Whether or not this is the case, there remains, I think, a sense in which no attempt to categorise Jesus in either political or religious terms is going to succeed. The Gospels seem to suggest, at least, that there is a certain inevitability here, quite apart from any malicious intention on the part of the opponents of Jesus. It seems to me quite certain that any idea that there was simply a lamentable misunderstanding which could have been avoided by a little clarification, has to be just wrong.

Consider, for example, the story of the tribute to Caesar. The tribute was, naturally, unpopular but especially with the

---

6. Ibid., p. 309.

Pharisees who see it as an insult to the Lord, the only king of the universe, for his special people to acknowledge the lordship of this primitive idol-worshipper in Rome. So if Jesus had said: Yes, the tribute should be paid, he would alienate true and devout Jews. On the other hand the Herodians, who were also present, were not so traditionalist and felt that God's law would allow them to come to an accommodation with Caesar for practical purposes; so had Jesus said that the tribute was not to be paid he would have been speedily reported to the police as a subversive.

Clever; but not so clever as Jesus. In the first place he makes the Pharisees produce a coin with Caesar's image stamped on it: thus acknowledging that they are prepared to handle and use an abomination, a graven image, an idol specifically forbidden by the Law. But then he says: 'Render to Caesar the things that are Caesar's and to God the things that are God's'.

Now, if he had meant by this that there are two areas, one the world of coins and trade and secular life which is the business of Caesar, and another, a spiritual realm separate from this which is the preserve of religion and God, he would simply have been opting for the Herodian side, for they were the nearest thing a Jew could get to such a bizarre idea. (This is, need I say, the interpretation taken by all modern liberal individualists: churchmen should not meddle in public politics, nor politicians in private matters of religion.)

It might be that Jesus was taking this position: one area of life where God held sway and another for Caesar, but it seems unlikely that his theology was as bad as that. More importantly, it would not account for the punch-line of the story where it says (in all three synoptics) that when they heard his reply the crowd were astonished at it. If he had opted just for one side of the argument they might have approved or disapproved but hardly have been astonished.

I suggest that they were astonished and perhaps delighted by the ingenious way Jesus evaded the trap set for him. He has devised an ambiguous answer which could satisfy either party, for what he said could have another opposite meaning which would be satisfactory to Pharisees. 'Render to Caesar what is Caesar's and to God what is God's' could also mean: Caesar, under God of course, is welcome to the rest of the world and may lay it under tribute, but this land is Eretz Israel and it belongs only to God and was bestowed by God on his own people, the Jews. This concrete interpretation is, in fact, much more obvious than the abstract separation of sacred and secular aspects of human life. It is, of course, one congenial to the Pharisees rather than the Herodians.

There is, then, no formula within which Jesus and his mission can be encapsulated. For Luke, remember, his public life begins with the boy who runs away from home, explaining, when they find him in the temple, that his parents did not understand him.

Jesus, then, was not, we may say, interested in politics or in acquiring political power (Jn 6:15 represents him as actively avoiding it), but the striking thing is how very much politicians and others concerned with power were interested in Jesus. 'The chief priests and pharisees gathered the council and said: 'what are we to do? For this man performs many signs. If we let him go on thus, everyone will believe in him, and the Romans will come and destroy both our holy place and our nation' (Jn 11:47).

The kingdom of God, as Jesus tells Pilate in John's Gospel, is not 'of this world' but it is nevertheless of great interest and importance to this world, and more especially if 'this world' is taken in the sense in which it is most commonly used by John: this corrupt world. This world will hate Jesus and, so he warns his followers, it will hate them as well. The preaching of the kingdom of heaven is threatening to the kingdom of this world – what John the Baptist calls 'the sin of this world'.

It is time now to take a quick look at the implications for ecclesiology of the picture of Christ that I have been sketching. To try to answer the question: 'In what sense was Jesus a political figure?' is also to point to an answer to the question: In what sense is the Church a political institution or related to such institutions? Since I am going to restrict myself to the Roman Catholic Church, I will begin with a word about what is called 'Catholic social teaching'. I do not think that there is a Catholic social teaching in the sense that there is an accepted Catholic teaching about, say, the Trinity or the Eucharist. Instead there have been an important series of responses on the part of representative Catholics to contemporary social and political situations and doctrines.

Let us start with *Rerum Novarum* (1891). It has, I think rightly, been said that Pope Leo XIII did not address the social injustices of his day: that had already been done by Karl Marx and others. *Rerum Novarum* was addressed centrally to what it described as the socialist response to and critique of liberal capitalism. That liberal capitalism was a disaster for a large proportion of the human race was obvious, and common ground to socialists and the Pope. That it was not a natural disaster but one made by human beings and perhaps curable by human beings was also common ground.

What that highly intelligent and humane man, Leo XIII, saw was that the only serious available critique of the abominations of nineteenth century liberal capitalism was nineteenth century socialism and that this would not do. For a majority of European socialists, 'socialism' was an oversimplified doctrine hopelessly in thrall to ideas left over from the Enlightenment, in particular, the Enlightenment's view of religion: the odd phenomenon that we should call bourgeois atheism.

Leo's problem was to preach the gospel in the face of capitalism without allowing the gospel itself to be oversimplified in a similar way. It was, of course, because Catholics had been slow to preach the gospel in the face of capitalism that when they began they found this rival in the field who had to be coped with. This indeed, was the reason why they (or a small minority of them) began at all. Anyway, whether or not you read *Rerum Novarum* as I do, you may perhaps agree that it was a response to concrete circumstances rather than the handing down of an already developed traditional doctrine. It was simply a matter of preaching the gospel as best you can in a certain time and place.

I do not want, here, to argue this same point for the great succeeding 'social encyclicals'; but it seems plausible to see *Quadragesimo Anno* as a rather similar reaction to the thirties world of fascism, and *Centesimus Annus* as a response to the collapse of state capitalism in Eastern Europe – or rather, as with *Rerum Novarum*, a critique of what is perceived as an oversimplified response (in this case of the Western 'market economy') to these events.

I would like now to look briefly at four models of the relationship between church and society: as alternative, as model, as social cement and as challenge.

First, then, the model of the Church as *alternative to political society*, even a way of escaping from political society. This model has been popular in our time mainly as an object of abuse, under the name of 'otherworldly Christianity'. The Church is seen as pointing the way to a kingdom of God which is quite distinct from this world. The view is that we should not be too concerned about this world and its problems. Provided they live by the rules, the members of the Church will shortly be leaving this vale of tears and inhabiting an altogether better and quite distinct place. It is no concern of the Church to change the world. We need, of course, to change our individual selves, and this, naturally, involves changing our behaviour towards our neighbours, making sure that we treat them with charity and justice. But that is a very different matter from trying to bring about a just world order. It is an illusion (and perhaps sinful vanity) to suppose we could do any such thing.

The world, on this view, is still in the power of the Prince of this World. True, he has been cast out of the heavens, where he is no longer the Accuser of humankind and has been replaced there by the Advocate, the paraclete. Satan has indeed fallen from heaven, but fallen to earth; and all that the faithful Christian can expect from this world is persecution at the hands of his agents. Christ's kingdom is not of this world and he reigns only in the hearts of his faithful, secretly. There will be a time when his kingdom will become manifest, but it is not yet.

The illumination I think we might detect in all this is a proper scepticism about the finality of any human achievement. It seems to me that a central contribution that Christianity makes to our understanding of humankind is its understanding of, and ability to cope with, failure. From one point of view, this is exactly what the cross is.

We see this theoretical model concretely represented in the early monastic movement. Here we had groups of people deciding that the life of the gospel could not easily, if at all, be lived in the cities. They went out into the countryside, not because they wanted to be close to 'nature', nor because of its beauty (to which, I imagine, they were wholly indifferent, if not hostile), but because it was not the city, it was not society. Whether in the unstructured groups of desert fathers, or, in a different way, amongst the Irish monks, or in the organised communes of continental monasticism, we find the idea that the Christian life can best be lived in a church which is an alternative society and an alternative to society.

It is, of course, true that the great monastic communities of the West fairly soon themselves became centres of society; became, in fact, great undying corporations which, by their accumulation of wealth, formed the backbone of medieval rural capitalism; but by that time the model had changed somewhat. So the Church as alternative to the world or to society had respectable and interesting supporters.

I turn, now, to another model, derived, I think, from the first: this is the model of the Church itself as *model for society*. The idea is that, especially in a society consisting largely of Christians, organisations such as parishes or religious communities could be, for example, pioneering testing grounds for projects of social welfare. This is not an absurd idea for, after all, the state-run schools and hospitals of modern Europe are directly descended from such Church activities in the past, as, indeed, are the universities and the structures associated with marriage. Whatever we say of this, though, and however centrally we place the option for the poor, it is hard to see such good works as the defining function of the Church or its principle relevance to society and politics.

I would like to move on to the third model: the metaphor of *social cement*. The Church might be thought to provide the social cohesion upon which, in the end, society rests. This, too, has a highly respectable and ancient background. Aristotle seeks to identify the difference between the links that may be formed between separate states and the bonds which unite the citizens of the same state. There can be trade agreements and pacts, he says, between separate states and their individual members, but no amount of such contracts will constitute them as one state or superstate.

The reason Aristotle gives is that the citizens of a state are bound together, not fundamentally by commutative justice, fairness and law, but by what he calls *philia*, political friendship, a recognition that they belong to each other and are responsible for each other. Friendship, he maintains, is much more than mutual benevolence, it involves a certain sharing, a *koinonia*, what Aquinas calls a *communicatio*, a sharing of life between friends.

True friendship, moreover, has to be based on more than a sharing of pleasures or of commercial interests, it has to be a sharing of the most fundamental human requirement, the virtues. Virtues, for Aristotle, are an absolutely necessary (though not a sufficient) condition for human happiness; for virtues are just the cluster of acquired dispositions necessary for living a flourishing human life. So, unless the citizens care about and seek to foster virtue, and thus happiness, in each other and in the community in general, there is no true polis: there is just a crowd of businessmen making honourable agreements in order to further their own particular interests. For this reason, Aristotle put at the basis of the state the kind of common life that is expressed in festivals and games and cultural life in general, for it is these things that foster friendship, and, as we should say, a common identity.

Now, if you think that Aristotle has got a point here, then it will not be difficult to, so to say, transpose *philia*, friendship, into a new key. As Fergus Kerr has shown, Thomas Aquinas proposed to treat *caritas* (primarily the love of God for us) on the analogy of *philia*, *amicitia*, and not, as generations of theologians had done, following Augustine, on the analogy of *amor*, the passion of love. *Caritas* means that God shares his life, his Holy Spirit with us, and that consequently we can share it with each other. In Aquinas the model for the plan of salvation is the establishment of a political community: but a political community understood in Aristotelean (rather than, say, Thatcherite) terms. For Aquinas the Church is the sacrament of this community-in-charity: as *Lumen Gentium* put it succinctly, 'the sacrament of union with God and the unity of humankind'.

The Church, then, is the symbolic visibility of God's outpouring of the Spirit in the world. In the world, please notice, not just amongst the members of the Church. The unity sacramentally symbolised and realised in the eucharist is not the unity of the church, as such, but of humankind; and it is a unity manifestly not yet achieved; though to love in charity is to have a foretaste or glimpse of it.

It is important to be rather clear about this. What corresponds to the *philia* without which there can be no true political society, is the divine *agape*, *caritas*, that is required if there is ever to be a true humankind: that future unity in charity that will mark humankind's coming of age. It is not the unity of the Church; for this is simply the sacramental sign of human unity. What the sacramental life of the Church is about is the

future unity of humankind (and our foretaste of that), not the
unity of this or that human society at any point in history. If the
sacramental life is the social cement that binds together a
particular society, it is merely in the way that festivals and games
and a common culture bind it together. One concrete exemplar
of the church as social cement is what we have come to call the
'establishment' of a church.

We have looked, then, at the Church seen as alternative, as
model, and as cement for society. Let me turn now to what I see
as a more promising model than any of these: the Church as
challenge to society. The parallel between this ecclesiology and
the christology I sketched earlier will, I hope, be plain. To put it
simply: Christ was not interested in political power, but
powerful politicians were very interested in him because they
felt threatened. Similarly, the Church (in its sporadic periods of
health) is not interested in political power, but these are the very
times when those with political power come to take the same
kind of hostile interest in the Church.

When Leo XIII spoke of the market economy of capitalism
laying on the masses 'a yoke little better than slavery itself', he
spoke from within a moral tradition that has much in common
with the socialist moral tradition but is not identical with it.
The socialist critique of capitalism is based on a fundamentally
Aristotelean version of human society, which you can simplify
by saying that it is about people before it is about products,
though it is about both. The making of people into
commodities was noted by both Pope Leo and Karl Marx, who
acknowledged his debt to Aristotle more than once.

The difference is partly one of perspective. The socialist is
analogous to a doctor who prescribes the right treatment for
some baneful disease – working within, let us call it, the
'hippocratic tradition' where he learnt his craft and science. The
socialist like the doctor, is concerned with a particular virulent
disease – in his case the chronic condition of capitalism. He is
no more concerned with the coming of the kingdom of God, or,

indeed, with the coming of any kind of utopia on earth, than is the doctor with curing his patient of death. They are both tackling a specific job, presented to them by a particular juncture in history.

The preaching of the gospel (although of course it takes place at a particular juncture of history) has its perspective not on an immediate and particular objective but on the *eschaton*, on the ultimate destiny of human beings and humankind. That is why, unlike socialism as such, the gospel is not a programme for political action: not because it is too vague and general or too private, but because it is also a critique of action itself, a reminder that we must think on the end.

Central to the gospel is the revelation that our salvation, in the end, comes not by our achievements but by the failure which is the cross, a failure accepted out of Christ's loving obedience to his mission from the Father and for love of his fellow men and women. So if I think (as I do) that all my fellow-Catholics should support a socialist immediate programme, it is not because I am a Catholic but because I am a socialist.

The Christian socialist, as I see her, is more complex, more ironic, than her non-Christian colleagues because her eye is also on the ultimate future, on the future that is attained by weakness, through and beyond the struggle to win in this immediate fight. But even short of the *eschaton*, the Christian is also more vividly aware, not only of the need to avoid injustice in the fight for justice (as any rational non-Christian socialist would, of course, be) but also of the need always to crown victory, not with triumphalism but with forgiveness and mercy, for only in this way can the victory won in this fight remain related to the kingdom of God.

Without that opening onto a future (and, as yet, mysterious) destiny what begins as a local victory for justice becomes, in its turn, yet another form of domination, another occasion for challenge and struggle we have seen time and time again in the history of the Church and the history of all liberation movements – remember that even the capitalist revolution could once be regarded rightly as a liberation struggle.

To return to the Church, the sacrament of the divine life in humankind. The sacraments belong, Aquinas reminds us, to the time between, the epoch between the cross, on which our salvation was won, and the *eschaton*, when the fruits of that great sacrifice of love will be plainly, and not just sacramentally, revealed. When there will be no longer faith but vision, no longer a church but just human beings in and through whose human lives God will be manifested, no longer in alienated, distant form but in our own lives. God will be all in all. For Aquinas, the sacramental and all that belongs to religion and the church as we know it, is part of the time before that, the time of sin.

Like Karl Marx, Aquinas knew that religious cult belongs to human alienation, and that the passing of this alienation would mean the withering away of the church. But unlike Marx, he knew that the passing of this alienation needed more than the establishment of socialism, or even of communism; it meant a revolution in our very bodies, a death and resurrection.

CHAPTER THREE

Living the Death of Christ Until He Comes

NICHOLAS PETER HARVEY

> Dying, he destroyed our death;
> Rising, he restored our life...

It is worth noticing the weakness of the second claim compared with the first. This weakness springs from an atomised notion of the Paschal mystery wherein the death of Jesus has to be said to accomplish one thing and his resurrection another. This generates the notion of restoration as the best that resurrection can do; whereas the image of a death which destroys death has considerable potency. If death is in any significant sense destroyed we are already participants in a transformation-scene for which the word 'restoration' is both impoverished and misleading. Give me rather Ariel's song:

> Full fathom five thy Father lies:
> Of his bones are coral made.
> Those are pearls that were his eyes.
> Nothing of him that doth fade,
> But doth suffer a sea-change
> Into something rich and strange.

Here we touch more nearly on the mystery of life through death which is the theme of this paper.

Our faith has as its central act of worship the proclamation of a particular death, as if the world's whole destiny hinges upon it. The original context for faith was a bereavement, and there is an abiding strangeness about a faith that arises from the experience of a death; though the strangeness of this faith, as we find it chartered in the New Testament, has nothing in common with that of a seance. There is further strangeness in the fact that this was a particularly nasty and ignominious death, without any of the obvious dignity or shape found in martyrological stories or heroic sagas. Yet this is a death which, if the foundational witnesses are to be trusted, it is appropriate to proclaim, to celebrate, to live with a view to the consummation.

The New Testament books proclaim a memory, the memory of a man who both *chose* and *dreaded* a horrible and shapeless death. His dread is not disguised; yet his death is not remembered as a tragic necessity, nor yet as an act of resignation in the mood of our tubercular poet who found himself 'half in love with easeful death' and wanted 'to cease upon the midnight with no pain'. No. Jesus' death is remembered as something positively chosen, an act of love, a freely chosen identification in compassion with the deepest human anguish. It is a choice of victimhood, of the worst, of the unthinkable, a self-determined immersion in the tortuous and tortured ambiguities of created life.

This last phrase could suggest a form of masochism, but Jesus' perspective on his death is startlingly different: 'I have a baptism with which to be baptised, and how I am straitened until it is accomplished' (Lk 12:50). This sense of being strait-jacketed, hemmed in, limited, short of his death pervades the story. It does not merely succeed upon the outward-going ministry in Galilee but is interwoven with it. The thrust of his whole life is towards his death, as something desired, chosen, embraced in love out of a fullness of humanity. Here is the story of a man stretching life to its limit and so seeing death as the real limit. This man is alive to what death is and free to surrender his short-of-death life to it as the way to consummation. It is helpful here to recall Wittgenstein, 'Death is not an event of life.

Death is not lived.' Theologies of liberation and of healing will fall short of their creative potential if they fail fully to register the fact that mind and body die. Short of this recognition they will yield to the temptation to continue to think in terms of preparing for a future which is not God's, a future which we can plan.

That most dangerous adversary, the jovial simplifier, would already be interrupting to suggest that I am unduly complicating things: 'What's all this fuss about death? Death is a fact of life. Jesus faced up to it in faith. Then came the resurrection, which made things all right after all. It is the resurrection which is the proper focus of our praise and of our living. That really is something to celebrate.' This approach suggests that the death of Jesus was somehow undone by the resurrection, while the tradition, by contrast, shows his resurrection as declaring the true meaning of Jesus' death and, by implication, of all death. Death is writ large in the resurrection, for it is there seen as the gateway to an otherwise unimaginable fullness of life. It is in the light of the resurrection that the death of Jesus is hailed as having nothing less than cosmic significance. That which was accomplished in the death is declared in the resurrection.

The celebration of this de-death in the spirit of the resurrection broaches a range of sharp questions. What is specific to this death that it can have such resonance? What is specific to this death which makes it appropriate to speak of proclaiming it and living it with a view to the consummation? What is it about this death which changes the shape of all human living and dying; or, if you will, declares and promotes the true shape of all human living and dying? We need to notice, as theology so often fails to do, the way in which the early belief in Jesus' resurrection points back insistently into his death.

There is a view, associated with a former Bishop of Durham among others, that to accept as they stand the Gospel narratives of resurrection appearances and empty tomb would be to underwrite the notion of a selectively interventionist God. The image is of a God who takes positive action in this instance but allows horrendous suffering at Auschwitz and elsewhere to take its course. No doubt this unease is in its turn a reaction to a tendency to commend the resurrection in terms which do not point to the death, rather as if what happened at Auschwitz is somehow all right because Christ is risen. For such a view the raising of Jesus means that all issues have been resolved, and it seems to me obviously right to have reservations about this conclusion. But the anxiety about selective divine intervention forgets that Jesus' Passion is allowed to take its course: 'Having loved his own, he loved them to the end' (Jn 13:1). The resurrection in no sense undoes the suffering of the Passion, but makes it overtly scandalous. I am arguing that what the resurrection of Jesus gave to his chosen ones was precisely the sense of the overwhelming and abiding significance of his suffering and death, and that not merely in their lives but in the whole human story.

Of course there is no Christian story without the Resurrection; but our faith is in the raising up of this *particular man who has died a particular death*. Jesus is the one who *became obedient* unto death, even unto the death of the cross, *and so* has been raised in sign of the destiny of all humanity. He has been raised *from the dead*: the force of this image is that what is in store for all human beings has already happened to him. The implication is that it has happened to him not arbitrarily but in connection with his death in loving obedience. The reality of Jesus' anguished dying is in no way impugned by any statement about resurrection.

All four evangelists give a preponderant place to narrative of the Passion. This conviction that Jesus has been raised does not lead them to lose interest in the form taken by his movement into death, but rather the reverse. All is interpretation, of course; but what is being interpreted, and offered to the neophyte as saving, is the death. Paul says that we are baptised into Jesus' death (Rom 6:3). The letter to the Colossians even tells its readers: 'You have died, and your life is hidden now with Christ in God' (Col 3:3). Identification with the death of Jesus could hardly go further.

In a recent paper David Ford comments on 2 Corinthians 4:6: 'For it is the God who said, 'Let light shine in darkness,' who has shone in our hearts to give the light of the knowledge of the glory of God in the face of Christ.'[1] Ford argues that this face, which is neither separable from historical contingencies nor reducible to them, 'has also been dead. Yet it is seen as the manifestation of the glory of God, so that in future the glory of God and this death *cannot be thought* without each other'. The sense of an indissoluble conjunction between the death and the glory sharpens our questions. What is it that is specific to this death which has power to set at naught the worst that can happen? What is it about the death of Jesus which makes it to be the case that what Paul calls 'the last enemy' (1 Cor 5:26) will be destroyed?

In order to try to answer, or even properly to understand, those questions we need to recognise that our sense of death is distorted. I suggest that for us death is somehow off limits, repressed and therefore having about it an odd combination of remoteness and inevitability. Some effort of introspection therefore seems necessary to pick up the contrast between the vibrancy of Jesus' expectation of life through death and on the other hand 'death's magnet', that curious suction which the repressed thought of death otherwise exercises in the human adventure. Ernest Becker even argues that the whole human enterprise is conducted in flight from death, in denial of death. In so far as Becker is right we find here a prime example of that law of the psyche which says that anything which is merely repressed returns to threaten our stability.

---

1. D. F. Ford, 'Tragedy and Atonement', in *Christ, Ethics and Tragedy: Essays in Honour of Donald McKinnon*, ed. K. Surin (Cambridge: 1989), pp. 117-130.

The nuclear bomb, for instance, is the fruit of repression. The possession of such a weapon arises from and intensifies the illusion that there need be no end, while at the same time threatens our world with unprecedented catastrophe. I suggest that the anxiety which makes us mistrustful of life rules death out of court. It is as if we have not learned to live and so cannot die. The bomb then, shows us to ourselves, prompting Gerry Hughes SJ to write in *God of Surprises* 'the facts are kind'.[2]

The Gospel offers an alternative to this repressed sense of death. What is distinctive is that we discover in this story of a death a capacity for offered suffering and an invitation to us to live this way. An unrepressed sense of death makes of it something both desired and dreaded: desired in fulfilment of our destiny, dreaded as meaningless. In the story of Jesus there is evidence both of such desire and of such a dread. His approach to death seems to spring from a place in himself where life and death are not at enmity. E. C. Hoskyns draws attention to a dialectic in the story between Jesus' movement of response to the immediate needs of others and his movement towards his death.[3] It is dismaying that most theology is undisturbed by this dialectic. What do we suppose happened subsequently to those whom he healed or fed or delivered from evil spirits or raised from the dead? How does his dealing with them relate to his journey to Jerusalem to die? If we miss the underlying movement into death this question will pass us by, despite the recorded dismay, fear and disapproval of the disciples.

It is worth adding that the cutting edge is blunted if we make the journey to Jerusalem a campaigning thrust rather than a sacrificial one. Then his death becomes no more than an unfortunate consequence of his stance towards life. It would be something Jesus risked rather than something he deliberately embarked upon in his whole way of living. To take that view

---

2. G. W. Hughes, *God of Surprises* (London: 1996).
3. E. C. Hoskyns and F. N. Davey, *Crucifixion, Resurrection: The Pattern of Theology and Ethics in the New Testament* (London: 1981), Ch. 8.

would be to tell a very different and much less interesting story than the New Testament books, whatever else they differ on, consistently tell. It can even be said that the wonders Jesus worked were in sign of his death, for death is where he was heading as 'he set his face towards Jerusalem' to the consternation of those who accompanied him.

Jesus' approach to his own death comes through in the story as incomprehensible to everyone else but in harmony in his own mind with his work of teaching and healing. This, I argue, is how he sees it and lives it. This was not clear to me when I wrote my book *Death's Gift*, where I argued that for Jesus his death was totally at odds with his characteristic sense of burgeoning life and with his life-affirming mission.[4] His death was entered upon, I then claimed, in the conviction of faith that things would work out but with a sharp sense of a disjunction between life and death. I could find no place for a victimhood passionately chosen in loving identification with the predicament of others. The key thing, I think, was that I could find no such capacity in myself, and was therefore constrained to project onto Jesus an obedience not free of the taint of stoicism.

A connected point is the insignificance, in terms of the inner dynamic of the story, of the people who plot against Jesus and those who bring him to his death. The story stresses that his is a chosen destiny in the sense of something in preparation throughout his life and willingly entered upon at every step. Jesus is presented as having the freedom so to prepare and so to choose: 'My hour is not yet come' (Jn 2:4) or, more vividly, in his message to Herod: 'Go and tell that fox, 'Behold, I cast out demons and perform cures today and tomorrow, and the third day I finish my course" (Lk 13:32). In other words 'I shall be brought to book, but not now, and not by him.' This is not like choosing a university course or what to buy for supper. It is a

---

4. N. P. Harvey, *Death's Gift: Chapters on Resurrection and Bereavement* (Epworth Press: 1985; Eerdmans Grand Rapids, Michigan: 1995), passim.

chosen destiny, the enactment of which comes from within in the form of surrender seen as consummation. While at the time this freedom to obey put Jesus in a place equally inaccessible to friends and enemies, it is remembered by early believers in the conviction that his way has become our destiny, our gift and our call.

It would seem to be our hopelessness which makes of death the ultimate hopelessness. This anxiety, this hopelessness, is, I think, a central symptom of the condition which the tradition attempts to pin-point in the doctrine of original sin. What the Gospel affirms is that this condition is less than human, and that our vocation is to discover the normality of Jesus' way of life through death.

Original sin understood as a condition in which the whole human race finds itself has been described by Sebastian Moore as a universal condition of arrested development.[5] It is an inertial condition, a condition of non-growth, a stunted state involving a flight from understanding and therefore from reality. This state lands us with a range of distorted perceptions and has no proper place for death. Whenever we find ourselves thinking or saying, 'Things can't ever be much different from the way they are', it is this condition which speaks in us. Then there is nothing to hope for and death is no more than the logical end of all our striving. In this sense sin can only expect death, and so expose us to being negatively ruled by death. There is nothing else for sin to expect, and the death it expects is unthinkable because it is without meaning. Sin then has to deny death, which in its repressed state shadows all our projects and threatens our whole life's course with lack of meaning. The surrender invited by death is the polar opposite of the sinful condition. The fairy-tale meaning of 'the wages of sin is death' is that the wretched sinner deserves to die at the hands of a supremely just God. The deeper meaning is that the voice of sin

---

5. Moore, *Let This Mind Be In You: The Quest For Identity Through Oedipus to Christ* (London: 1985), pp. 84-6.

at work in us sets up a hopeless image of death, as indeed of God.

Woody Allen said, 'I'm not afraid to die. I just don't want to be there when it happens!' It is not the death of Jesus, looked at on its own, which is distinctive. It is the place this death has in his life. It is this death as the meaning of his life: as such it changes the shape of all human living and dying, for ever. It is, most strangely and yet most fittingly, the act of obedience towards which his whole life moves and in which the world is changed. The spirit of this death is quite other than either martyrdom or death-wish. In this man who journeys toward death we find someone who is living his own life. Discovering the capacity to live your own life is, I believe, more central to conversion than any sense of sin. Jesus, after all, was believed to have been without sin and yet his baptism in the Jordan has the hallmarks of a conversion experience. From there, you might say, he never looks back to the 'hidden' or subject life. Only as we come upon and act out this freedom to live our own lives can death find its proper place, without morbidity or despair.

Two examples are to hand. The first is a forty-year-old woman emerging from a long depression, who has this to say:

> The world has not changed, there is so much evil and meanness all around me, and I see it even more clearly than before. Nevertheless, for the first time I find life really worth living. Perhaps this is because, for the first time, I have the feeling that I am really living my own life. On the other hand, I can understand my suicidal ideas better now – it seemed pointless to carry on – because in a way I had always been living a life that wasn't mine, that I didn't want, and that I was ready to throw away.[6]

---

6. Alice Miller, *The Drama of the Gifted Child* (New York: Basic Books, 1981), Ch. 1.

Only the life of someone living his or her own life can become a story of true self-love and therefore of self-gift. My second example makes this rather more explicit. It is from the diary of Etty Hillesum, a Dutch Jew in her mid-twenties as the Nazi occupiers' drive against Jewish people in Holland moved into top gear.[7] She is surrounded by people in the grip of fear, resentment, fatalism, or the illusion, clearly recognised as such by Etty, that the allies will somehow prevent the cataclysm which looms. Here are her words:

> I only want to try to be true to that in me which seeks to fulfil its promise. …I have matured enough to assume my 'destiny', to cease living an accidental life. …It is no longer a romantic dream or the thirst for adventure, or for love, all of which can drive you to commit mad and irresponsible acts. No, it is a terrible, sacred, inner seriousness, difficult and at the same time inevitable.

Later, and cheerfully, she went to Auschwitz, where she died, having been a tremendous encouragement to others.

Jesus' approach to his death as something desired, as something short of which he was constricted, left his friends in total disarray. They could not cope with the deathward direction of this life which they could only interpret as life-affirming in an unredeemed sense, stopping short of death. There was for them an appropriate disillusionment. They came to see the force of Jesus' searing words to the sign-seekers that the only sign that mattered was the sign of Jonah: that is to say, himself dead, Jesus in the heart of the earth. That is precisely the movement of chosen and offered victimhood. That is how he became, in being raised from the dead, the burning centre of this universe, the one in whom our cosmos finds its godward meaning, no longer bound in any sense by death.

---

7. E. Hillesum, *Etty: A Diary 1941-43* (London: 1983).

My argument is that Jesus died the first properly human death, that horrible death chosen and offered in love being the enactment of his sinless perception of the human predicament. In the dying of that death the human flight from reality is put into reverse: the death of Jesus unlocks in humanity our freedom to obey. Through his death the Spirit is ready to open up in us that capacity freely to embrace our vocation. Thus is Paul led to exclaim: 'Having nothing, we possess all things' (2 Cor 6:10).

Obedience is the key: 'my meat is to do the will of him that sent me' (Jn 4:34). Not 'my duty' or 'my obligation' but 'my meat', is my nourishment, my very life's blood, that which makes me who I am, is the doing of this will. This will itself remains opaque to the outsider, for there is no frame of reference to which appeal can be made to check out Jesus' reading of it. This obedience is vocational. The word has strong connotations of listening, of honouring the other as other, of attentivity and receptivity, of an observant wakefulness, of being attuned to the fundamental dynamic of things.

To say that there is no obvious frame of reference for Jesus' obedience is not to say that there is no context for it. The choice he makes is not at all the context-free 'authentic decision' of the existentialist, without historical formation or future. The New Testament gives the impression that Jesus saw himself as very much part of his people's story and in particular as the fulfilment of the prophecies in the Jewish scriptures. Some biblical scholars, finding difficulty with this picture, have taken it to be a later construction by the evangelists. I find myself wondering whether this suggestion is one way of denying the centrality of Jesus' death. Without such a personal sense of a particular historical destiny with universal consequences the story of Jesus would lack any distinctive coherence. If we cavil at his life and death consciously taking that history a decisive step further to become the story of redeemed humanity, then we baulk at that obedience which brought him to his death.

Any failure to make Jesus' death central leaves us with a de-centred theology. This de-centring may result in a hortatory Jesus, an exemplary Jesus, a Jesus of confrontation, a justice-and-peace Jesus, or a blandly resurrected Jesus. All of these christologies assume, mistakenly to my mind, that the Gospel is about the good life rather than life with the living God. Missing from them all is any real sense of Jesus as the one who died the saving death, that death which both is and promotes the consummation of all things if we can find it in ourselves to hear his call and to live his gift. It is possible, I suppose, for theology to be in an original sinful state, in which case we very much need to hear the word of life through death: 'Choose life, says the Lord, I will not the death of a sinner, but that he be converted and live'.

CHAPTER FOUR

Mary at the Margins:
Christology and Ecclesiology in Modernity

SARAH JANE BOSS

You have to understand what it is that you want to leave behind.

–PIERRE BOULEZ

Every published history of Marian doctrine claims that Francis Suarez was the founder of modern mariology; and this claim is more or less true.[1] But there are other, less well-attested claims about Suarez, and one of these concerns the process for his canonisation. According to oral tradition, when Suarez's body was exhumed for examination, it was found that there were scratch marks on the inside of his coffin. This raised the possibility that the holy man might have suffered the sin of despair before he died, and for this reason, he could not be canonised. I suggest, however, that if Suarez really did suffer from despair, then this was most probably a reaction to some of the developments in mariology which had occurred since the time of his burial. Indeed, it would be surprising if all the great Marian theologians of Western Christianity were not now turning fairly vigorously in their graves and reliquaries. This

---

1. Heinrich Stirnimann, *Mariam: Marienrede an einer Wende* (Freiburg: 1989), p. 134. Michael O'Carroll, *Theotokos: A Theological Encyclopedia of the Blessed Virgin Mary* (Dublin: 1982), p. 334. Hilda Graef, *Mary: A History of Doctrine and Devotion* (London: 1985), part 2, p. 21. Marina Warner, *Alone of All Her Sex: The Myth and the Cult of the Virgin Mary* (London: 1978), p. 39.

paper is largely concerned with identifying what it is that has gone wrong with mariology and what needs to be done to soothe the unquiet graves.

In 1963, René Laurentin published a book entitled *La Question Mariale*, 'The Marian Question'.[2] I offer this paper partly by way of contribution to *une réponse* – an answer. Because although *La Question Mariale* was written more than thirty years ago – even before the Fathers of the Second Vatican Council had taken the decision to include the Blessed Virgin in the schema on the Church – it seems to me that the situation which Laurentin then described has not radically altered. Laurentin presented a picture in which there were two competing schools of thought about Mary: On the one hand, there were the 'maximalists', whose mariology was sometimes called 'christotypical', since it understood Mary principally in terms of her likeness to Christ the Redeemer. Inspired by passionate devotion, the maximalists were constantly pressing for new Marian feast days and the declaration of new dogmas, such a Co-redemptress and Mediatrix of All Graces. In opposition to them were the 'minimalists', who, adopting a narrowly intellectual stance, wished to do away with many strands of Marian devotion, and favoured an 'ecclesiotypical' mariology: one which saw Mary in terms of her likeness to the Church, the recipient of redemption. Laurentin saw good and bad in both camps, and argued that the *Via Aurea* consisted in regarding Mary as 'entirely relative to God' and 'entirely correlative to the Church', 'in Christ, by Christ and for Christ'.[3]

If for the present we accept Laurentin's diagnosis, then we can say that in the years following the publication of this work, Marian maximalists have been largely suppressed, and a mixture of minimalists and Laurentinians have been in the ascendant. Yet a deep-seated problem which Laurentin himself identified

---

2. R. Laurentin, *La Question Mariale* (Paris: 1963). The British edition is *Mary's Place in the Church* (London: Burns and Oates, 1965).
3. Ibid., pp. 101-2.

has scarcely been affected at all in the last thirty years, namely, the separation of mariology from the rest of Catholic theology. Laurentin's analysis does not show how this separation is to be overcome, and it is this problem which the present paper is intended to address. Laurentin considered that the legitimate practice of specialising in various sub-disciplines of theology had in the case of Mariology become distorted into something which was unrelated to the rest of the discipline.[4]

I shall argue with particular reference to Christology that the malaise which Laurentin described still affects not only mariology, but Catholic theology in general. Like some nightmare of modern bureaucracy, the parts have become disengaged from one another, and have lost sight of the whole. In this situation, a question such as whether Mary should be understood in the context of Christology or of ecclesiology amounts to little more than rearranging the deck-chairs on the theological Titanic. The task that faces us is a radical reassembly of Christology, mariology, ecclesiology, and any other stray parts of the theological edifice. I shall identify one of the points at which it seems to me that this edifice has drifted asunder, to wit, at the point of reflection upon Mary's physical conception and gestation of God incarnate. And I shall argue that it is at this point that the work of reconstruction should begin.

The word 'mariology' seems to have first come into use around the turn of the seventeenth century,[5] referring to a systematic theological discipline which in practice had been underway since at least the 1580s.[6] Mariology was a child of the

4. Ibid., pp. 26-43.
5. Laurentin considers that the first use of the term was in Nicolas Nigido's *Summa sacrae mariologiae* (Palermo: J. A. de Franciscis 1602) (Laurentin, *Marie: L'Église et le Sacerdoce: I, Essai sur le développement d'une idée religieuse* [Paris: 1952], p. 211).
6. Suarez's *Questiones de Beata Virgine Maria* were composed in 1585 (J. A. de Aldama, 'Piéte et Système dans la Mariologie du "Doctor Eximius"', in Hubert du Manoir, *Maria: Études sur la Sainte Vierge*, Tome II [Paris: 1952], p. 978). An Englishman, Henry Annesley, had a theological work on the

Counter-Reformation and, more specifically, of the Society of
Jesus. It had a noble infancy, but has frequently failed to live up
to its youthful promise. Some comparisons between the
writings from the decades immediately following the Council of
Trent and writings from the decades immediately following
Vatican II will illustrate the kind of shift that has occurred in
theological perceptions of the Virgin.

In 1573, the Jesuit Gaspar Loarte published a book of
meditations on the rosary. The Jesuit historian John O'Malley,
in his book *The First Jesuits*, seems anxious to play down the
extent of early Jesuit devotion to the Virgin, and he comments,
'Loarte's meditations on the rosary... dealt more explicitly with
the life of Christ than with Mary.'[7] This assertion is not only
untrue, but it presupposes an opposition between the figures of
Christ and Mary which Loarte would certainly have rejected.
For in the Preface to the meditations, Loarte explains to the
reader that his original intention had been principally to write a
work on the life of Christ; but when he realised that meditations
on the complete mysteries of Christ's life would be too long, he
decided instead to write only upon the mysteries of the rosary,
since the chief points of the life of Christ are contained in
them.[8] Loarte thus chose a Marian devotional practice as the
vehicle for meditations upon the Lord. Furthermore, Loarte's
concluding prayers for each of the meditations are addressed to
the Virgin, even when she does not take any physical part in the
particular mystery concerned. This clearly suggests that for
Loarte there is no competition between Christocentric and
Mariocentric devotion. On the contrary, meditation upon the

Virgin published at Ingolstadt in 1589 (Gerard M. Corr, *Devotion to Our Lady
among English Catholics in the Seventeenth and Eighteenth Centuries* [London:
CTS, 1992], p. 10).
7. John W. O'Malley, *The First Jesuits* (Cambridge Mass and London: 1994),
p. 270.
8. Gaspar Loarte, *Instructions and Advertisements, how to Meditate on the
Misteries of the Rosarie of the most holy Virgin Mary* (Rouen: Cardin Hamillon,
1613), pp. 18-19.

Mother of God is something which is undivided from meditation upon God incarnate.

Yet the notion of some theological or devotional opposition between Christ and Mary would not have been unknown to Loarte. For Protestants had for a long time been complaining that Catholics elevated Mary too highly in relation to Jesus. The year 1577 saw the publication of the vast *Opus Marianum* of Peter Canisius. This work was written as a response to Lutheran propaganda, and is frequently concerned to demonstrate that the Catholic Church's teaching about Mary means not that she eclipses Christ but, on the contrary, that her graces and privileges reveal the vast extent of his goodness and wisdom.[9] The praises that are heaped upon Mary are in no way a diminishment of her son.

Nevertheless, in the Catholic Church itself, the separation of Christ from Mary in both worship and theology has tended to increase over time down to the present day. This is seen very vividly in the liturgy, where a rigid distinction is drawn between feasts of the Lord and feasts of the Virgin, and the Annunciation is designated as Dominical rather than Marian. In the calendars and martyrologies of the earlier Middle Ages, the Annunciation is sometimes called 'the conception of the Lord' or 'Mary the Mother of God's conception of the Lord'; but in other places it is called 'the conception of St Mary'. Likewise, the feast of Mary's conception in the womb of her mother St Anne is sometimes called 'the conception of St Mary', but sometimes 'the conception of St Anne'.[10] This strongly suggests that the conception of a child in the womb was understood as an event which involved mother and child equally, and would not be regarded in terms of one to the exclusion of the other.

---

9. This, for example, is one of the arguments in defence of the Immaculate Conception. Peter Canisius, *De Maria Virgine Incomparabili, et Dei Genetrice Sacrosancta* (Ingolstadt: David Sartorius, 1677), p. 39.
10. Mary Clayton, *The Cult of the Virgin Mary in Anglo-Saxon England* (Cambridge: 1990), pp. 27-29; 38-43.

But in later discussions over the Immaculate Conception, a distinction in this matter came to be made very firmly, when it was argued that the sinlessness of Mary's conception did not pertain to St Anne's actively conceiving her daughter, but only to the Virgin's passive conception in her mother's body. A similar distinction was made by authors who considered that although Mary's active conception of Christ was miraculous, his passive conception in her womb was natural. This distinction between the passive conception of an infant and the active conception of the mother has become an occasion for wrenching the two apart in the designation of the Annunciation as a feast of Our Lord and not of Our Lady. For the mystery which is the source of all Mary's other privileges is now excluded from the Marian liturgy.

For much of the Middle Ages, however, the Annunciation was the Virgin's principal feast day. Over the centuries it was gradually supplanted by the Assumption, and the new calendar's effective designation of the Assumption as the Virgin's principal solemnity, together with the exclusion of the Annunciation from the Marian list altogether, constitutes an official ratification of this state of affairs 'with brass knobs on'. Lady Day, the feast which celebrates the most perfect and intimate union between Christ and his mother, has effectively been replaced by the Assumption, which, by comparison, can easily be construed in such a way that Mary is set at some distance from her son. This liturgical development also has the consequence of creating the impression that Mary does not belong in the Bible so much as in the Apocrypha.

And at this point, one can spot a gentle irony. For a very great devotion to the Assumption might be taken as a sign of so-called 'Marian maximalism'. But any devotion which sets Mary apart from Christ has an implicit tendency to make Mary marginal to the primary focuses of Christian worship. For Christianity is centrally concerned with Christ, and so the more closely we associate Mary with Jesus, the more deeply ingrained she will be in all aspects of Christian life. Conversely, if we hold elaborate festivals for the Assumption, Our Lady's Birthday and the Immaculate Conception, but do not honour Mary equally on Lady Day, Christmas and Candlemas – that is, on the feasts which she shares with the Lord – then she is constantly vulnerable to being pushed out of the main body of Christian liturgy and teaching. So perhaps the decline in Marian festivities which occurred after Vatican II was in some measure a case of the devotional 'maximalists' being hoist by their own petard. This implies that at least to a limited extent the term 'maximalist' is something of a misnomer. Marian 'maximalists' and Marian 'minimalists' can both turn out to be Marian marginalists.

Yet if we turn back to Mariology's founding father, and see what Suarez considers to be important about the Virgin, then we find that she is not only placed close to Christ but is, of course, a pivotal figure in the whole economy of salvation. Since God chose the Incarnation as the means for salvation, the woman who gave Christ his humanity is of key importance for our redemption. Suarez's Mariology derives entirely from the doctrine of the divine motherhood, that is, the fact that Mary is Mother of God. Modern authors are sometimes careful to point out that the term 'Mother of God' signifies more than Mary's physical conception and childbearing. They state that the condition of motherhood entails caring and educative functions, and that in Mary's case, it might also be taken to include her consent to Gabriel's message.

In Suarez's writing, however, although he almost always uses the term *Mater Dei* – Mother of God – the sense in which he uses it means that it can rarely be distinguished from the terms *Dei genitrix* and *Deipara* – conceiver and bearer of God. That is to say, Suarez attaches great importance to Mary's physical conception of Christ, and to the fact that Christ's flesh was the flesh of the Virgin. He quotes words of Gregory Nazianzus, 'If anyone does not believe St Mary to be the Godbearer, that

person is without divine understanding.' For this reason, says
Suarez, the Fathers call the Virgin, 'throne, bridal chamber,
tabernacle, and temple of God'.[11] He goes on to lay great
emphasis upon the dignity which accrues to Mary because her
flesh was shared with Christ, and because her blood and her
milk nourished him, and thus were united to the Word of
God.[12] He concludes by saying that the Virgin retains a supreme
and excellent degree of dignity, because of her singular union
with and closeness to God.[13] Elsewhere, he enumerates three
ways in which the Blessed Virgin has assisted in our salvation.
The third of these is 'by conceiving Christ, the author of our
salvation'.[14]

Suarez raises a doubt, a *dubium*, about the merit of Mary's
physical conception of Christ. He says: surely what counts is
Mary's moral action of accepting the word of the Lord and
keeping it, rather than her physical maternity? To the woman in
the crowd who cried out, 'Blessed is the womb that bore you
and the breasts that gave you suck', Christ replied, 'Blessed
rather are those who hear the word of the Lord and keep it.' And
in this respect, Mary is surely no different from any other saint?
All the saints have done God's will in their own lives, and Mary's
virtue likewise resides in her acceptance of God's word.

In reply to this, Suarez insists that the divine motherhood is
of a different order; first, whilst all the saints are adopted
children of God, Mary alone is his mother, and divine
motherhood is a condition which is outstandingly different
from adoptive filiation. Suarez then wittily observes that the
woman who spoke of Mary's womb as blessed was not thinking
of Christ's divinity! Nevertheless, he says, the saints also
conceive Christ in a spiritual manner by hearing the word of

---

11. Francis Suarez, 'Commentarii et Disputationes in Tertiam Partem D.
Thomae', Q. XXVII, Disp. I, Sec. I:9, in *Opera Omnia*, ed. Charles Burton,
vol. XIX (Paris: 1860), p. 5.
12. Suarez, 'Commentarii', Disp. I, Sec. II:2, p. 7.
13. Ibid., p. 8.
14. Suarez, 'Commentarii', Q. XXXVIII. Art. AV, Disp. XXIII, Sec. I:4, p. 331.

God and keeping it.[15] Thus, Mary simultaneously has a unique and essential part to play in the work of salvation, but is also one of the saints. Her divine maternity is an unparalleled honour, but her response to the Word of God is an example for everybody else. There are occasions in Suarez's writing when Mary seems to occupy a mediate position between Christ and the Church; but in general, she is not placed at a distance from either. She belongs to both: on the one hand, bound to Christ with a unique intimacy; on the other hand, the most eminent member of the communion of saints.

The sense that Mary is exceptionally privileged and closest to Christ, yet also one of the redeemed, pervades the Marian writings of Counter-Reformation theologians. Canisius calls her our Mediatrix because she constitutes the connection between Christ and ourselves.[16] The bond between God and humanity is established in Christ, but in this union of divinity and creation, it is Mary who gives Christ his flesh and thus connects us to God in her son.

It was frequently by way of replying to Protestants that authors such as Canisius and Suarez developed their refined understanding of Mary's place in the scheme of salvation. Martin Luther's commentary on the Magnificat provides an instructive contrast to the writings of the Catholic apologists. Luther continually emphasises Mary's lowliness, and states:

> the masters who so depict and portray the blessed Virgin that there is found in her naught to be despised, but only great and lofty things – what is it they do but contrast us with her instead of her with God? Whereby they make us timid and afraid, and hide the Virgin's comfortable picture, as the images are covered over in Lent.[17]

---

15. Suarez, 'Commentarii', Disp. I, Sec. 11:3-5, p. 8.
16. Canisius, *De Maria Virgine incomparabili*, Book 5, Ch. XII, p. 615 *se seq.*
17. Martin Luther, 'The Magnificat Translated and Explained', trans. A. T. W. Steinhaeuser, *Works of Martin Luther*, vol. III, (Michigan: Grand Rapids, 1982), pp. 156-7.

Mary, Luther says, should be an example of the grace of God, encouraging us to believe that he will regard us also as he once regarded her.

The phrase that 'they... contrast us with her instead of her with God' reveals the relationship which Luther assumes to exist between God and humanity: it is one of distance and separation. There is a gulf between God and ourselves which was once crossed in the life, death and resurrection of Jesus Christ, but which otherwise remains present. Mary must therefore be either on God's side or on ours. So those who greatly elevate Mary necessarily make her too distant from us. For Canisius and Suarez, on the other hand, Mary is precisely the figure who assures us that in Christ, the gulf between God and humanity has been permanently overcome – that the way is always open. To illustrate this, they use the Patristic and Mediaeval images of Mary as the bridge between God and humanity, or as the neck between the head, which is Christ, and his body, which is the Church. According to the writings of the Counter-Reformation, when we look at Mary we see God's glory active and manifest within the created order. For Luther, when we look at Mary we see only a moral example of someone who 'leaves herself out and ascribes everything to God alone'.[18]

Much contemporary Catholic writing gives the impression of having gleaned its mariology as much from Luther as from Suarez. Almost all contemporary authors contrast Mary with God and show little interest in her relationship with anybody else. She is not seen as the great Mother of God who is an object of reverence, she is merely a faithful disciple 'and an example to us all'.[19] Michael Evans, in a recent document on Mary which was commissioned by the British Methodist/Roman Catholic

18. Ibid., p. 138.
19. Some authors have suggested that it is Mary's discipleship which should be used as the basic principle of modern mariology; Joseph Paredes, *Mary and the Kingdom of God: A Synthesis of Mariology*, trans. Joseph Daries and Josefina Martinez (Slough: St Paul Publications, 1991), pp. 154-170.

Committee, states, 'Mary is nothing apart from the grace of God.' This is an odd thing to say, because it is true not only of Mary, but of everyone and everything that exists. Apart from the grace of God, everything is nothing. So why bother to specify this of Mary? Well, the context in which this statement is set might lead us to suspect that what is surreptitiously being suggested here is that even with the abundance of God's grace, Mary is still nothing, at least in the sense that she is of no importance. Certainly, this document contains no words of wonder before the All-Holy Godbearer.

Evans continues, 'Everything in her says to God, "Not to us, Lord, not to us, but to your name give glory"'. And this deployment of a scriptural quotation subtly creates the impression that the glorification of the Mother of God is not itself an act of praise in honour of the Blessed Trinity, but might in some way be a distraction from the proper object of Christian devotions.[20] So, rather as John O'Malley assumes that a devotional focus upon Mary is in opposition to such a focus upon Christ, so Michael Evans seems to suspect that the act of praising Mary is in competition with praising God. When we look back to Suarez, then, we might reasonably ask, 'What has now become of the Godbearer, the 'throne, bridal chamber, tabernacle, and temple of God'?' Or, to put the question more accurately, 'What has become of Catholic perceptions of her?'

The current tendency to keep Christ and his mother well away from one another is in part a consequence of what seems to me to be the single greatest difference between the mariology of the Counter-Reformation and that of more recent modernity, namely, a change in attitude towards the physical conception of Christ and the flesh of God incarnate.

We have already seen that Suarez attributed the greatest importance to the physical conception and to the fact that

---

20. British Methodist/Roman Catholic Committee, *Mary, Mother of the Lord: Sign of Grace, Faith and Holiness* (London and Peterborough: CTS Publications and Methodist Publishing House, 1995), p. 6.

Mary's flesh was Christ's flesh. The power of this idea is dramatically demonstrated by the following anecdote. On 13 August 1621, a young Jesuit scholastic died, who was later canonised. After his death, a piece of paper was found on which he had written the following words,

> I, John Berchmans, most unworthy son of the Society of Jesus, do declare before you and before your Son, whom I believe and confess to be here present in the most glorious sacrament of the Eucharist, that always and everywhere, in so far as a decision of the Church does not oppose it, I will profess and defend your Immaculate Conception. As testimony to this, I have signed in my own blood, and traced below, the sign of the Society of Jesus. The year 1621. John Berchmans, IHS.[21]

To follow the logic of Berchmans' actions, it is necessary to understand that the Virgin's conception was often understood as preparation for the Incarnation. Thus, Robert Southwell, in his poem *The Conception of Our Ladie*, wrote, 'Earth breedes a heaven for God's new dwelling-place'. Mary's conception is the beginning of the same flesh which is eventually to be united with the eternal Word of God in Christ. It is this flesh of Christ's which is again made real in the host on the altar. Thus, the fact that it was in the presence of the Blessed Sacrament that Berchmans made his profession of faith in the Immaculate Conception, has a significance that is greater than purely personal piety. The conception of the Virgin, the eucharistic host, and the name of the incarnate Lord – IHS – are all constituent parts of a single mystery, whose unity resides in the body of the Virgin: Christ's first earthly dwelling-place, whose flesh and blood he took for his own.

---

21. E.Villaret, 'Marie et la Compagnie de Jesus', in *du Manoir: Maria*, Tome 11, pp. 948-9.

Yet by the time of John Berchmans' death, a quite different understanding of the human condition, and consequently of the Incarnation, had taken root in European thought – an understanding in which flesh was accorded a much lower status. In 1618, the Spanish theologian Ferdinand Quirino de Salazar – an influential mariologist who also became an important figure at the court of Philip IV[22] – published a work which included Mary's co-operation in the work of redemption. Suarez and others had argued that the act of conceiving Christ was one of the ways in which she contributed to our salvation. Salazar rejected this, stating that this act of engendering was of itself 'a work of nature and consequently neither free, nor meritorious'.[23]

This opinion was not new. The notion that a physical condition could not be regarded as being of intrinsic moral worth is found in Mediaeval philosophy. However, in modern times, the opinion that Mary's physical conception of Christ was, in the words of Salazar, 'a work of nature and consequently…[not] meritorious' has become well-nigh universal. Furthermore, it has been accompanied by a loss of any sense that Mary's conception of Christ and her pregnancy are events of grandeur and wonder.[24] The importance of the Annunciation is now considered to reside almost entirely in Mary's acceptance of God's will.

It is true that theologians of the present century such as Edward Schillebeeckx, Karl Rahner and Joseph Ratzinger agree that Mary's free consent to become Christ's mother and the physical motherhood itself must be understood as a single

---

22. Laurentin, *Marie, L'Église et le Sacerdoce: I*, pp. 232-3.
23. Ibid., p. 244; quotation from *In Proverbiis*, 1618 (ed. Paris: 1619), vol. 1, VIII, 206-7, p. 62 1.
24. A notable exception to this, and to much that follows, is A. M. Allchin's *The Joy of All Creation: An Anglican Meditation on the Place of Mary* (London: New City, 1993). The concern of the present paper is with Roman Catholic theology and practice.

event.[25] It is the consent which makes the conception come about, but without the conception the consent would be of no salvific value (except perhaps for Mary herself). But these authors are clear in their conviction that the physical conception of Christ is not in itself a cause for praising Mary. Conversely, many contemporary authors attribute the utmost value to Mary's fiat, her free acceptance of God's will, which is considered to be of the highest moral worth. Adrienne von Speyr, for example, makes the notion of assent the dominant motif of her Marian writing.[26]

It should be noted here that the emphasis on Mary's assent to God's will is a feature which unites the Marian maximalists with the Marian minimalists. Both groups of authors place primary importance on Mary's co-operation with God's plan, and I suggest that this tendency is connected to the fact that both groups in practice understand Mary predominantly as a type of the Church. If one were to set out to construct a rigorously christotypical mariology, then it would be reasonable to base the parallel between Christ and Mary upon the fact that they shared the same flesh. The physical union could provide the foundation for union of a moral and salvific kind. In practice, however, modern Marian maximalists have not always done this. Rather, they – either explicitly or implicitly – associate Mary with the Church, and regard her as Mediatrix and Co-redemptress not so much because they want to make Mary similar to Christ, the Mediator and Redeemer, but because they consider these attributes of cooperation to be

25. Edward Schillebeeckx, *Mary, Mother of the Redemption* (London: Sheed & Ward, 1964), p. 70. Karl Rahner, 'The Immaculate Conception', in *Theological Investigations*, vol. I, trans. Cornelius Ernst (London: Darton, Longman & Todd, 1974), p. 203. Joseph Ratzinger, 'On the Position of Mariology and Marian Spirituality Within the Totality of Faith and Theology', trans. Graham Harrison in *The Church and Woman: A compendium*, ed. Helmut Moll (San Francisco: Ignatius Press, 1988), p. 75.
26. Adrienne von Speyr, *Handmaid of the Lord* (San Francisco: Ignatius Press, 1985).

proper to the Church. It is the Church which assents to God's will and co-operates in the work of salvation. The difference between Marian maximalists and minimalists is perhaps not a difference between a christotypical and an ecclesiotypical mariology, it is rather the difference between a high ecclesiology and a low ecclesiology. When the Church is seen as a source of redemption, then Mary is elevated. When the Church is seen as the recipient of redemption, then Mary is merely mundane.

Amongst those authors who might loosely be termed 'maximalist', central elements in their mariology derive from the work of Matthias Scheeben.[27] Scheeben considered that at the Annunciation Mary became not only God's mother but also his bride, since she and the incarnate Word were one flesh. Scheeben did not intend to suggest that a parallel relationship obtains in the case of any other human pregnancy, and the idea of Mary's bridal motherhood (*gottesbräutliche Mutterschaft*) is an allusion to the Pauline idea that the Church is the bride of Christ. Scheeben considered the bridal motherhood to be the fundamental principle of mariology. Otto Semmelroth, in the 1960s, drew on Scheeben's work to produce the most thoroughgoing ecclesial mariology, when he argued that it is Mary's function as *archetype of the Church* which is the basic principle from which all mariology derives.[28]

God required a receptive human co-operator in the work of redemption, and thus willed that the Church should exist. The Church, like a bride, gives her free agreement to be the Lord's helpmeet in the work of redemption and makes his work her own. All that is true of Mary follows from the basic principle that she is archetype of the Church. So at the Annunciation she becomes God's bride by her *fiat*, and simultaneously co-operates in the redeeming work of the Incarnation by becoming his

---

27. A summary of Scheeben's mariology is given in Graef, *Mary: A History of Doctrine and Devotion,* part 2, pp. 118-126.
28. Otto Semmelroth, *Mary, Archetype of the Church,* trans. Maria von Eroes and John Devlin (Dublin: Gill and Son, 1964).

mother. Semmelroth writes, 'In the divine motherhood, Mary was given the most perfect opportunity to pre-figure the Church in a co-redemptive way.'[29] Thus, Mary's co-redemption depends not on her likeness to Christ, but on her likeness to the Church. Moreover, Mary's status as archetype of the redeemed ecclesial body is ontologically prior to her actual motherhood, either physical or moral.

Yet surely Semmelroth's argument inverts the proper ordering of things: it is Mary's physical and moral motherhood which makes possible the Church's existence. John Berchmans' witness reminds us that the Church is entrusted with the responsibility of making Christ's flesh real again in the Eucharist: the true body, born of the Virgin Mary. What Mary once did for all time, the Church re-presents in the Mass. And it is at this point above all that the Church must keep in mind her closeness to Christ's mother, for without Mary we will forget the incarnate source of our own life, and hence fail to recognise Christ in the suffering flesh of the world we inhabit. The Church will then become an empty parody of redemption, cut off from the mystery which sustains her.

Now, the subordination of Mary's conception and pregnancy to her moral will has a Christological correlate, for what is of central theological concern here is the enfleshment of the divine Word, and much contemporary Christology has a tendency to attend only fleetingly to this fundamental aspect of Christ's human condition.

Amongst theologians of the twentieth century, it is perhaps Rahner whose Mariology is in its essentials closest to the mariology of the Counter-Reformation. He argues that, in giving her obedient consent to be the mother of Christ and in conceiving him in her womb, 'the co-operation of the Blessed Virgin in the Incarnation is, in a true sense, an immediate co-operation in a soteriological event, at the level of objective

---

29. Ibid., p. 117.

redemption'.[30] From the first moment of the Incarnation, the course of God's redemptive action in history was fixed, because in taking the flesh of Adam, the Son of Man was necessarily destined to die. His saving death was already inscribed in his human conception. So Rahner says of Mary, 'For us and for our salvation, she opened the way into our flesh of sin for the Eternal Word'.[31] Yet Mary is able to do this only because she has already received the grace which flows from the merits of her Son's death and Resurrection. In conceiving the eternal Son for the redemption of the world, Mary is herself most perfectly redeemed. Thus, in one action she makes a necessary contribution to the universal history of salvation and simultaneously accepts her own subjective redemption, thereby becoming 'the first of the redeemed'.[32]

However, Rahner does not quite maintain the balance between the unique character of Mary's task within the economy of salvation on the one hand, and her likeness to the rest of the saints on the other. For although he states that the difference between her and the rest of the redeemed is not one only of degree, this statement does not seem to have many consequences for the rest of his mariology. In Rahner's writing, the uniqueness of Mary's actions is often overshadowed by her likeness to the other saints. She becomes 'the best possible Christian' rather than the object of our gratitude and devotion. We have already noted Suarez's observation to the effect that 'hearing the word of the Lord and keeping it' is something which all the saints do, whilst the divine maternity is Mary's unique privilege. And it may be that Rahner's slight tendency to pull Mary into line with the rest of us is related to another tendency, which I have already referred to – that of emphasising the importance of Mary's consent to Gabriel's message, which is

---

30. Karl Rahner, 'Le Principe Fondamental de la Théologie Mariale', in *Recherches de Science Religieuse* 42 (1954), p. 491.
31. Rahner, 'The Immaculate Conception', p. 204.
32. Rahner, 'Le Principe Fondamental de la Théologie Mariale', pp. 498-9 and passim.

the action that she holds most in common with the other saints, at the expense of paying attention to her conception and childbearing. Rahner stresses the insufficiency of what he calls the 'purely biological' aspect of Mary's maternity when it comes to accounting for her importance in the salvation of the world. Indeed, the insufficiency of the 'purely biological' is a point which Rahner dwells upon, so that at certain moments it almost undermines his insistence upon the redemptive value of the Word taking mortal flesh.

It is not surprising, then, to find a similar tendency present in some of his Christological writings. For here again, he formally insists that the union of the eternal Word with human flesh is necessary if the possibility of redemption is to be offered to all humanity, but it is not clear that this has immediate consequences for his understanding of Christ's particular humanity. To illustrate this point, I shall take his essay 'The Two Basic Types of Christology'.[33] Rahner's contention here is that all Christology can be reduced to two basic types, the first of which he calls the 'saving history' type, and the second the 'metaphysical' type. The first, he says, takes the experience of the man Jesus as its point of departure and develops 'upwards' from below, whilst the second, a 'descending' Christology, proceeds from a doctrine of the Trinity and the Logos, who then make themselves known in Jesus. Rahner considers that Christology needs both these approaches, although in more than one respect he gives preference to the *saving history* type over the *metaphysical.*

However, this preference seems to be based upon a misrepresentation of what he calls 'metaphysical' Christology. If we assume that *saving history* Christology had a distant ancestor in Antioch, and that *metaphysical* Christology had a distant ancestor in Alexandria, then we must protest at Rahner's

---

33. Karl Rahner, 'The Two Basic Types of Christology', in *Theological Investigations,* vol. XIII, trans. David Bourke (London: Darton, Longman & Todd, 1975), pp. 213-223.

characterisation of the latter. For however much this Christology may be concerned with the pre-existing Son of God, it understands the union of God with humanity to be first and foremost 'the Word made flesh', or *incarnation*. When Cyril of Alexandria defends the divine motherhood against Nestorius' objections, he refers almost constantly to the fact of Christ's flesh since it is incarnation which underlies and sums up the whole of Christ's humanity. Cyril says,

> scripture does not say that the Word united a human person to himself, but that he became flesh. The Word's becoming flesh means nothing else than that he partook of flesh and blood like us; he made our body his own, and came forth a man from woman without casting aside his deity, or his generation from God the Father, but rather in his assumption of flesh remaining what he was.[34]

And this emphasis on flesh, rather than on other aspects of humanity, has an important consequence for our understanding of the scope of Christ's redemption. For our *flesh* is that aspect of humanity which we have in common with other aspects of the physical creation. Anyone who first sees a human body that has suffered a particularly violent death, and then looks in the window of a butcher's shop, will have no doubt about humanity's likeness to other animals, or about the transience of our mortal flesh. We are made of dust, and to dust we will most assuredly return. So it is partly because God bound himself not only to the human spirit and intellect, but also to our corruptible flesh, that we know that when God became man, he was not only redeeming humanity but uniting himself to the whole created order. And we know that the Word was truly made flesh because he was born of the Virgin Mary. Even when there is no explicit reference to flesh, it is still Christ's

---

34. Norman P. Tanner, ed., *Decrees of the Ecumenical Councils*, vol. 1 (*Council of Ephesus*, pp. 36-74), (London: Sheed and Ward, 1990), p. 43.

conception in the womb of the Virgin which is the most
common focal point for reflection upon his cosmic significance.
Gregory of Nyssa, 'the Father of the Fathers', addresses Mary in
a homily on the Annunciation,

> The Lord is with you! He is in you and in every place, he
> is with you and of you... The Son in the bosom of his
> Father, the Only Begotten Son in your womb, the Lord,
> in the way known alone to him, all in all and all in you!
> ...you have received within you the One who is so great
> that nothing in the world could him contain, you have
> received him who fills all with himself, for you have
> become the place in which has come to pass salvation.[35]

In the whole of the Christian mystery, there is no moment
that is better suited than the Annunciation for considering the
wonder of God's presence throughout the creation. For in this
event, the Second Person of the Trinity, through whom the
cosmos came into being, comes to dwell in the tiny space of the
Virgin's womb and thus, in this unique wonder, reveals to us his
sacred presence in all things.

However, this is not the only way in which theologians have
understood the relationship between Christ and the material
creation. One alternative understanding takes as its starting-
point Genesis 3:17-18, when the Lord curses the ground
because Adam has eaten the forbidden fruit. The earth, which is
subject to Adam's dominion, is cursed because of Adam's sin.
Hence, when Adam is redeemed in Christ, the curse is likewise
lifted from the earth. So instead of a doctrine of God's presence
throughout the cosmos, we have here a teaching that the natural
order is cursed and restored in dependence upon humanity's Fall

---

35. Gregory of Nyassa: PG62, 766. Translation (amended) from Constante
Berselli and Giorgio Gharib, *In Praise of Mary: Hymns from the First
Millennium of the Eastern and Western Churches,* trans. Phil Jenkins (Slough:
St Paul Publications, 1981), p. 25.

and Redemption. This seems to be the theology implicit in one of Anselm's prayers to St Mary. He says,

> Heaven, stars, earth, waters, day and night, and whatever was in the power or use of men was guilty; they rejoice now, Lady, that they lost that glory, for a new and ineffable grace has been given them through you. They are brought back to life and give thanks.[36]

Again, it is not by chance that the restoration of the natural order is set within the context of a prayer to the Virgin. For this restoration is dependent upon the redemption of humanity, which in turn is dependent upon the humanity of Christ. And Christ's humanity was given him by his mother. So Anselm can say to Mary,

> by you the elements are renewed, hell is redeemed... O woman full and overflowing with grace, plenty flows from you to make all creatures green again.[37]

In this way the conception of the Lord in his mother's womb is again the crucial moment of connection between Christ and the rest of the created order.

The question underlying this discussion is of course, 'What does it mean to be human?' It was by taking human nature that the Word brought universal salvation; hence, our understanding of human nature will determine what we consider to be essential about Christ's particular humanity. Likewise, our understanding of the person and natures of Christ will probably influence our perception of our own human condition. Now, for many hundreds of years it was taken for granted that the primary

---

36. St Anselm, 'Prayer to St Mary (3)', in *The Prayers and Meditations of St Anselm*, trans. Benedicta Ward (Harmondsworth: Penguin Books, 1973), p. 118.
37. Ibid., pp. 119-120.

defining characteristic of Jesus' humanity was his physical birth from Mary; but this is implicitly denied in many contemporary theological works. In his essay 'The Two Basic Types of Christology', Rahner suggests that the two types are rooted in 'the two poles of our basic understanding of humanity', namely, 'transcendentality' and 'historicity'. *Metaphysical* Christology derives from our awareness of the transcendent, and *saving history* Christology from our sense of being bound within the confines of historical process. But at this point, we must raise a query. For if our basic understanding of humanity is truly set out along a line between two poles of which one is *transcendentality*, then the other is not *historicity*. Christ's historical actions and their significance for salvation depend upon his first being a physical human being. The Word was made flesh. It is not historicity but *carnality* that most deeply determines our condition within this transient, limited, material order. And when we seek transcendence, what we seek to transcend in the first place is the fleshly state of suffering pain and mortality.

If we think that historicity is one of two poles in our basic understanding of humanity, then we need to ask who are the 'we' who are doing this understanding. The tiny baby and the adult with a severe mental handicap experience the world as human persons, yet it is fairly certain that they do not have a sense of themselves as participating in history. None the less, they are aware of every physical sensation and every fluctuating emotion, and it is these aspects of humanity which are evidently common to all of us. It is as though Rahner had edited the doctrine of Christ so as to include the historical man who was 'born under the Law' and 'suffered under Pontius Pilate', but so as to leave out the fragile infant who was 'born of woman', 'born of the Virgin Mary'.

A further illustration of modern Christology's marginalisation of the flesh is found in Gerald O'Collins' recent monograph *Christology*. As with Rahner, O'Collins wants to establish the importance of our physical being but, like Rahner, he fails to do so satisfactorily because he does not start by recognising that what it is to be human is to be 'born of woman'. With regard to Christ's humanity, O'Collins asks the direct question, 'What is it to be human?' and he suggests 'five essential characteristics: organic bodily existence, coupled with rationality, free will, affectivity, and memory'. He goes on to say, ' 'Dynamic' and 'social' could be the next themes to come to mind'.[38] After this, O'Collins observes that '[t]he polarity limited/unlimited catches essential aspects of the human condition.'[39] By 'limited', O'Collins means that we are confined to particular times, places and cultures, that we do not have infinite powers of any kind, and that our existence is dependent upon other people and upon God.

It is instructive to compare O'Collins' understanding of what it is to be human with that which is found in the Scriptures. For the authors of the Bible, the defining characteristics of the human condition include being born of woman, made from the dust of the earth, being in the image and likeness of God, being dependent upon the earth and our own toil for survival, and having dominion over other species. And this list seems to have a considerable amount in common with that of O'Collins. But it differs significantly from his in that every term in it is one of relationship: relationship with other human beings, with God, or with the earth, for example. In the Scriptures, being 'social' is not something which is merely additional to other human attributes, but is the mode in which all human attributes exist and through which one learns what it is to be a human person. To be fair to O'Collins, it must be said that he does try to convey the impression that society is of central importance to human life. He writes, 'Human beings,

---

38. Gerald O'Collins, *Christology: A Biblical, Historical and Systematic Study of Jesus Christ* (Oxford: Oxford University Press, 1995), p. 229.
39. Ibid., p. 230.

for all their capacity to live autonomously... are through and through beings in community.'[40]

But what is this supposed 'capacity to live autonomously'? Very many human beings – small children, and people who are severely sick or disabled, for example – have almost no capacity for autonomous living. Is O'Collins calling into question their full humanity? And what about the rest of us? For as a matter of fact, none of us would survive beyond a few days old if we were not constantly cared for by other people – typically, our mothers. And even if we are fortunate enough to be healthy adults who might, in extreme circumstances, be able to live independently of other human beings, we are always utterly dependent upon the air we breathe, the water we drink and the earth which feeds us. We are in no measure self-sufficient. Moreover, this shows that the state of being limited is not something which is grafted on to a more fundamental list of human characteristics: it is inscribed in our mortal flesh from the moment of our conception and defines our lives entirely. 'Organic bodily existence' necessarily entails relationality and limitation.

It is of course the case that other items on O'Collins' list, such as rationality, free will and memory, are human characteristics which Christ, as a human being, possessed (and neither does this mean that Christ's redemption is only for the benefit of people who have a full set of mental faculties). But we must insist that Christ's humanity is in the first place physical, emotional and dependent, because these are the fundamental characteristics of our human lives, and all other qualities rest upon them. O'Collins is evidently aware that these characteristics are of great significance, but he fails to convey their importance adequately because he begins his consideration of the human condition by thinking about analytical categories, rather than by turning his mind to the fact that Christ was born of Mary – that he was made of flesh and was dependent upon a mother's milk for his survival.

---

40. Ibid., p. 230.

Mary's physical motherhood of God is the assurance that Christ is human, and that all creation is sacred. At the same time, it reminds us of the fundamental characteristics of our own humanity: of our dependence and mortality, as well as of our likeness to the Creator. We need to be constantly attentive to the doctrine that Mary is *Dei genitrix*, and no amount of talk about Mary's 'yes' to God can be a substitute for this.

At this point, I think it is helpful to draw a distinction between the terms *flesh* and *body* as they are used of human beings. I am not saying that the terms are mutually exclusive: on the contrary, their meanings include a considerable area of overlap. Neither am I saying that the words are never interchangeable, they frequently are. Nevertheless, Catholics and others tend to use them in sufficiently distinct ways that it is worth noting some differences.

Flesh is a term which tends to be associated with sin, pain, pleasure, decay and mortality. *Body*, on the other hand, is often associated with redemption, integrity and eternity. A saint who has practised mortification of the *flesh* – and especially sexual abstinence – may turn out after death to have an incorrupt *body*. A secular parallel to this may be the woman who acquires what is supposed to be a beautiful *body* by starving her *flesh*. Sins of a sexual nature are called 'sins of the *flesh*'; but in Gerard Manley Hopkins' poem *At the Wedding March*, the author prays that the bride may be blessed 'With lissome scions, sweet scions, Out of hallowed *bodies* bred.' It is often said to be *flesh* which rots in the grave, but *bodies* which are resurrected on the last day.[41] This last example also illustrates another difference between the two terms, which is that *body* sometimes refers to a whole person, whilst *flesh* very rarely does. The pair 'body and soul' can sometimes be used interchangeably with 'spirit and flesh'. But whereas the term spirit almost never includes the meaning *flesh*, and vice versa, *body* quite often includes soul, as soul includes

---

41. It is worth noting that where the Apostles' Creed gives *resurrectio carnis* the English translation is almost always 'resurrection of the body'!

body. Thus, if a priest has five hundred souls living in his parish, these are not likely to be disembodied spirits. Conversely, if I say that the saints are resurrected as glorified *bodies* I do not mean that they are zombies.

I suggest that within Christian teaching, there is an understanding of what constitutes the proper relationship between flesh and body. Flesh is something which can occasion sin and which suffers the consequences thereof; but because Christ has taken our sinful and suffering flesh upon himself, and through the Cross and Resurrection has redeemed it, each person's flesh is sanctified and incorporated in its own body. However, Christians do not always keep the totality of this relationship between flesh and body in view, and at a given period of history they may tend to emphasise one aspect at the expense of another. In the later fourteenth century, for example, many people were understandably preoccupied with flesh. The Black Death and other calamities generated a distressed mood of anxious despondency which was expressed in an intense concern with the suffering of Christ, the sorrows of his mother and the fleshly torments of Purgatory and Hell.

Modern mariology, by contrast, is dominated by the image of the redeemed body. Mary has for many centuries been the principal example of such a body. Much iconography suggests that Christ retains the marks of his five wounds in eternity, and is thereby a constant reminder to us of our own mortality and of our sins which are the cause of his suffering. Mary, on the other hand, is the personification of bodily integrity: the perpetual virgin who is assumed, body and soul, into heavenly glory. Her Immaculate Conception has similarly been understood to signify bodily perfection and, even though the philosophical points which this involves have been disputed, modern Catholics do seem to regard an unblemished body as the icon of a spotless soul. In the Middle Ages, Mary's conception was usually represented either by the embrace of her parents, Anne and Joachim, or else by the figure of St Anne with the infant Mary visible in her womb. Both of these might be seen in one respect as belonging to the category which I have called 'flesh', since they are both attempts to represent an earthly, physical conception.

Since the sixteenth century, however, these representations have been replaced by the now familiar images of the Virgin standing alone, often at prayer as in Velasquez's *Virgin of the Immaculate Conception*, the Miraculous Medal, or the statue of Our Lady of Lourdes. This iconography was partly inspired by the visions of the Portuguese seer Beatrice de Silva,[42] and is supposed to show the Virgin conceived in the mind of God from the foundation of the world. Thus, these are images of a body, but not of those things generally associated with flesh.

In the case of John Berchmans' vow to defend the doctrine of the Immaculate Conception, I argued that an internal connection was implied to exist between the body of Mary and the flesh of Christ. Mary was exempt from the taint of sin so that she would be a fit dwelling-place for God incarnate, and so that her flesh would be worthy to be united with the eternal Word. Yet at the same time, it was only as a consequence of the death and Resurrection of this son whom she had not yet conceived, that Mary's preservation from original sin was brought about. Christ's flesh and Mary's body – Christ's body and Mary's flesh – could hardly be more intimately connected. Similarly, the Virgin's bodily Assumption was for centuries understood to be a consequence of her physical motherhood: the body which had been the bearer of God incarnate and had given him his flesh would not be permitted to suffer decay. Yet in modern mariology, this bond between fleshly conception and bodily redemption has been increasingly severed, as the redeemed body has come to predominate over transient flesh.

---

42. Marina Warner writes: 'Francisco Pacheco (d. 1654), Velasquez' father-in-law, laid down the orthodox iconography [of the Immaculate Conception] in his *Arte de la Pintura*, inspired by the visions of the Portuguese mystic Beatrice de Silva (d. 1490).' (*Alone of All Her Sex*, p. 246.)

The Annunciation is not now celebrated on a par with the Assumption.

The tendency to present Mary as a redeemed body which has forgotten its connection with the flesh is expressed with particular clarity in much current mariology which presents the Virgin principally in terms of her relationship with the Church – the Christian body *par excellence*. The notion that Mary is a representative or symbolic figure for the Church is of course ancient. The explicit identification of Mary as type of the Church seems to have been made first by St Ambrose,[43] but a similar association had been implied by earlier authors. Patristic and Mediaeval theology never forgot the connections between Mary and the Church, but it regarded the divine motherhood as more fundamental. Modern ecclesio-mariology is distinctive in that it makes Mary's identity with the Church the key to the interpretation of the whole of Marian doctrine. As I have already indicated, this trait is manifested in the work of theologians who in other respects are very different from one another.

In a modified ecclesio-mariology, Latin American liberation theologians such as Virgil Elizondo[44] or Ivone Gebara and Maria Clara Bingemer[45] have given precedence to Mary's typification of the redeemed community. Gebara and Bingemer see Mary as the community of Israel whose divine motherhood means that God's salvation is present in her midst.[46] The work of redemption has already begun in her. These authors present the doctrines of Mary's perpetual virginity, Immaculate Conception and Assumption as signs and realisations of the redemption which God intends for the oppressed. At various times and places, the peoples of Latin America have been raped and

43. Graef, *Mary: A History of Doctrine and Devotion*, part 1, pp. 84-5.
44. Virgil Elizondo, 'Mary and the Poor: A Model of Evangelising Ecumenism', in *Concilium* 168 (1983), pp. 59-65.
45. Ivone Gebara and Maria Clara Bingemer, *Mary, Mother of God, Mother of the Poor*, trans. Phillip Berryman (Tunbridge Wells: Burns & Oates, 1989).
46. Ibid., p. 100.

massacred, and dispossessed of their land and culture. In this context, Mary's virginity, her sinlessness and her bodily preservation are all taken as signs of God's promised kingdom in which people's health and dignity will be restored, together with the integrity of the land, and that violence and oppression will be forever brought to an end. In this way, a powerful association is made between present physical suffering and the hope for bodily redemption.

Furthermore, Gebara and Bingemer understand the doctrine of the divine motherhood to mean that 'it is in the frailty, poverty and limits of human flesh that the ineffable greatness of the Spirit can be adored'.[47] They thus present a more serious attempt than many other theologians to understand the flesh in the light of redemption. However, the almost exclusive association of Mary with the community of the redeemed means that the carnal connection between mother and son tends to get overlooked when the specific topic under discussion is something other than the divine maternity. Yet it is only this Incarnation which can make possible the salvation which liberation theologians are hoping for.

If we do not attend to the fact that Christ was born of Mary, then we can easily imagine the Church to be an ethereal body which has drifted apart from its origins in physical birth and death. We also forget the integrity of the human person; and we avert our gaze from the truth that God in Christ united himself with the very entrails of the material creation. Consequently, we construct an anthropology, an ecclesiology, a Christology and a theology of creation which are all awry.

It is perhaps the mariology of Rahner which again comes closest to maintaining the integral vision of the first mariologists. This is seen in his work on the Assumption. When writing of Mary as 'perfectly redeemed', and therefore as 'type of the Church', he asserts that what this means concretely is that Mary is the Mother of God. That is to say, if we ask the

47. Ibid., p. 98.

question, 'What would it mean to be perfectly redeemed?' the answer is, 'To conceive Christ in faith and in the flesh.'[48] The body which is glorified at the Assumption is the same as the flesh whose redemption was realised in Christ's conception; bodily assumption is the consequence of fleshly redemption. It is because Mary's redemption takes place in the flesh as well as in faith that the Assumption is the glorification of the body as well as the soul.[49]

Yet Rahner's argument implies an interesting line of enquiry which he never follows up. If what it means to be perfectly redeemed is to conceive and bear Christ, then what does this signify for the state of redemption in general? Consider the following poem by Dinah Livingstone,

The Eschatological Dimension

Pregnant woman cannot reach her feet.
She is a barrel.
Her fellow carefully rolls her about.
He's in bed with a whale.
He likes her like that.

On a good day she can understand
the astonishing thought
that Origen taught
that glorified bodies are perfectly round.[50]

If redeemed flesh is flesh which is pregnant, then will a resurrected body not still bear the signs of its conceiving and childbearing? The resurrected body of Christ still carries the

---

48. Rahner, 'Le Principe Fondamental de la Théologie Mariale', pp. 499, 511.
49. Karl Rahner, 'The Interpretation of the Dogma of the Assumption', in *Theological Investigations*, vol.1, pp. 215-227.
50. Rosemary Palmeira, ed., *In the Gold of Flesh: Poems of Birth and Motherhood* (London: The Women's Press, 1990), p. 28.

marks of his mortal wounds – redeeming flesh transformed into a redeeming body. Likewise, it is the same flesh which conceived and bore Christ for the salvation of the world, which is assumed as a resurrected body into heavenly glory.

With that, then, let us return to the mortal remains of Francis Suarez and to the scratch marks in his coffin. Are these marks truly a sign that he might have suffered the sin of despair? Well, I don't think so. On the contrary, I suspect that you just can't keep a good man down. So I will let Suarez have the last word. Writing of the Virgin's Assumption, he says,

> in as much as the body of Christ is taken from the body of the Virgin, they can be said in a certain measure to be one flesh. For this reason, just as Adam said, 'This now is bone of my bones, and flesh of my flesh', so Christ can say the converse: 'This now is flesh of which is my flesh'. Therefore, since it befits the flesh of Christ to be blessed and incorrupt, so it also befits the flesh of his mother, whose glory abounds in this honour.[51]

---

51. Suarez, '*Commentarii*', Q. XXXVIII: Art. IV, Disp. XXI, Sec. II.6, p. 317.

CHAPTER FIVE

Creation and Salvation: Green Faith and Christian Themes

JOHN MCDADE

In 1961, after speaking with Buddhist theologians, Paul Tillich remarked that 'the main characteristic of the present encounter of world religions is their encounter with the quasi-religions of our time'. It is in these quasi-religions that we see the quests of the human spirit for wholeness; they may be inchoate and confused, but they are intentional in character. His point is valid thirty years later, because the principal Western quasi-religion which has evolved during this period is not a frivolous transmutation of decadent capitalism. It is not 'what we do with our solitude'; nor is it a version of 'how to be a full human being by being a mellow Californian'. It is forensic, deeply extroverted – which makes a change from further hermetic burrowings within the psyche – and responsibly ethical. It is now the only discourse which can adopt the tone of serious moralism without provoking ridicule: both political rhetoric and Christian language do well to avoid the tone of sermons in their public utterances. It is gradually acquiring the status of the shared humanistic creed in which everyone can feel involved, the stem of 'natural religion' common to people of all creeds and none, the common feature shared by radically distinct perspectives.

This quasi-religion, which I shall call 'green faith', is a deeply serious response to the crisis of our relationship to the world in which we live. I intend no disrespect to its various manifestations by labelling it a 'quasi-religion': this term carries none of the dismissive connotations of 'pseudo-religion'. Green faith asks how human identity relates to the rest of the natural order – what Christian theology considers under the rubric of 'creation' – and, in the light of this, it proposes that only by living according to the constraints of this relationship is authentic personhood within a perfected creation attained – what Christian theology traditionally considers within the category of 'salvation'. Formal religious belief in the West may be quiescent, but an intra-mundane religiosity like this is an appealing alternative. I am tempted to say that green faith has taken the 'a' out of agnostic, and offers a contemporary variation on gnosticism's character as a phenomenology of human identity within a network of forces and powers.

The popular narrative of green faith offers its own mythical narrative of paradise (harmony with nature, still seen in pre-technological cultures), fall (the *hubris* which detaches human beings from harmonious relationships with nature), inherited sinfulness (an ecological concupiscence which threatens at the same time to destroy our very existence), a present crisis of apocalyptic dimensions (the death of the planet) and its moral and spiritual resolution (conversion and *metanoia*, leading to a new ecological future).

We should also recognise the theological hand of Joachim da Fiore and a green Marxist vision behind Thomas Berry's delineation of 'the historical sequence of cultural periods': the passage through 'the tribal-shamanic period, the neolithic village period, the classical civilisational period, the scientific-technological period, and the emerging ecological period'.[1] But, as with Christian linear and mythical patterns, accounts of this

---

1. The quotation is from Berry's 'Twelve Principles for Understanding the Universe and the Role of the Human in the Universe Process' in *Thomas Berry and the New Cosmology*, eds. Anne Lonergan and Caroline Richards (Mystic CT: Twenty-Third Publications, 1987), p. 107. This volume contains two articles by Berry himself and appreciations by others of his work. Further articles by Berry are contained in *Cross Currents* 37 (1987), pp. 178-244.

kind require questions which the simple narration presupposes but cannot satisfactorily answer.

Green faith argues that the balance between the human and non-human dimensions of the world is seriously disturbed by our human failure to live within proper limits, and that this is not only destructive of the eco-system without, it is also destructive of the quality of humanness within. It rejects the anthropocentric arrogance of human beings who behave as the lords of creation, in favour of recovering – for this faith, although prophetic, is also nostalgic and Romantic in impulse – a modest estimate of human beings participating responsibly in the network of life. Human *rights* over creation are replaced by human *responsibility* to recognise the rights of the other life forms in creation. Green faith seeks to work out a consonant anthropology, with ethical and spiritual consequences, in which human identity is located within a wider pattern of significant life. I would regard it as an attempt in the ethos of post-Christian culture to develop a secular spirituality of human life within the coherence of the natural order:[2] it is a valuable counter-balance to the now weary liaison between Christian spirituality and psychology which identifies introspection and psychological integration with the search for God and the redeemed life.

Green faith takes the human order, not as central, but as a function of the broader processes of the earth's character and development: if we are able to restore the order of creation, through an asceticism and modest human presence on the planet, this will be the required 'saving work'. Restoration, balance and harmony are the terms used to envisage a creation which has found its way back to an integrated identity. I would

---

2. An angry dismissal of this spirituality is expressed in a recent Evangelical publication, *What is the New Age?* by Michael Cole, Jim Graham, Tony Higton and David Lewis (Hodder and Stoughton, 1990). For a more entertaining and positive guide, cf. the editorial in *The Month* (August/September 1989), pp. 296-7.

suggest, then, that salvation is envisaged by green faith as an harmonious equilibrium of creaturely rights, which human beings ought to create and share in. The point to note is that the salvific process is located within the dynamic of creatureliness. Human identity is recovered, not in the tradition of 'inwardness' which has been so strong in Christian spirituality, but in participation in the cosmic process, harmony and energy. This might be our first clue for the working of the same themes within a Christian context.

We might also reflect that, in part, green faith is a reaction to the failure within Christian secularity to maintain the insight that the natural order is constantly under God's action. The tendency towards deism, as Eastern Orthodox theologians point out, may be indigenous to theological approaches which relegate the role of the Holy Spirit to a Christological postscript, rather than as the very condition of divine life *ad extra*. In addition, there is a repeated concentration on creation as a protological conception – what takes place in the first few milliseconds of the Big Bang – rather than as the condition of the whole natural order sustained by divine action. This has fostered the mistaken idea that the doctrine of creation is about what happens at the beginning: Stephen Hawking's *A Brief History of Time* seems to suggest that the question of God is to be raised principally in this context, as though God is more present, more real, more active *then*, in those first milliseconds, than at any other point in time. In addition, as I shall suggest later, we have allowed the balance between the two poles of 'creation' and 'salvation' to be weighted in favour of the latter: theology 'at the foot of the Cross' has assumed a dominance which inhibits a fuller development of creational themes.[3] It is significant that the agnosticism of green faith has offered a more sensitive response to the current ecological crisis than has Christian sensibility.

3. The most notorious critique of 'redemption-centred' spirituality is that of Matthew Fox in his books *Original Blessing* and *The Coming of the Cosmic Christ*. Cardinal Ratzinger probably made a wise decision not to accept Fox's

In addition to promoting an ecological wisdom within different established religious traditions, Jonathan Porritt speaks of 'the need to find ways of letting people reconnect with the Earth', especially those of no religious faith. Our human alienation from nature must be healed, he says, through presenting 'the abundance and diversity of the natural world as the primary revelation of the Divine to most men and women'.[4] This is a point which the Passionist Thomas Berry makes in his 'Twelve Principles for Reflecting on the Universe':

> The universe, the solar system, and the planet earth in themselves in their evolutionary emergence constitute for the human community the primary revelation of that ultimate mystery where all things emerge into being.[5]

One of the characteristics of green faith is shown by its reference, not to God, but to 'the divine as revealed in the universe'.[6] It is in 'the cosmic process' that the divine is encountered, and the self chasteningly rediscovered, within a continuum of creation that acts as the primary revelation of the divine. The status of what is meant by 'primary' is, of course, central: does it mean 'first', 'fundamental', 'archetypal', or

---

invitation to 'dance Sara's circle' in California. In spite of the misleading simplifications which Fox offers, there is no doubt that he has identified a serious weakness in our inherited tradition. Recommended holiday reading by Fox: *On Becoming a Musical, Mystical Bear: Spirituality American Style*, and *Whee! We, Wee all the Way Home: A Guide to Sensual, Prophetic Spirituality* (Santa Fe: Bear and Company).

4. J. Porritt, quoted in Cole et al., *What is the New Age*, p. 84.

5. Lonergan and Richards, *Thomas Berry and the New Cosmology*, p. 107. Cf. Berry's remark in the same volume (p. 38), '...it should not be difficult to accept the universe itself as the primordial sacred community, the macrophase mode of every religious tradition, the context in which the divine reality is revealed to itself in that diversity which in a special manner is "the perfection of the universe"'.

6. Thomas Clarke, 'Creational Spirituality', *The Way* 29 (1969), p. 78. Clarke's article is a valuable critique of Berry and Fox.

'unsurpassable'? But before we leap too quickly to assert that it is the Incarnate Son of God who is the 'primary' revelation of God, and that the world is a secondary manifestation, we should notice that Aquinas saw the very diversity of the world as a created sign of divine goodness. Individual creatures may be inadequate signs of God's perfection, but the complexity of what we would today call the 'ecosystem' is to be accorded a high status as a mediating representation of divine goodness:

> For God brought things into existence so that his goodness might be communicated to creatures, and be represented by them; and because it could not be adequately represented by one single creature, he produced many and diverse creatures, so that what was wanting in one expression of the divine goodness might be supplied by another. For goodness, which in God is simple and undivided, in creatures is manifold and divided. Hence the whole universe participates in the divine goodness more perfectly, and represents it better than any single creature. (S. T., la. 47,1)

The mediating role of the non-human creation as the corrective and authentic context in which human identity is to be lived points Christians in the direction of re-examining elements in our tradition in which the status of the created order is given high value as a 'mediation' of divine reality. Raimondo Panikkar's description of Christianity as essentially an 'iconolatry', the worship of the visible manifestation of the divine, is worth pondering. The visibility of the Son, to whom the Father gives everything that He 'is', arises from God's eternity. If 'in him' all things are created, then the visible universe is a constitutive feature of that divine imaging, 'emanating' from the God who cannot be seen, but who communicates existence and blessings in the joint visibility of Son and creation. The universe then, as a creation of God, is also a divine mediation. This is given iconic expression in Hildegard's great vision of the Trinity, where the visible Son, human and creaturely, emerges from the unseen ('geometric') depths of Father and Spirit.

We have lost the Aristotelian and Thomist sense that the whole of contingent reality is an active participation, an *energeia* or *actus*, through which the world has its own being in all its proper autonomy, integrity and worth only in the degree to which it is totally and immediately grounded in the creative agency of God. Equally, we have lost sight of the interaction of God and the creation which the Eastern orthodox *theologoumenon* of the divine energies offers: the creation participates in the sphere of the divine energies in which God is present to and in the creation without there being a confusion of the two orders of being. As Kathryn Tanner puts it:

> Non-divine being must be talked about as always and in every respect *constituted* by, and therefore *nothing apart from*, an immediate relation with the founding agency of God... One must say created being becomes what it is and this all the more fully, not by way of separation or neutrality from God, but within the intimacy of a relationship to divinity as its total ground.[7]

For the Chalcedonian tradition which Maximus the Confessor represents, the relationship between God and the creation is a 'communion of energies', a reciprocity between the Creator and a creation whose 'dynamic character testifies in itself to the freedom of God's presence in things, being in the whole of creation in its differentiation and yet not being

---

7. Kathryn Tanner, *God and Creation in Christian Theology* (Oxford: 1988), pp. 84-85. Tanner's work is a careful analysis of the regulative character of our language about the God-world relationship, building on George Lindbeck's approach in *The Nature of Doctrine: Religion and Theology in a Postliberal Age* (London: 1984).

divided, but holding it all together in Himself as Being'.[8] Maximus regards the distinction and interdependence of created things as a function of God's action:

> For God who made and brought into existence all things by his infinite power contains, gathers, and limits them and in his Providence binds both intelligible and sensible beings to himself and to one another. Maintaining about himself as cause, beginning and end all beings which are by nature distant from one another, he makes them converge in each other by the singular force of their relationship to him as origin. Through this force he leads all beings to a common and unconfused identity of movement and existence, no one being originally in revolt against any other or separated from him by a difference of nature or of movement, but all things combine with all others in an unconfused way by the singular indissoluble relation to, and protection of, the one principle and cause.[9]

Maximus goes so far as to speak of God's relationship to the creation as stages in the process of divine incarnation. Picking up the patristic theme of the relationship between God's truth (the Logos) and the dynamic intelligibility of creation (the *logoi* of creation), he speaks in terms of a threefold embodiment, almost a gradual incarnation of God's Logos within creation. The French Dominican Alain Riou summarises Maximus' approach which presents all the works of God within the framework of God's 'embodiment' (*ensomatosis*):

• The incarnation of the Logos in the *logoi* of created

8. Lars Thunberg, *The Vision of Maximus the Confessor* (St Vladimir's Press, 1980), p. 140.
9. 'The Church's Mystagogy, I' in *Maximus Confessor: Selected Writings*, *The Classics of Western Spirituality*, (London: 1985), p.186.

beings at the time of the creation of the world and of the four elements, when the Spirit of God covered the waters.

- The incarnation of the Logos in the *logoi* of Scripture and the four Gospels, when the Spirit inspired the 'prophets'.
- The incarnation of the Logos in our flesh, in the man 'of our kind', in the humanity that is ours, realising the fullness of the four cardinal virtues, when the Spirit covered the Virgin with his shadow.[10]

This approach points us in the direction of considering human salvation within the wider framework of the pluriform activity of the Logos in the world, and it shows points of contact with the pattern of green faith. As I indicated earlier, green faith presents salvation as the restoration of creaturely equilibrium, and subordinates human reality within the framework of the world's natural processes. In the language of Christian theology, salvation is placed within the overarching framework of the processes of creation. The drama of God's engagement with human freedom what we call 'salvation' – takes place within the context of the Creator's sustaining presence to the creation, as the moment of intensity which focuses the Creator's love. God's engagement with human freedom and responsiveness (the process that we label 'redemption') is the supreme focus of God's sustaining presence to the whole of creation.

If the themes of creation and salvation act, within the Christian tradition, as two poles corresponding to the broader context of God's relationship to the world, and the particularity of the divine action in Jesus two dimensions of 'context' and 'focus', perhaps there can be a partial tension between them simply because of the difficulties of holding the range of connotations together within the one account. Barth's approach is to hold creation and salvation together as the outer and inner dimensions of God's love, but it is in expounding redemption

---

10. A. Riou, *Le Monde et l'église selon Maxime le Confesseur* (Paris: 1973), pp. 62-63.

that his theology finds its true voice. Within the Reformed tradition, redemption is the necessary restoration of proper creaturely existence, so much has sin destroyed our capacity for blessedness. Less responsible writers such as Matthew Fox, for example, and to a lesser extent Thomas Berry, present a radical disjunction between the strands of creation and redemption: the tension has been lost in favour of a simpler model in which the theophanic status of creation takes precedence over the significance of the death of Jesus. As green faith points out, the dominant emphasis in Christianity is on the processes of redemption from sin, rather than on the inherent blessedness of creation. Within the complex structures of Christian theology, a choice is perhaps inevitable about which theme is to be accorded the greater importance.

Karl Rahner, in an interview in 1974 raises the question of what is 'the fundamental and basic conception within Christian theology'. His answer is neither Incarnation nor soteriology – neither Christocentrism nor the saving efficacy of the death of Jesus – but 'the divinization of the world through the Spirit of God, within which Incarnation and redemption arise as inner moments'.[11]

This approach locates the particularity of God's action in Jesus (Christology), and the engagement with human freedom which that represents (the death of Jesus), within the broader context of the God-world relationship. The specific history of God's action in Jesus is, therefore, the focus of intensification, the moment within the process which illuminates the whole, and which exemplifies the nature of the Creator/creation relationship. With regard to soteriology, it is significant that perhaps alone out of the great theologians this century, Rahner makes minimal use of the metaphors of soteriology: where Barth, you feel, cannot wait to proclaim reconciliation and regeneration in the *Church Dogmatics*, Rahner is reticent. The

---

11. P. Imhof and H. Biallowons, eds., *Karl Rahner in Dialogue: Conversations and Interviews 1965-1982* (Crossroads: 1986), p.126.

accusation against him, by von Balthasar and nearly every student of theology, is that he does not have an adequate account of salvation because his approach does not need a salvific moment and process. The reason, I would suggest, is that he opts for a structure of theological exposition which eschews the priority of the soteriological voice within Christian theology. His great work, *Foundations of Christian Faith*, is refreshingly free from the great metaphors of salvation. His is a modern attempt to locate Christian discourse within a philosophical account of 'the nature of reality' which reworks the patristic theme of the relationship of the Logos to the signs of divine presence within creation (the *logoi*). For Rahner, what takes place within the relationship between God and the diverse world of creatures is given exemplary expression in the Incarnation of God's Logos in the person of Jesus. Maximus the Confessor, with his version of a progressive 'embodiment' of the Logos within the processes of creation, is not far from the same line of thinking.

Those versions of the ordering of Christian truth which treat salvation as the central Christian theme are guilty, it seems to me, of being irreducibly anthropocentric, of placing human ambivalence at the centre of the theological scheme around which the other themes are deployed. Such a concentration on the human condition cannot but subordinate the status of the non-human order. The centre of divine action becomes the event of the Cross and the subjectivity of the individual (the detached, introspective subject) who is faced with the dialectic of judgment and mercy. The self-disclosure of God in the hiddenness of the crucifixion is elevated as the sole *locus revelationis*, the centre of all *authentic* theology, with a consequent relegation of the divine presence in the rest of creation. The *pro nobis* of the redemption occupies centre stage, with the rest of the created order as the backdrop to the real drama between God and sinners.

This strand, which is characteristic of the Augustinian

Reformed tradition, manifests little appreciation of the mediating role of created reality in the individual's relationship with God – indeed, in its most extreme statements, there is an explicit denial that any created reality other than the humanity of Jesus and the words of Scripture can mediate God.

Neither is it an accident that it is this tradition which is most tempted to treat the death of Jesus as an event which 'affects' God: the death of Jesus is taken to be the divine experience of 'perishing', 'nothingness', the creation's annihilating dimension. Because the constraints which regulate the difference between God and the world have been weakened, and because there is a tacit uncertainty about the mode of divine presence to the whole creation, the crucifixion becomes an event in which the Trinitarian God is affected by death. It is as though there has to be a divine presence in the death of Jesus as the point of contact between divine compassion and the suffering of the world, because there is no adequate account of the divine presence to the creation: God has to be the 'subject' of a human death to have any real relation to the world.[13]

But if the primacy in the relationship between creation and salvation is given to the Creator-creation relationship, there are some corrective principles which regulate how the death of Jesus is to be interpreted. For one thing, the distinction between God and the world may not be dissolved in a way which interprets the death of Jesus as a pathology of divine suffering, a set of experiences which affect the Trinitarian life by introducing something 'new'. The primordial and mysterious relationship

---

13. Moltmann and Jüngel are the best known presenters of this theme in which the death of Jesus marks a moment of division or separation within the Trinitarian life: 'Here, in the relationship between the Father and the Son, a death was experienced which has rightly been described as "eternal death". If we take the relinquishment of the Father's name in Jesus' death cry seriously, then this is even the breakdown of the relationship that constitutes the very life of the Trinity' (J. Moltmann, *The Trinity and the Kingdom of God* [London: 1981], p. 80). Does not this collapse the distinction between God and the world and simply make God the biggest, suffering thing within the world?

between God and the non-divine is not breached by the death of Jesus: although the significance of this death can be explored metaphorically in, for example, the Anselmian scheme of the intrinsic demands of justice, its significance from the point of view of a doctrine of creation lies in its being the deepest communion of God with the creaturely distance and freedom which the Logos has assumed. In the language of patristic Christology, the death of Jesus affects only his human nature: there is no monenergist event of 'divine dying', such as some contemporary process theologians present. The patristic theologoumenon of the Logos and the *logoi*, Maximus' theme of the reciprocity between the divine *energeia* and the diverse *energeia* of the creation and the Chalcedonian distinctions between the divine and created natures should still be operative in our treatment of the death of Jesus.

There is no adequate language for this distinction-in-communion of God and the world. Peter Geach's image for this relationship is simple: 'God sustains the world as a singer sustains his/her song'. Classically, the relationship is best described negatively, through the adverbs of the Chalcedonian definition: the natures of Christ are said to exist 'without confusion, without separation': never confused – as though the divine and the human can be fused like wine and water in a

---

Jüngel is even more hermetic, and certain, about the mode of divine experience, 'Talk about the death of God means, accordingly…: a) that God involved himself with nothingness; b) that God involved himself with nothingness in the form of a struggle; c) that God struggles against nothingness by showing it where its place is; d) that God gives nothingness a place within being by taking it on himself…. God is that one who can bear and does bear, can suffer and does suffer, in his being the annihilating power of nothingness, even the negation of death, without being annihilated by it' (*God as the Mystery of the World* [Edinburgh: 1983], p. 219). With language like this we are back in the mythical primal sea where God wrestles with the dragon of chaos (Psalm 74:13-14). For a refreshingly sane Thomist alternative to these mystifications, cf. H. McCabe, 'The Involvement of God' in *God Matters*, ed., T. Radcliffe (London: 1987), pp. 39-51; cf. also, J. McDade, 'The Trinity and the Paschal Mystery', *Heythrop Journal* 29, (1988), pp. 175-91.

pantheist mingling – and never separated, as though there is an autonomous creation which is outside God's action. These adverbs regulate also the two orders of God and the whole creation. The adverbs identify an indefinable 'x' between God and the non-divine, identified negatively, but not explained; and in this way, the formula preserves the distinction between the two orders of existence in their closest proximity in the Incarnate Word. What takes place in Christ is the supreme instantiation of God's presence to, and in hypostatic relationship to, created reality. The goal of the Incarnation is to be the point of intensity in which there is, in the language of Maximus the Confessor, a communion between energies, the divine self-bestowal to the creation and the responsiveness of the creation which in humanity has developed to the point of reflective and responsible activity.

And this active freedom between God and the creaturely identity of the Incarnate Son is the supreme focus of what takes place at Calvary. The Incarnation itself is the supreme act of divine grace, which manifests and carries into effect the creative communion between God and the creation. The nadir of the Son of God's creatureliness is, I would suggest, not the physical fact of his dying, but his obedient creatureliness, the orientation of his mind, heart and will towards God, in which, as von Balthasar puts it, 'he can give to his love the character of obedience to such a degree that in it he experiences the complete godlessness of lost man'.[14]

I want to propose that the mistake which is made in approaches such as those of Moltmann and Jungel is the assumption that death is the point of vulnerability within creation. But the point where destructiveness is operative in creation is not in the fact of death, but in the moral evil associated with human freedom: this is the point at which the engraced creation acquires the ability to appropriate its divinely sustained identity, with the corresponding capacity to deny and

---

14. H. U. von Balthasar, *Elucidations* (London: 1975), p. 51.

refuse it. It is sin, not death, which is evil; death is a biological fact of all organic life. At the level of our metaphors, death and sin interact, and death stands as the symbol of sinful destructiveness; at the level of actuality, they are separable and ought to be distinguished. Death is not the supreme countersign to divine goodness; it is not the obverse of 'being'. That status is to be assigned to human malice which has so ravaged both the human and the non-human spheres that we can no longer separate the world from the effects of its destructive presence. The human will has malevolently and indelibly inscribed itself on the world's experience – a point which is often ignored in our estimates of 'natural evil'. Paul Ricoeur makes the point succinctly, and we should, in all justice, extend his principle to the impact of human malice on the non-human order:

> If we were to remove the suffering inflicted by people on other people, we would see what remained of suffering in the world, but to tell the truth, we have no idea of what this would be, to such an extent does human violence impregnate suffering.[15]

We badly need to ask if the weight of metaphorical connotations which death has acquired for us prevents us from accepting its naturalness. I will die, not because I am a sinner, but because I am an animal and because dying is what all animals do. We cannot envisage the creation without death – it is part of organic nature – but in the person of Jesus we are asked to consider the creation without sin: creation, ultimately, is defined, not by its resistance to God, but by its self-determining responsiveness to God. The very witness of martyrdom is an assertion that there is, in all seriousness, a more destructive reality than death, namely, the possibility of rejecting God's love; it also reaffirms that human identity is

15. P. Ricoeur, 'Evil: A Challenge to Philosophy and Theology', *Journal of the American Academy of Religion* 53, no. 3 (1989), pp. 635-48.

determined ultimately, neither by its mortality, nor by its inherited and wilful sinfulness, but by the exercise of its freedom in response to God.

If such a distinction is permissible, and I make it only to dramatise the point, it is the event of free obedience in Gethsemane, not the shedding of blood on Calvary, which is central: putting it another way, it is not the physical dying of Jesus but the attitudes of love and obedience with which he commits himself to God in his death that are of primary significance. The physical death of Jesus is the outward sign, the sacrament of the union between creaturely dying and divine presence, the reciprocity between the *energeia* of God and the *energeia* of a creature, the interchange between God and created freedom which is perfected in the death of the Son. This takes place in the context of human malice and violence, the obverse of the loving obedience with which Jesus endures his passion.

In this perspective, the drama of the cross is not God's entry into death, but is rather the most intense focus of union between God and the creation when the Incarnate Son raises created existence to a pitch of responsiveness and identity by committing himself to the God whose Kingdom he mediates. The Paschal Mystery, with its dialectic of death and blessedness, would then mark the perfected reciprocity between the creation and the Creator, each expressing a self-giving love ('*kenosis*') for the other: Jesus entrusting his life to God in the midst of hatred and violence, and the Father bringing his Son into God's Sabbath rest, when all creation rejoices in the divine presence, and attains the fulfilment of its creaturely identity.

Jesus' death, like the death of all of us, is disclosed to be, not the entry into the 'nothingness' which the God-forsaken imagination fears, but the deepest entry into the condition of creatureliness, distinct from God but established by him as the constantly precious object of his love. Death does not mark a window on 'nothingness' within creation; it is not the annihilating dimension; it is not a surd within an otherwise ordered creation. Death marks a moment of deeper union between the Creator and the creature, an intensification of the creaturely relationship rather than a hiatus, a deeper blessedness rather than a curse. E. M. Forster's dictum, 'Death destroys a man; the idea of death saves him' can be reversed with more truth than we might expect.

I have deliberately avoided the soteriological narratives which have been such a central part of Christian theology: the condition to be reversed (alienation, sinfulness, frustration), the metaphorical treatment of the death of Jesus as the Archimedean point which changes or reverses the previous condition (ransoming, saving, freeing, atoning), and the subsequent open horizon which his death opens for us (filiation, intimacy, liberation). Soteriological narratives of this kind are necessary because they are the articulation of the Church's symbolic self-expression in Eucharistic worship, and they provide an endlessly complex and rich characterisation of the mediation of Jesus in the drama of God and the free creation. They dramatise the interchange of God and the human order in an indispensable way, but it may be no accident that reverence for the non-human order has been culpably weak in a Christianity which has become, I would suggest, more and more dominated by its soteriological narratives, at the expense of the creational current. Green faith may be of value in correcting the balance.

Whatever the merits of green faith, almost by definition it cannot have an inner narrative in which a focus within the context is a supreme instance of what applies to the whole. Christian theology says that what happens here – in the person of Jesus – is an intensification of the character of God and the character of creation, a co-presence of divine love and a creation brought to a pitch of freedom and response.

The Christian account is a complex circuit of 'contrasting structures': an overarching framework that goes from Genesis to Apocalypse, from origin to fulfilled destiny, and, within this, a tighter compressing and focusing of the elements in Jesus' experience. Wallace Stevens, in his poem, 'Angel Surrounded by Paysans', pictures the arrival of 'the angel of reality' who speaks to the peasants:

> I am one of you and being one of you
> Is being and knowing what I am and know.
> Yet I am the necessary angel of earth,
> Since, in my sight, you see the earth again,
>
> Cleared of its stiff and stubborn, man-locked set...

For us, Jesus is that angel of reality, the necessary angel of earth, the imaging of God in full communion with the world and so real in his expression of God's love that he is the radical blessedness of creation: the freshness of its innocence and the victim of its rage against God; the first-born of many brothers and sisters who live and die. He also belongs within the world of stones cast aside only to become keystones in holy places; he belongs within the world of trees of life which build temples and arks, and trees of death which become gallows and racks; within a world of seeds which fall into the dark earth to give life, rocks that stand against evil forces, temples of creation where every person is taught by God. He is the pearl of great price that the world brings forth, first as an irritant on its surface, and then as the thing of beauty by which the creation praises God.

CHAPTER SIX

Trinity and 'the Feminine Other'

JANET MARTIN SOSKICE

The notion of 'the feminine Other' is a vexed one for feminists. In the opening pages of *The Second Sex* Simone de Beauvoir asks, 'Are there women, really? Most assuredly the theory of the eternal feminine still has its adherents who will whisper in your ear: "Even in Russia women still are *women*"'.[1] For de Beauvoir the verbal symmetry of 'masculine' and 'feminine' is merely a matter of linguistic form. In the real world of work and love – in life in general – man is the norm and woman is man's 'other', thus her famous remark, 'He is the Subject... she is the Other', the 'not man' defined by men.[2]

Levinas may be a 'recent read' for many of us but already, writing in 1949, de Beauvoir quotes him; 'Otherness', says Levinas, 'reaches its full flowering in the feminine, a term of the same rank as consciousness but of opposite meaning.' 'I suppose' de Beauvoir comments, 'that Levinas does not forget that woman, too, is aware of her own consciousness... But it is striking that he deliberately takes a man's point of view. When he writes that "woman is mystery", he implies that she is mystery *for man*. Thus his description, which is intended to be objective, is in fact an assertion of masculine privilege.'[3] And one which, we can note with de Beauvoir, can stand in a long

---

1. Simone de Beauvoir, *The Second Sex* (London: 1988), p. 13.
2. Ibid., p. 16
3. Ibid., footnote.

line of philosophical evocation of 'the female' and 'the feminine' from the pre-Socratics to Nietzsche and beyond.

In the existentialist rubric of *The Second Sex* de Beauvoir sees the problem as this – a woman, like anyone else, is an autonomous freedom, yet she discovers herself in a world where men force her to assume herself as the 'Other'. Woman, philosophically speaking, lacks her own subjectivity. The subject of philosophy is male, whether consciously or not, and 'woman' is constructed as man's 'other'. 'One is not born, but rather becomes a woman'.

This styling of 'woman' as man's other is, for de Beauvoir, only one example (we might say the paradigmatic one) of a philosophical tradition which can only see otherness as opposition.

The existentialism of *The Second Sex* with its 'boot-strapping' approach to liberation has not worn well, particularly as a tool for the emancipation of women, but de Beauvoir's suggestion that 'woman' is largely a construct, man's 'other', has had an important place in what is known as 'second wave feminism' – feminist thought from the 1960s onwards.[4] It is not entirely a new insight. Perhaps the most droll and best written account of woman as man's 'mirror' is given in Virginia Woolf's *A Room of One's Own*, published several decades before *The Second Sex*.

It is sometimes said, usually in criticism of feminism, that it is a product of the 1960s. If there is truth in this it may be not because, as is often suggested, the sixties were a period of great freedom for women (a thesis many feminists would dispute), but rather that the late fifties and sixties were a period in which

---

4. Michelle Le Doeuff gives an amusing and insightful account of the 'miracle' that any kind of feminism might be based on a Sartrean existentialism in her excellent book *Hipparchia's Choice* (Oxford: 1989). Briefly, 'choosing a freedom which invents its own ends' is a difficult philosophical aspiration for the Peruvian peasant woman whose husband has left her with eight children to feed. Le Doeuff speaks of Sartre's 'megalomanical voluntarism' (p. 127).

many western and educated (and thus vocal) women, bombarded by advertising and the media, began to realise how many and how insistent were the ideals of womanhood held out before them – the beach-doll beauty, the stiletto heel, the whiter wash, the germ-free toilet bowl. The early sixties were a time in which such women were told all the time what women were like. But by whom?

Kate Millett's successful book, *Sexual Politics*, gave expression to this question in literary terms. Published in 1970, this book's first chapter included long, raunchy excerpts from Henry Miller's *Sexus*, a book published in France in the forties but censored in the United States until its publication in the mid-sixties. Kate Millet asks her readers to note, in Miller's extensive and excruciating account of sexual conquests (by the man) and degradation (of the woman), that the events narrated are physically impossible, for instance, with regard to the ease with which certain female garments could be shed and so on. Miller's narrative is a particularly vicious fantasy of male potency and female degradation. Following the lifting of censorship and the publication of this book in English, women reading Henry Miller's book (especially if they had also read Kate Millet's) might well ask,

> 'Is this what Miller thinks about some women? Is this what Miller thinks about all women? Is this what many men think about many women – or wish to think about them?
>
> And who are, or rather what is 'woman' anyway – amidst the flood of media representations – visual, verbal, commercial, even those of children's cartoons (remember Wilma in *The Flintstones*)?
>
> Are there any women in Henry Miller's novels? There are female characters, but he has composed them. Are there any women in Dickens' novels?
>
> Who, in the end, speaks for women?'

Largely in the history of western culture, and not just there, it has been men. And what versions of 'woman' are they that we get from largely male sources?

Around the same time similar questions were asked of the texts of theology. In 1960 Valerie Saiving Goldstein published an article entitled, 'The Human Situation – A Feminine View'. In this she made the uncontroversial observation that the soteriology of a theologian much depends on his 'doctrine of man' – that is, his anthropology. Descriptions of the nature of salvation are dependent on what one thinks people are like and what they are being saved 'from'. Focusing on the writings of Reinhold Niebuhr and Anders Nygren she argued that their anthropologies, far from being neutral, were much more appropriate to men than to women. Sin was identified in terms of 'the' human temptations to pride, self-assertion and self-centredness – salvation correlatively in terms of humility and self-abnegation. But these, Goldstein argued, might not necessarily be the temptations of women. The sins of women, she suggested, might be better suggested by terms like triviality and diffuseness, dependence on others for one's own self-definition and so on – what she called an 'underdevelopment or negation of the self'.[5]

We need not take Goldstein's article as proposing an essentialism in which men are universally selfish and arrogant, and women submissive. Nor, as she insisted, was she saying that women do not sin as much as men do. Rather what her article did point out, and graphically for many of its readers, was that the texts of modern theology have spoken with inappropriate ease of 'the human condition' and invoked without sufficient caution a putatively universal subject who was in fact far more local than was customarily allowed. Generalisations about *the* human condition are found throughout the historical texts of philosophy and theology. The tendency is exacerbated in

5. Valerie Saiving-Goldstein, 'The Human Situation–A Feminine View', *The Journal of Religion* 40, (1960), p. 201.

Enlightenment texts given to wide declarations on 'Man' and 'his nature'.

We might summarise Saiving Goldstein's insight, and Kate Millet's, as the recognition that texts are 'sexed' or sexuate.[6] 'Man', the subject of so many modern and early modern texts of economics, politics, and even theology is not in fact neutral but already placed by race, class and by gender. And, most importantly, this is so not only when the texts in questions (whether they be literary, theological or philosophical) say depressing things about women but even when the texts are, like those of Niebuhr and Nygren, ostensibly neutral – in theory speaking for 'everyman'.

Here we might note shared concerns of some feminist theology and some French philosophy.[7] The point of congruence lies in the shared questions, 'Who is the subject?' and 'How can the Other speak?'

'Woman' and 'the feminine' are considerable topics in French philosophy, and not simply or even mostly topics for women. Foucault, Levinas, Lyotard, Deleuze, Barthes all discuss 'woman'. We need to add in haste that 'woman' here does not necessarily have reference to actual women, but rather functions as a philosophical cipher, representing what has been called 'a new rhetorical space', sometimes also called void, excess, the unsaid, unknowable lack, the uncontained – all that is 'woman'.[8]

The nature of this 'space' seems to vary from theorist to theorist, as do reasons why it should be called 'woman'. For some, most notably Lacan and those affected by him, it is the impact on French thought of psychoanalysis.[9] Others, like

---

6. 'Sexuate' is a neologism now common, because useful, in feminist writings.
7. Although, with a few exceptions, practitioners in these two areas show little interest in, or awareness of, the existence of each other.
8. See Alice Jardine, *Gynesis* (Ithaca, 1985), p. 25.
9. Stephen Heath makes these observations, summarising Lacan's position in *Encore*. For Lacan, 'the woman is that which relates to the Other. Woman and Other, 'locus of the signifying cause of the subject' (*Encore*, p. 841), are not-all,

Derrida, undertake critiques of western philosophy as a system in which the One dominates and triumphs over the other. This philosophical tendency to reduce everything to 'the same' is seen by some theorists, women and men, as having a masculine logic (and again this does not mean that it is exclusively males who engage in it). Irigaray, for instance speaks of philosophy's *position of mastery* and says that 'this domination of the philosophic logos stems in large part from its power *to reduce all others to the economy of the Same*'.[10] Attention to 'woman' is thus a strategy by means of which one can criticise what Stephen Heath has called 'the indifference of the existing order, the sameness it asserts through that very fixing of difference'.[11] As Naomi Schor sees it, the feminine becomes an emblem for a new kind of subjectivity which 'does not constitute itself by simultaneously excluding and incorporating others'.[12]

These questions return us to territory which has parallels in mainstream English-language philosophy. The socalled 'Cartesian subject' and more generally modern western philosophical notions of 'self' and 'subject' have come in for attack from Wittgenstein, Iris Murdoch and Charles Taylor, no less than Foucault or Irigaray. And in French philosophy the 'death of man' would seem to refer not to the end of the human race, nor yet to the demise of the male but rather to the extinction of this particular philosophical fiction. Described in pastiche by Irigaray, what ails this 'cartesian cogito' is that it 'is conceived as auto-effective, auto-affecting and solipsistic'. By doubting everything, this 'singular subject' is 'charged with giving birth to the universe all over again, after he has brought

---

more and less of the order of the phallus, radically other...' Heath continues, theologians might take note, 'Thus (the jouissance of) the woman is (in the position of) God. The Other is the only place left 'in which to put the term God' (SXX, p. 44). Stephen Heath, 'Difference', *Screen* 19 (1978), p. 59-60.

10. Luce Irigaray, *This Sex which is not One* (Ithaca, 1985), p. 74.

11. Heath, 'Difference', p. 112.

12. Naomi Schor, 'This Essentialism Which Is Not One: Coming to Grips With Irigaray', *differences: A Journal of Feminist Cultural Studies* 1 (1989), p. 56.

himself back into the world in a way that avoids the precariousness of existence as it is usually understood.'[13] By generating himself in an act of rationality, this cogito, or 'Disengaged Man' (to use Charles Taylor's term) detaches himself and is transcendental in the sense of transcending his own material base, even his own body which becomes one more 'object' of study.[14] And because it is, figuratively, '*Man*' who is dead, and indeed the 'Cartesian man' who constitutes himself by the denial of the '*mater*-ial' (that is, the 'feminine') – that other is named 'woman'.

It should be clear that, as Rosi Braidotti insists, 'French theories of the feminine' such as the above, cannot be equated or confused with 'French feminist theory', although the latter is informed by the former.[15] And it is not surprising that feminists have been cautious in welcoming this new-found invocation of 'the feminine' and the so-called 'becoming woman' of French philosophy. It is unsurprising that some women philosophers have responded by casting off the whole neo-Nietzschean, neo-Freudian clabber, with all its unfortunate residual dualisms of male and female.[16] One can sympathise. However some of the most interesting theoreticians of French feminism, notably Luce Irigaray and Julia Kristeva, have not, and for reasons which should interest the theologian and to which I shall return.

Contemporary English-language philosophy and French philosophy share an interest in language and linguistics, although they develop it in different ways. In particular modern French philosophy has been influenced in ways the English empiricist tradition has not, by both psychoanalysis and cultural

---

13. Luce Irigaray, *Speculum of the Other Woman* (Ithaca, New York: Cornell University Press, 1985), p. 181-2.
14. Rosi Braidotti, *Patterns of Dissonance: A Study of Women in Contemporary Philosophy* (Oxford: Polity Press, 1991), p. 254. See also Charles Taylor, *Sources of the Self* (Cambridge: 1989), passim.
15. Braidotti, *Patterns*, p. 11.
16. This is true of some Anglo-American critics but also, to some extent, of the French philosopher Michelle Le Doeuff, for instance.

anthropology, and accordingly importance is given to questions
of image, symbol, and the powers of figuration.[17] More
specifically within feminist critical theory the contrast has
sometimes been drawn between the concern of English and
American feminists with the 'oppression of women', and the
concern of French theorists with the 'repression of the
feminine'. This is recognised, increasingly, as not an 'either-or'.[18]
Women's problems, Irigaray's work suggests, are both *real* and
symbolic [19] – we need better employment legislation, workplace
creches and so on, but we also need to change at a profound
level the manner in which we think about self and other, about
'man' and 'woman'. French feminists may be wary of the
'becoming woman' of philosophy while finding some truth in
the diagnosis of western modernity as unable positively to think
'difference' or otherness except as 'the other of the same'. On the
practical level, any serious attempts to think seriously about
difference could not but affect the lives of actual women.

The importance accorded to questions of symbolism means
that French feminist theorists are less likely than their Anglo-
American counterparts to suppose one can affect lasting change
or achieve 'equality' while ignoring the sexed nature of texts
which, historically, have informed western intellectual culture
and whose values have been exported round the world. (This,
too, should make them important reading to feminist
theologians who have even more reason than secular feminists to
be aware of the enduring influence of symbols on present day
life.) Irigaray, for example, is suspicious of the rush to
androgyny she detects in some feminist thought. The so-called
'androgynous ideal' will still be male-formed. What other ideal
have we, whether we be male or female in this society, in which

17. Jean-Joseph Goux makes this point in 'The Phallus: Masculine Identity
and the "Exchange of Women"', *differences* 4.1 (1992).
18. See Elizabeth Gross, 'Philosophy, subjectivity and the body: Kristeva and
Irigaray' in *Feminist Challenges to Social and Political Theory*, eds. Carole
Pateman and E. Gross (Boston: 1986), p. 133.
19. Braidotti, *Patterns*, p. 252.

to think? And when enunciating feminist aspirations to equality we must also ask, as Irigaray does, 'equal to whom?' If the answer remains 'to men' then the male is still supplying the norm around which the female or the neuter is constructed, with the further disadvantage that this andromorphism is concealed.[20] What we need, according to Irigaray, is to rethink sexual difference.

The thesis that the texts of philosophy are 'sexed', while perhaps initially curious, becomes far more convincing on re-examination of some of the texts of ancient philosophy. Let me illustrate this by reference to an article by Jean-Joseph Goux, 'The Phallus: Masculine Identity and the "Exchange of Women"'.[21] While the 'phallus' is a common notion in modern ethnography and psychoanalysis, Goux reminds us of its place in ancient philosophy. Citing Herodotus and Plutarch, he reminds us of the place of the phallus in ancient myth and cult and its close (and obvious) association with a masculine principle of generation. As such the phallus has close association with intelligence, or formative word (logos). The sexual imagery of Plato's allegory of the cave, with its movement from the womb-like *mater*-ial, through representation to the Forms has, of course, been obvious to philosophers long before Freud.[22] Plutarch writes, 'Plato is wont to give the conceptual the name of idea, example, or father, and to the material the name of mother or nurse, or place of generation, and to that which results from both the name *offspring* or *generation*.'[23] Intelligence or reason is that which transcends matter and the material (*mater*). Thus, says Goux, the 'inaugural opposition of metaphysics', a major metaphysical opposition between 'a male principle which is intelligible reason (ideas, model, father) and

---

20. Luce Irigaray, *Je, Tu, Nous: Towards a Culture of Difference* (London: 1993), p. 12.
21. In *differences* 4.1 (1992).
22. Irigaray explores Plato's allegory at some length in *Speculum of the Other Woman*.
23. Plutarch, *Moralia*, cit. Goux, p. 46.

a female principle which is matter' is quite overt in Plato and Aristotle (46). The female (nurturing, womb-like matter) is that which the male, rational principle transcends.

The Neoplatonists revived these generative metaphors in their idea of the One as first principle, fertile power, and source of all life. (And I would draw the theological reader's attention to the obvious appropriateness of such a paternal metaphor to peoples whose biological conviction and contemporary science told them that only males, as bearers of seed, were truly generative.) In the Stoics 'the masculine sexual signification of the organizing principle stands out even more sharply... in the unambiguous notion of *logos spermatikos*... the power of sperm fashioning each thing in accordance with its species...' (48). Logos may be no more gender-neutral a term than is 'father' in these texts, linked as it is to metaphors of male generation.

Goux's target is metaphysical dualism, and that tradition of metaphysics which emphasises presence versus absence, the One and the Other of the same, but theologians with some knowledge of the use of the term *logos spermatikos* in early Christian texts should also sit up sharply. It is almost impossible not to see here, for instance, another reason why, for those whose biological beliefs and symbols were of such an order, the notion of the ordination of women would be out of the question, quite literally 'inconceivable'. For it is not only Jesus of Nazareth who is humanly male, but God as source of generation, and Logos, as seed of generation, who are symbolically male. In a scheme where only males are truly generative then, in a sense, only males can truly give birth. The only true parent is the father, source of seed which it is the female task to nurture. Lest we think this all just 'mere metaphor' we can note that one reason given by Aquinas in the *Contra Gentiles* why we ought not to speak of the first person of the Trinity as Mother, is because God begets actively, and the role of the mother in procreation is, on the other hand, passive (IV. 11).

Perhaps I have said enough to suggest why investigations into sexual and procreative metaphors in the texts of philosophy should interest not only French philosophers and critics of 'the western tradition of metaphysics',[24] but also theologians and students of trinitarian theology. Let me turn now directly to discussion of the doctrine of the Trinity.

There would seem to have been, over the last three hundred years of Western Christianity, equal numbers of theologians who think either that the doctrine of the Trinity has outworn its usefulness and might now be scrapped, or that the doctrine is at the very centre of the Christian faith. If we start from the recognition that the doctrine was developed by Christians, not in order to reject their Jewish ancestry, but to demonstrate why they could claim to stand in continuity with it, we may see why. Trinitarian language, developed for particular purposes, can so often appear to suggest their opposite. For instance, we speak of the One God's 'triunity', but it readily appears to be tritheism. Walter Kasper writes with great caution and accuracy of the absolute unity of God *despite* the distinction of persons, and the absolute equality of the persons *despite* the dependence of the second person on the first and the third on the first and the second, and so on. To many people in the pews, and not just to them, this 'despite' language sounds a little like Orwell's *Animal Farm*: all animals are equal but some are more equal than others. Trinitarian language may be introduced, historically, as a corrective to the tendency of idolatry, but how successful has it

---

24. To speak so generally of '*the* western tradition of metaphysics' or '*the* onto-theological constitution of metaphysics', as though the same old story could be told across 2,500 years. It is more accurately one particular, and we could say in the modern period particularly dominant, tradition of western metaphysics that is being criticised. Those who speak of 'the western tradition' often seem forgetful, in a way one hopes theologians are not, of medieval philosophy. Indeed, part of the argument of this paper is that recollection of the delicate philosophical arguments on the Trinity itself might be a sovereign cure against any system which degenerates into *oppositional dualisms*.

been? How frequently, as Ann Loades has reminded us, do we hear such phrases as 'divine fatherhood does not have masculine characteristics but …'?[25] Christians are good at rejecting heresies they never found very attractive anyway, like tritheism, and less successful at rejecting those they quite like, such as various and related forms of subordinationism, monarchianism and deistic sexism, all in their way idolatrous.

Recent years have seen a number of feminist criticisms of classical formulations of the doctrine. These vary from simple rejection of what sounds like a three-man club, to more nuanced critiques of the way in which, despite best efforts, the Father always seems accorded a status superior to the other two persons, with the Holy Spirit as a distinct third. The Trinity appears still hierarchical, still male – maleness, indeed, seems enshrined in God's eternity.

One line of thought has been to emphasise the putatively female characteristics of the Spirit. We can readily uncover a tradition of regarding the Spirit as the maternal aspect of God-brooding, nurturing, bringing new members of the Church to life in baptism. There is, too, the early Syriac tradition of styling the Spirit as feminine, following the female gender of the noun in the Semitic languages, but these evocations have failed to convince feminist and other theologians of their enduring merit for women or, for that matter, for the Trinity. Consider the implications of these remarks of Yves Congar,

> The, part played in our upbringing by the Holy Spirit is that of a mother – a mother who enables us to know our Father, God, and our brother, Jesus… He (the Spirit) teaches us how to practise the virtues and how to use the gifts of a son of God by grace. All this is part of a mother's function.[26]

---

25. In a paper given to a conference on 'The Trinity', Trinity College, Dublin, May 1992.
26. Yves Congar, *I Believe in the Holy Spirit* (London: 1983), vol III, p. 161.

Along with deifying one particular, and particularly western, version of 'a mother's function' (why is it not a mother's function to raise the crops so that her family may eat?) the Spirit by implication is ancillary to the other two persons who are the ones really to be known and loved.

Even less satisfactory, as Elizabeth Johnson notes, is the valiant effort by the process theologian, John Cobb, to align the Logos, as the masculine aspect of God, with order, novelty, demand, agency and transformation, while the feminine aspect of God, the kingdom or Spirit, is linked with receptivity, empathy, suffering and preservation.[27]

Feminists are surely right to reject what Sarah Coakley has called 'mawkish and sentimentalised versions of the feminine' as both providing warrant for a particular stereotype of the feminine and at the same time feeding the unorthodox suggestion that there is sexual difference in the Trinity. Furthermore this kind of feminising rhetoric does nothing to counteract the genuine neglect of the Spirit in modern theology, in which the Spirit appears a sort of 'edifying appendage' to the two real persons, those who have faces, the Father and the Son.[28] We must avoid, as Coakley says, subordinating 'the Spirit to a Father who, as "cause", and "source" of the other two persons, remains as a "masculine" stereotype with the theological upper hand.'[29] It is this covert monarchianism which is perhaps the main fear of feminist theologians: a patriarchal 'father-god' who exhibits an exclusive and narcissistic love for the Son. Unfortunately the history of theology resounds with just such deficiencies.

God, we all know, is not male but God's 'fatherhood', equally obviously, has been used to underwrite patterns of male dominance in marriage, family, state, and Church. So what do

---

27. Elizabeth A. Johnson, 'The Incomprehensibility of God and the Image of God Male and Female', *Theological Studies* 45 (1984), p. 459.
28. Ibid., p. 457.
29. '"Femininity" and the Holy Spirit' in *Mirror to the Church,* ed. M. Furlong (London: 1988).

we do? One strategy ready to hand is to desexualise the language of the Trinity altogether and speak instead of Creator, Sustainer and Redeemer. But while this is acceptable and at times necessary as an alternative liturgical usage, it does not carry the relational content of Father, Son and Spirit. The Creator is not the Creator of the Sustainer, and so on. Creator, Sustainer and Redeemer are three names of what God is 'for us' in the economy of salvation but say nothing of the eternal mutuality of the Three-In-One. They can also suggest, misleadingly, that it is only the First Person who creates, the Second who redeems and the Third who sustains when, for instance, creation is properly the action of all three persons. Taking a page from the French feminists, we need furthermore to ask whether neutering texts simply makes their sexual imagery less easy to spot and to recognise as imagery.

I am suspicious of attempts to purge offensive metaphors and 'tidy up' the stories. They veil the historically placed nature of the biblical texts and are especially misleading if, by purging, we think we will achieve a theology that is 'pure': scientific and free of fable. Scientific or ostensibly 'value-free' fables are the most deceptive of all, since they conceal their own interpretive and cultural biases.

In the realm of Trinitarian theology one cannot cease to tell stories, or to remember that they are stories. A refreshing aspect of the great Trinitarian treatises are the admissions of inevitable inadequacy by authors in the face of the divine mystery. Patristic texts like those of Athanasius and Augustine exhibit great precision in thought, while at the same time throwing out a profusion of models, or Trinitarian stories – as though they are saying, 'imagine it is like this, or this, or this…'

Let me then seek not just to comment on previous formulations of the doctrine but also to tell a Trinitarian tale which takes seriously the language of the economy, with all its gendered relational and procreational imagery.

We can start with the title 'Father'.[30] In a suggestive article on 'fatherhood', Paul Ricoeur notes that whereas God is called 'father' 170 times by Jesus in the Synoptics, God is styled as 'father' only 11 times in the entire Hebrew Bible, and never there invoked as 'father' in prayer. Ricoeur also points out that 'father' is a semantically dependent title – it is because there is a child that someone is called a father. It is, in short, in this *technical* sense, a *relational term*. So the advent of the child, in a sense, 'gives birth' to the father. Ricoeur suggests that in the Christian narrative it is with the Son's death that the distinctive nature of God's fatherhood is established for Christians, for the death of the Son is in some sense also the 'death' of the Father who is one with the Son. The French philosopher, Jean-Luc Marion, makes a similar suggestion, 'Upon the Cross, the Father expires as much as the Word (Son) since they expire the same Spirit. The Trinity respires from being able to breath among us.'[31] The death of the Son then, and separation of God from God in the cry of dereliction on the Cross, gives way to a new birth, the *ekstasis* which is the mission of the Spirit. It is through the Spirit (and here we can say: styled as feminine) that there is resurrection and the Church born to newness of life.

The trinitarian narrative of the economy, in this telling, moves both ways – The Father begets the Son. The Spirit proceeds from the Father and the Son. Yet we can also say that the Son is raised in the Spirit. And the Father is Father in virtue of the Son – because it is the child who 'makes' someone a father. The father in this story can no longer have the property, within the economic Trinity, of innascibility (the attribute of being independent of birth) prized by some trinitarian theologians but predicated only of the Father. In this telling of

---

30. The following remarks are a precis of another paper, 'Can a Feminist Call God "Father"?' which appears in *Women's Voices in Religion*, ed. Teresa Elwes (London: 1992) and also in *The Holy Trinity and the Challenge of Feminism*, ed. Alvin Kimmel (Eerdmans, 1992).
31. Jean-Luc Marion, *God Without Being* (Chicago: 1991), p. 142-3.

the economy the father, too, 'is born' – or better 'becomes father' – with the Son, and in the Spirit.

This is a vision of a Trinity of complete mutuality, yet it is not one in which all three persons become the same, as three sides of an equilateral triangle. The First person, as Unoriginate Origin, begets the Son (and is thus named 'Father' or we could say equally 'Mother'), and from these two proceeds the Spirit. The Son, by being Son, is the one who makes God Father/Mother. The Son gives birth to the Church in the Spirit, represented figuratively in the high tradition of western religious art by the water and the blood flowing from Christ's pierced side on the Cross – clear birth imagery from which medieval artist did not shrink. The Spirit is the Lord, the Giver of Life, in whom the Son is raised in resurrected Life.

From the economic point of view, this story has an exitus-reditus structure: Father – Son – Spirit, Spirit – Son – Father, but at the immanent level it is a story of the perichoretic outpouring of love and birth between the Three who only *Are* in relation one to another. All three persons, figuratively, give birth – the First person as Unoriginate Origin begets Son and gives the Spirit, the Second as Son 'makes' God the father and 'gives birth' to the Church on the Cross, and the Holy Spirit, the Lord the Giver of Life, animates the Church in the world. The activity of all three can be styled in the procreative imagery of the human feminine and of the human masculine.

Theories of complete mutuality are not unknown in the history of trinitarian thought, and I am not sure whether this one is another version of those which speak of God as Patreque, Filioque and Spirituque (Patreque indicating that the Son proceeds from the Father and the Spirit, Filioque that the Spirit proceeds from the Father and the Son, and Spirituque that the Father proceeds from Son and Spirit, and the Son from Father and Spirit.) If so I may attract the ire of Catherine La Cugna whose helpful, recent book, *God for Us*, is an extensive defence of the primacy of the economic (soteriological) Trinity over what she regards as intellectualising, immanent accounts of God *in se.* Her criticism of Patreque, Filioque, Spirituque accounts (at least as deployed by Leonardo Boff) is that it outstrips anything we know of the economy of salvation and as such is, she says, 'an extreme version of scholastic trinitarian theology' (not a criticism one thinks of as usual for Boff) with a 'highly reified account of divine substance'.[32]

I am not so sure. Indeed I am not so sure that the much decried scholastic trinitarian theologies were remote from the economy of salvation. But in any case this retelling of the economic narrative seems to fit the Biblical witness and imagery quite well – indeed it draws our attention, in a way neither mawkish nor sentimental, to the extensive and hugely neglected repertoire of birth images in the New Testament, often associated with the Spirit. Might not the theological neglect of this birth imagery and the persisting inability to find a proper place for the Spirit in so much modern theology be connected?

If as Aquinas suggests, 'relation' is the key to the Trinity, and the To-Be of God is To-Be-Related,[33] then the Son cannot be what the Son is except by relation to Father and Spirit, and the Spirit cannot be what the Spirit is except by relation to Son and Father, and the Father cannot be what the Father is except by relation to Son and Spirit. As many classical theologians point out, God is not called 'Father' because he is our father – rather it is because God is 'Father' to the Son that we are able to pray, 'Our Father.'

The divine persons cannot be thought of as separate from one another. This full integration of the Holy Spirit, the Lord, the Giver of Life, would go a long way to rectifying treatments in which the Spirit does indeed seem, in Elizabeth Johnson's phrase, to be no more than an 'edifying' (perhaps female) 'appendage' to the self-absorbed life of the Father and the Son, the One and the Other, exhausted in their dualism.

---

32. Catherine Mowry La Cugna, *God For Us: The Trinity and Christian Life* (New York: 1991), p. 277.
33. Ibid., p. 153.

The criticisms of western metaphysics I discussed earlier are critiques of a philosophy governed by inexorable dualisms, economics of the One and the Same. This, I hazard, could never be a Christian metaphysics, although it might be a particular neo-Platonic heresy. It could only be a metaphysics forgetful of the great efforts made by theologians and philosophers to give account of God's Being as *To-Be-Related*. We may now stand at a moment of evangelical opportunity in the West, a time in which people not only need to hear a fully relational account of the trinitarian life of God, but may also be receptive to it.

We frequently read in the texts of modern theology that we need the doctrine of the Trinity in order to teach us how to be relational beings. This often sounds a kind of utilitarian apologetics – 'the doctrine doesn't mean much anymore but at least it's socially useful'. But, we might ask, what does the Trinity tell us of human relational experiences? Personally I think something has gone seriously wrong if theologians can even ask that kind of question in the way they so often now do. I must emphasise, then, that the sense in which I discuss relation in the Trinity is here a *formal one*. To give a mundane example, a man becomes a father in a technical sense when he has a child. Even were he to have no idea of the child's existence and thus no 'relationship' (in the vernacular sense) with it, he would nonetheless be related to this child as father. 'Relation' is a useful technical term in trinitarian theology, and the water is muddied if we forget the several senses, including the modern psychological ones, in which the term can be used.[34]

As to the way the modern theologians invoke 'relation', I was surprised to find Walter Kasper drawing the following contrast between God and us; whereas God is relational, according to Kasper, we human beings only choose to be relational. He adds, 'relations are essential only to the full self-realisation of the being. A human being is, and remains a human being even if he

---

34. This does not mean, of course, that God cannot 'relate to us', in the vernacular sense of the term 'relate'.

selfishly closes himself against relations with others.'[35] What can this mean? Surely we need other human beings, notably parents, to come into being at all. Which human being is free of human relations? As infants we are entirely dependent on others for our existence. Those others teach us language, values, stories – in short, a world. Even our very limited capacity to 'close ourselves off from others, is only conceivable because we have *already* been socially constituted. I need other people even in order to shut myself off from them. We are constituted, not 'autonomously', not despite others, but because of and by others. The more we are 'in relation', the more we are likely to be our selves.[36] We *are* relational beings, and if this is not obvious to us then it only shows how deeply we are prey to that most insidious of modern myths, the myth of the self-constituting subject of so much modern thought.

But it is this atomistic, relationless agent, you will recall, who has been the target of some of the most sustained and persuasive philosophical critiques in our century. Wittgenstein showed him to be epistemologically threadbare, Charles Taylor and Alison Jagger show him to be morally and politically bankrupt – and sexist to boot – Foucault showed him to be a social-scientific non-sense, and Lacan and Irigaray present him as psychologically pathological.[37] As a model for human beings this 'disengaged man' is a nonstarter, for human knowing and human being not only are not but could not be self-constituted.

Is it then a coincidence that the period between the sixteenth and twentieth centuries in the West – a period Lacan has called the 'ego's era' – should be both one which has seen a precipitate decline in religious practice in the West and also one in which the affirmation of God as Trinity has again and again been challenged by theologians of deistic, rationalist, or empiricist

---

35. Walter Kasper, *The God of Jesus Christ* (London: 1983), p. 280.
36. This is one of the main thrusts of Charles Taylor's *Sources of the Self.*
37. On this theme in Lacan see Teresa Brennan's *History After Lacan* (London: 1993).

bent? We could even dare to say the popular image of God in the mind of many faithful Christians is deistic and Unitarian – the God who is One, and who perhaps has a very special friend, his messenger Jesus, who was sent to make things better for us.

In feminist critical theory (not feminist theology) 'God' gets short shrift. Secular theorists are not of the opinion that 'God' has been very good for women. But the 'God' one finds in their texts is a bit player who appears merely as a pretext for the authority of Man and men, the divine guarantor of the veracity of the insights of the Cartesian subject. This *'cogito'*, self-engendered through the denial of the other, the external world, even his own physicality, speaks in the place of and with the authority of 'God'. Rational 'man', viewing things from a 'God's-eye-view' separates self from other, but there is never any genuine other, always just the 'economy of the Same'.

But the theologian might well object (indeed, should object) that the 'God' thus described is not the Christian God, and not the God of Jesus Christ. This 'God' is a philosophical fiction created by 'Man' for man's purposes, the *'causa sui'*. At most this 'God' is a binity where the second person is not Jesus but 'Man' himself. Indeed 'Man' is the senior partner, establishing his 'God' as another self to whom he can relate.[38] This is indeed a culture of narcissism where the One (Man) gazes on the other he has made (God made in man's image). As Braidotti says, with more truth than she perhaps knows, this 'God himself is not an infinite Being, for the 'I' has accorded to him his essence and his existence, according to the order of Reason.'[39]

Unfortunately the 'God' of the philosophers is taken by many to be what Christians understand by God. The criticism of this idolatrous God of philosophy is at the heart of Jean-Luc Marion's philosophical essay, *God Without Being*. And it is at the heart, too, of Heidegger's criticisms of the 'onto-theological constitution of metaphysics' which Marion follows. The God of modern

---

38. See La Cugna, *God For Us*, p. 251.
39. Braidotti, *Patterns*, p. 255.

philosophy is *causa sui* but, as Heidegger says, only therefore an idol before which we can neither pray nor dance.[40] Heidegger rightly says that this 'God can come into philosophy only insofar as philosophy ... requires or determines that and how God enters into it.[41] But this is because this is not the true God, this 'God' is a precept of philosophy. Christians do not know God as *causa sui*, but as the God who reveals, as the Gift Given.[42]

The Christian doctrine of the Trinity has ever been a challenge to philosophies of the One, in both their ancient and modern forms. The trinitarian theology of the Cappadocians was formulated over and against just such a metaphysics of the One that contemporary philosophers find so oppressive. The name 'Father', the Cappodocians insisted, does not describe some kind of divine *ousia* but a relation to the Son.[43] Indeed if God's 'To Be' is 'To-Be-Related' then all our most seemingly substantive and static divine titles, including those of Father and Son, are really relational. Even to call the First Person 'unoriginate origin' is to indicate a relation to that which is originated or begotten. Trinitarian theology presents us with a God who cannot be dissected, reified, confined, materialised, controlled, but who is totally present to us, as totally Other. Paradoxically it is with such thoughts that this very Christian doctrine of God's otherness and nearness, the Known Unknowable, to speak in Barthian terms, that one feels also a closeness with our Jewish brothers and sisters. It is not surprising that some of the most productive current thought on a God who 'relates in and through difference' should come from a Jew.[44] 'Subjectivity', says Levinas, 'is not for itself, it is once again – initially for another'.[45]

---

40. Martin Heidegger, *Identity and Difference*, trans. Joan Stambaugh (New York, London: Harper and Row, 1974), p. 35.
41. Ibid., p. 34.
42. Marion, *God Without Being*, p. 36.
43. La Cugna, *God For Us*, p. 66.
44. See Morny Joy, 'Levinas: Alterity, the Feminine, and Women – a Meditation' in *Studies in Religion/Sciences Religieuses*, vol. 22, no. 2 (1994), p. 463ff.
45. E. Levinas, *Ethics and Infinity*, cit. Joy.

Let us return to de Beauvoir and her well-founded fears for the 'feminine other' – 'no group', she says, 'ever sets itself up as the One without at once setting up the Other over and against itself' (p. 17). These words sound bitterly across the history of religious sectarianism. Again, de Beauvoir: 'it is not the Other, who, in defining himself as Other, establishes the One. The Other is posed as such by the One in defining himself as the One' (p. 18). But according to the doctrine of the Trinity this is precisely what God does, what God is. God defines Godself as Other, it is through *Being-To-Other*, being related, that God is One. The doctrine of the Trinity tells us nothing of how men and women should relate to one another as males and females It does not show that all men should be like the 'father' and all women model themselves on a feminised Spirit. In this sense the doctrine tells us nothing of sexual difference. But it does let us glimpse what it is, most truly, to be. 'To be' most fully is 'to-be-related' in difference. This tells us a great deal.

CHAPTER SEVEN

Discerning Christ in the World Religions

GAVIN D'COSTA

The idea of truth as a grasp on things must necessarily have a non-metaphorical sense somewhere.

—EMMANUEL LEVINAS[1]

Recently in a number of disciplines such as anthropology, philosophy, literary and cultural studies there has been close attention to the dynamics involved in the representation of the other. While there is no single unified thesis emerging, there is an intriguing overlap, or family resemblance, of opinions that the non-European has been distorted in the western representation of the other, and that this construal cannot be detached from the colonial and imperial history of Europe.

In anthropology, for example, Bernard McGrane has asked whether the last four centuries of portrayal of the non-European amounts to much more than a distorted and negative mirror image of the European self.[2] In philosophy Emmanuel Levinas and Jacques Derrida each in quite different ways (responding to Heidegger) have challenged the western philosophical tradition regarding its totalising control and occlusion of the other.

---

1. In *Philosophy in France Today*, ed. Alan Montefiore (Cambridge University Press, 1983), p. 103.
2. See his *Beyond Anthropology: Society and the Other* (New York: Columbia University Press, 1989).

Hence, Levinas' challenge that ontology destroys otherness by assimilating it to sameness, and Derrida's criticisms of European logocentricism, which he writes is 'nothing but the most original and powerful ethnocentricism, in the process of imposing itself upon the world.'[3] In literary and cultural studies Edward Said's notion of 'colonial discourse' established in his major work *Orientalism*, has generated much debate and research centred around the construction of distorted visions of the other, the Oriental, within western colonial discourse.[4]

To take one example to illustrate some of the issues in slightly more detail, McGrane constructs a disturbing excavation showing that the portrayal of the other, the non-European within European history, says much about the horizon of interpretation employed by the European and the political social relationship of the European to this other. Obviously, very little about the other as really other is produced in this catalogue, but I will return to this in a moment. So for instance, the Renaissance was characterised by the other:

> interpreted on the horizon of Christianity. It was Christianity which fundamentally came between the European and the non-European other. Within the Christian conception of Otherness anthropology did not exist; there was, rather, demonology. It was in relation to the Fall and to the influence of Sin and Satan that the Other took on his historically specific meaning.[5]

McGrane's characterisation of this (and other) periods is far too generalised and neatly schematised but he nevertheless makes an important point. After the Enlightenment ignorance

---

3. Emmanuel Levinas, *Totality and Infinity: An Essay on Exteriority* (Pittsburg: Duquesne University Press, 1969). For Derrida see *Of Grammatology* (Baltimore: John Hopkins University Press, 1976), the quote given is on p. 3.
4. E. Said, *Orientalism: Western Conceptions of the Orient* (London: 1978).
5. McGrane, *Beyond Anthropology*, p. ix. McGrane's use of 'his' ironically adds to the occlusion of the other!

and error replace sin. With the slow erosion of religious belief, there developed a 'psychology of error and superstition, an ontology of ignorance, and an epistemology of all the forms of untruth and unenlightenment'.[6] Demonisation is replaced by ignorance, by a lack of enlightenment. Defoe's *Robinson Crusoe* (1718) emblematically reflects both these periods and anticipates the next in the representation of Friday; partly fallen, clearly ignorant, and definitely uncivilised.

In the nineteenth century the influence of geology (Lyell), evolutionary theory (Darwin) and anthropology (Tylor) provide the horizon of interpretation, so that the non-European other is organised in terms of stages of development, 'between the prehistorically fossilised "primitive" and the evolutionary advancement of modern Western science and civilisation'. The evolutionary ladder of savage, primitive, civilised is established and different groups positioned along its rungs with the European at the top.[7]

Finally, when McGrane comes to the twentieth century he fiercely contests the predominant episteme of cultural relativism in which difference becomes cultural difference alone, thereby masking the real challenge that the other poses. He rehearses the now well worn arguments against such relativisers (their absolute claim that all is relative must itself be relative, and their hidden imperialism in assuming a non-relative vantage point from which to make this observation about all cultures).[8] He argues that culture becomes the dominant paradigm for interpreting the other. Cultural relativity becomes the grand text into which difference is encoded; the non-European other is seen as 'fundamentally and merely, culturally different'.[9]

Ironically, in this mode of portrayal, difference is reduced to

---

6. McGrane, *Beyond Anthropology*, p. ix.

7. Ibid., p. x.

8. See, for example, Hilary Putnam, *Reason, Truth and History* (Cambridge University Press, 1981).

9. McGrane, *Beyond Anthropology*, p. x.

sameness and inoculated from any real interaction. So while in the sixteenth to nineteenth centuries there was a tendency of portraying the other in metonymic mode, a distorted mirror image of the European in the construction of the other; in the twentieth century the other is simply reflection, homogenised by assimilation, culturally relative, made same, rendered safe, and thereby, 'achieves' the respect of secular liberalism. While one excludes otherness as negative mirror image, the modern includes it by total assimilation. Both thereby distort, but in opposite ways.

So what of the Christian theologian involved in the question of the status and meaning of other religions? As one such, I would suggest that we have much to learn from these materials. To remain with McGrane for the moment.

First, McGrane's study alerts us to the horizon within which we proffer such portrayals. Second, the history of portrayal says much about the constructor and producer of such knowledge, their horizon of interpretation, and the power relations within which these constructions take place. Third, McGrane is not interested in theology as such, but the construction of the other has, since the Renaissance, been powerfully influenced by prevailing 'theologies of religion'. Hence this specific and very important element is not given the appropriate attention it deserves.

Fourth, and very germane to my main concern, McGrane's study indicates a tendency in the European history of the portrayal of the other to veer in one of two directions, but two directions held together by the same centrifugal force (which would be for Levinas: ontology; and for Derrida: logocentrism). The first direction is in terms of hierarchical inferiority, subjugation, power and control (be it in the categories of demonisation, unenlightenment or primitive tribe) so that otherness bears the opposite negative reflection of the image maker and can be subjected to that maker. The second direction is to make otherness sameness (be it in terms of cultural relativisation, liberal humanism's espousal of the universality of values such as justice and equal rights, or whatever) so that while it seems that equality is granted, it is always 'granted', that is, bestowed in terms of the portrayer's system of representation. The centrifugal force holding both these tendencies together is the Western Imperial Self, either destroying the other on the one hand or alternatively homogenising the other. Both movements of course collude in different types of destruction and effacement.

Fifth, McGrane, like Said, fails to really address the question of the relation of the other to the 'real' other, Orientalism to the Orient, the question of the possibility of the other being free to be other, and the possibility of representation without control, knowledge without coercive power. It would of course be impossible to have knowledge without power *per se*, but the real question as to the possibility of non-coercive representation still remains unresolved. I now want to focus more sharply on the fourth and fifth of these points: how to transcend the dichotomy of samenessotherness/assimilation-demonisation/total identity-incommensurable difference, and the underlying centrifugal force which in either direction results in distorted vision and the destruction of the other; and how to formulate a theology which allows for the possibility of non-coercive (self) re-presentation of the other.

To develop my argument, I will turn to Kenneth Surin, one of the few theologians who takes his cue from McGrane, Todorov and Foucault and like-minded thinkers to analyse the theology of religions.[10] Surin makes two very important points which will help focus my concern. The first is incisive and valid, the second problematic. The first is an argument showing how modern forms of Christian theological pluralism (in the work of

---

10. See Surin's main piece, 'A Certain "Politics of Speech": "Religious Pluralism" in the Age of the McDonald Hamburger', *Modern Theology*, 7, 1 1990, pp. 67-100, subsequently referred to as *MT*; (a shortened version of this appears in *Christian Uniqueness Reconsidered*, ed. G. D'Costa (New York, 1991), pp. 192-212.

John Hick for example) efface the other for the sake of homogenisation; despite the tolerant liberal rhetoric there is an imperialist occlusion. Here his argument follows McGrane's very closely.

Surin devastatingly shows how modern pluralism conforms to McGrane's typology of twentieth century representation of the non-European other and skilfully locates this representation in liberal capitalism's global pretensions, in the modernist grand narratives that allegedly acknowledge:

> heterogeneity and plurality, but this acknowledgement is always fatally compromised by [the] deployment of a homogeneous logic, a logic which irons-out the heterogeneous precisely by subsuming it under the categories of comprehensive and totalising 'global' and 'world' theology.[11]

If we see in pluralism the tendency to assimilate the other, to make same, we might expect to see the reverse in theological exclusivism; to reject by demonising the other in terms of a distorted self-image. And what of the midfield player, the theological inclusivist?

This leads to Surin's second point, which 123I find more problematic. Surin notes an important commonality between inclusivism and pluralism. He illustrates his point in regards to Las Casas' defence of the Indians against the Spaniards. Las Casas identifies the former as 'lambs' and as 'Christians', the latter as 'moors', 'wolves' and 'ravening wild beasts'. Hence, to quote Surin:

> so strong is Las Casas's commitment to equality that he will not characterise the Indians as 'different'. Good proto-Rahnerian that he is, he is prepared to see them as

---

11. Surin, *MT*, p. 92. I have replaced 'his' with 'the' in the citation.

'unwitting' Christians, and so, as Todorov points out, Las
Casas's 'postulate of equality involves the assertion of
identity'.[12]

It meant that Las Casas ended up knowing neither Indian nor
Spaniard, and it is this assertion of identity (the Indians were
unwitting Christians whether they knew it or not) that finally
makes inclusivism no different to pluralism in Surin's eyes. He
never properly locates exclusivism in relation to this question of
identity.

Now I want to contest Surin's claim, or rather, register a
qualification. Surin's criticism of Rahner's inclusivism as finally
and strategically aligned to pluralism's assimilation of the other,
raises the question (entirely untouched in Surin's paper)
between what I shall call a 'closed' and 'open' form of
inclusivism. As far as I am aware this distinction has not been
formally introduced into the discussion in theology of religions.
Surin's target is rightly a 'closed' form of inclusivism and again
here his textual paucity in regard to Rahner leaves unresolved
the question as to whether Rahner should be seen as an 'open'
or 'closed' inclusivist. What is disturbing is that in making this
point Surin fails to distinguish between these two forms of
inclusivism.

'Closed' inclusivists could be depicted as saying that in
Christ or/and the Christian Church we have the truth of God.
We can therefore recognise God in other religions in so much as
those others look like us, have our God, teach our doctrines.
And in this sense the term anonymous Christian (detached
from its Rahnerian context and used as a typology of
inclusivism) indicates that the Christian knows and recognises
God within the other, either despite the other or in keeping
with the other. The 'anonymous' here is related to the self-
consciousness of the other. Now this form of inclusivism does

---

12. Surin, *MT*, p. 77.

fall foul of making the other same, recognising the other only in so much as they conform to us. And Surin has a good point in thereby noting the affinity between pluralism and what I call a closed form of inclusivism.

But Surin fails to attend to 'open' inclusivism. Here a remark by Derrida will indicate the way in which I want to transcend the same-other dichotomy by transforming these terms by taking them up into a third term: God, both hidden and revealed. I want to replace the western imperial self with an eschatological trinitarian God. My project is certainly not Derridean, but what he says here of 'différence' is pertinent:

> The term 'différence' can't be stabilised within a polarisation of the same and the different. It's at one and the same time an idea rooted in sameness, and radical otherness... So I'd say that difference can't be enclosed within the same, or the idea of the radically other, about which nothing could be said. It's an enigmatic relation of the same to the other.[13]

It is this enigmatic relation of the same to the other that an open inclusivism seeks to retain and explore.

Hence, open inclusivists like myself can be depicted as saying that in Christ or/and the Christian Church we have the truth of God. *But* this truth is never our possession, but rather we are possessed by it. Now this is important for as we do not possess it we cannot control it or limit it or even claim to have a vantage point somewhere beyond it, by which we know it in its entirety. Furthermore, this truth is not closed in the sense that revelation is *eschatologically* oriented, so while the Church claims to have encountered God in the self-revelation of the Father in Jesus Christ, through his Spirit, it at the same time confesses an ignorance of this God. While we know God, we do not know everything about God. This point could be put in the form:

13. In Raoul Mortley, *French Philosophers in Conversation* (London: 1991), p. 99.

while the economic trinity is the immanent trinity, the immanent trinity is not the economic trinity until the eschaton.

It is in this surplus, this Derridean difference, that we find the possibility of avoiding either total assimilation, or total rejection and mirror-projection, or of course (for the more radical relativist – who remains silent in this paper) total incommensurability.[14] It is in this surplus that genuine otherness can become a question mark to my own Christian self-understanding, can become a question mark to the location of my questioning, can become the question mark that bears the trace of revelation.

In terms of the phrase 'anonymous Christian' the anonymous here does not relate to the self-consciousness of the other, but to the manner in which the Christian does not possess God or know God without remainder, so that there is a sense in which the anonymous relates neither to the self-consciousness of the other or the Christian, although in one sense to both, but rather to the mystery of God, who is known in Christ, yet still hidden. This approach I believe allows one to overcome the distorting dichotomy, because the centrifugal force at the centre is not homogenising, the one, the same. Rather it is relational and dynamic, revealed and hidden, known and unknown, unpossessable yet possessing, it is 'the enigmatic relation of the same to the other', the possibility of true communion with the stranger and the reality of our lack of such communion. This is the significance of proleptic eschatological revelation.

Let me flesh these comments out a little more to indicate the direction in which I would proceed and indicate some of the implications of such an approach. I cannot here develop the eschatological trinitarian theology I have begun to reflect upon elsewhere.[15]

---

14. I have not included this position in my analysis because of its internal lack of intelligibility.

15. See my 'Revelation and Revelations: Discerning God in Other Religions. Beyond a Static Valuation', *Modern Theology* 10 (2 April 1994), pp. 165-184; 'Christ, the Trinity and Religious Plurality' in *Christian Uniqueness Reconsidered*, ed. G. D'Costa, pp. 16-29.

First, the reason why I think an *open form of eschatological trinitarian inclusivism* is preferable to alternative approaches, including Surin's, is that it allows us to ask the question of God in our relations with the other, not excluding genealogical analysis, which would help make such theological speech more rigorously self-conscious about its coercive potential. It allows us to ask the question about God without this being a closed question and without it predefining the other a priori (as is the case with exclusivism, pluralism and to a lesser extent, closed forms of inclusivism).

In fact, when we believe that the God who reveals himself in Jesus Christ as Father, through the Spirit, is also only now known through a glass dimly (St Paul, 1 Cor 13:12) and who sends the Spirit so that we may come to grow in love and understanding of the mystery of God (St John 16:12ff), we are aware of that enigmatic relation between the same and other, between the God we know through our Christian tradition and that 'same' God (as God cannot be contradictory) who can yet be so 'other', who, we do not know and do not recognise, and who ceaselessly surprises us, and who, we may yet come to discover in the self-revealing of the other as other.

In this respect the eschatological trinitarianism I defend stipulates that in the name of the Father, Son and Spirit, we have only the parameters within which our encounter with God is guided, the grammatical rules that allow us to encounter real otherness without rendering it incommensurable, but without rendering it as same (positively or negatively). It leaves the question of God's presence in the world religions entirely open and thereby allows for the possibility of the other's self-definition as a question to us, not as an answer to confirm our theory. And the genealogical self-consciousness that is rightly enjoined upon us is required to question constantly whether we coerce the other in even inviting self-disclosure.

Let me give an example. In dialogues between Theravadin Buddhist monks and Roman Catholic Benedictine monks, there has been from the Roman Catholic side a growing sense of the presence of the apophatic possibility of the presence of the Father, but a sense of this presence which deeply challenges the all too anthropomorphic sense of 'Father' so often employed in Christianity.[16] It has called into question many traditional Christologies apart from a radical kenotic Christology, and has served therefore both in the *enhancement* and *destruction* of the Christian self engaged in this conversation. Now the reason for isolating this single example from many others that could be used is to isolate this dialectic between enhancement and destruction, in which the same is radically configured through the encounter with the other and its sameness is thereby rendered both familiar and strange, a commentary perhaps and a question mark.

What is important about this dialectic is that it reflects the tradition of the development of doctrine, the deepening of faith. It finds its narrative roots in the pious young man's question to Jesus: 'Teacher, what good must I do to have eternal life?' (Mt 19:16). The young man is of course devout and serious and follows the law sensitively and honestly as reflected in his reply after Jesus has told him to keep the commandments: 'All these I have observed; what do I still lack?' (v.20). It is of course his sense of something other, some as yet unfathomed trace present in his own keeping of the law, his sense of some 'lack' which draws him into this further questioning.

Jesus' reply is a deepening of understanding of those same commandments, yet it also acts to take him out of his understanding of it, so much so that the same is rendered so dramatically other that we find that the young man can no longer understand or bear the demands of the invitation to this fresh understanding and practice in which the same is transformed by the other, into something that is the same, yet

---

16. See Benedictine-Buddhist Dialogues; and also R. Panikkar, *The Silence of God: The Answer of the Buddha* (New York, 1989); D. Tracy, *Dialogue with the Other: The Inter-religious Dialogue* (Louvain/Michigan: 1990), ch. 4.

different: 'When the young man heard this he went away
sorrowful' (v.22).

In this encounter in dialogue we find the young man
incapable of hearing, although he has heard, incapable of the
practice required of him, although he has already successfully
practised and kept the commandments. It is little wonder that
Abraham's acceptance of the security of God's promise led him
out of his land, into insecurity, into the desert. And this can be
constructively contrasted with Ulysses' return to Ithaca, a
circular movement that returns always to its own starting point.[17]

If the church is really a pilgrim church, it has the curious and
disturbing task of seeking with the other a fuller sense of truth
through dialogue, while at the same time being the bearer of the
truth of Jesus Christ, but a bearer of a truth which is not fully
grasped and plumbed, and therefore never fully understood. I
should conclude with the recognition that in some respects all
visions of other religions are distorted visions.[18] The purpose of
this paper has been to argue for a theological view of other
religions which does not distort them into sameness or
otherness (as negative sameness), but abandons the binary logic
of identification and control, for a trinitarian logic of
relationship, freedom, love and service.

---

17. Levinas writes, 'To the myth of Ulysses returning to Ithaca, we would like
to oppose the story of Abraham leaving his homeland for ever for a still
unknown land and even forbidding his son to be brought back to its point of
departure.' Levinas, *En découvrant l'éxistence avec Husserl et Heidegger*, 3rd
edition (Paris, 1974), p. 191; as translated and quoted by S. Critchley, *The
Ethics of Deconstruction: Derrida and Levinas* (Oxford, 1992), p. 109.
18. This claim has serious implications for the suspect claim by 'Religious
Studies' to offer neutral methods of retrieval and representation. See my
article, 'The End of "Theology" and "Religious Studies"' in *Theology*
(September/October 1996), pp. 338-351.

CHAPTER EIGHT

Evangelisation and the Other: Response and Responsibility

MICHAEL BARNES

My intention is to ponder on the meaning of evangelisation in a multi-faith society; in particular, to offer some theological reflection on the experience of interfaith dialogue.

Eighteen months ago a large gathering of people of faith met in Westminster Cathedral to express their concern for peace in the Gulf. In his address Cardinal Hume said: 'An early and frequent casualty of war is human sensibility: that capacity to understand and respond to human feelings'.[1] On that occasion people of different faiths committed themselves to work for peace and understanding, that what was happening in Iraq might not exacerbate divisions at home.

A care for human sensibility is surely one of the most important demands of the Good News. At the very least, Christians have a responsibility to ensure that their work of evangelisation is fully aware of, and does not contribute to, the tensions inherent in a multicultural society.

These tensions are likely to be exacerbated by the way in which – so far – the Decade of Evangelisation has been handled. Last November the Open Letter to the bishops of the Church of England was published in the *Church Times*. It focused on an important issue, the appropriateness of interfaith worship, but

---

1. Published in the *Bulletin* of the Pontifical Council for Inter-religious Dialogue, vol. 76, pp. 39-42.

did so in language which raised once again the spectre of oppressive Christian exclusivism. At the same time, comments about the scope and intentions of the Decade were not calculated to lower public tensions. Wiser counsels have now prevailed. Operation Spearhead, as it was called, has been toned down and become the more acceptable Operation Springboard. In a world of many faiths, the language which Christians use to describe their relations with other communities is crucially important.

Nevertheless, many view the Decade with apprehension. They see it as a targeting exercise, with their youngest and weakest members as the targets. As Zaki Badawi put it in an interview he gave to *The Month* a year ago, 'My immediate reaction to the decade of evangelism was alarm and fear that the churches with all their financial, political and educational power would be engaging in an unequal battle. We do not have the organisation, the financial backing or the political power'.[2]

This is the perception which many people of faith have of Christianity in this country: a powerful force which, deliberately or not, is out to destroy non-Christian faiths and to break up the communities and cultures on which that faith depends. Is a stand-off between the faiths inevitable? Or is it possible to combine an integrity of commitment to one's own faith with openness towards the beliefs of others? Good-will is not enough. We tend to think of 'other faiths' in textbook terms, as a monolithic mass of more or less like-minded individuals who believe certain peculiar things. In practice, however, we are dealing with disparate communities whose identity is found in a sometimes highly sophisticated tradition of faith. Such traditions are no more easily understood than any individual – still less community – is understood.

To think of changing the faith of another is fraught with risk. There is a moral issue here, and perhaps one of justice too. If we want to argue that communities of faith have a right to exist in

2. *The Month*, vol. CCLII, no. 1485-86, pp. 370-1.

this country and to be free to follow and practise their ancient beliefs and ways of life, do we not also have some responsibility to see that they are not overly threatened by forces which they are powerless, in many instances, to withstand? In which case, how is the Gospel to be freely proposed to people who already feel their freedom circumscribed and limited?

If we would proclaim the Gospel we must be prepared to take responsibility for the possible consequences of evangelisation. What we see as Good News may be very bad news to those who perceive their fragile family and community structures being broken up. And yet the Gospel message of the love of God made manifest in Christ is not a Christian possession, to be jealously preserved within the Church. It is for all peoples. To make it anything less would turn the Church into a sect and Christianity into a tribalism.

Much, of course, depends on the manner of witness that Christians make to the Good News which is within us. The presentation of our beliefs must be sensitive to the feelings of others. Thus we find lots of talk now about dialogue and considerable hesitation about proclamation. Has the former been adopted as a politically correct version of the latter, an acceptable form of co-existence in a pluralist society? Do we not also need to think seriously about the meaning of the language of mission?

That there is a great need for developing a more nuanced vocabulary is clear. But that is not the only issue. There is more to interfaith than a gentle style. It demands a reflection on the experience of speaking 'inter-faith' – between the faiths. Anyone who would dare move into these border realms, on the edges where the outlines of Christian identity can easily become fudged, is forced to think seriously about how that identity is formed, how it grows and how it may change.

All too often proclamation is presented as the duty, if not the birthright, of the Christian, demanding unthinking obedient compliance rather than humble reflection before the mystery it seeks to communicate. But what if that mystery is already present to the other? And through the other to us? At that point proclamation becomes bound up with the total response which is made by the Christian to the action of God – in the other as much as in oneself. Hence responsibility *and* response: the willingness to ponder at some length on the experience – and mystery – of the other and what is to be learned from the encounter with people who profess a very different faith.

I shall return to that issue at the end of this paper. First, however, something needs to be said about the ambiguity with which the word evangelisation is used. I shall say nothing about its Protestant counterpart, Evangelism. From a Roman Catholic perspective a useful starting point is the recent document on dialogue and proclamation from the Pontifical Council for Inter-religious Dialogue.[3] There it is pointed out that in Paul VI's *Evangelii Nuntiandi*, evangelisation sometimes means 'to bring the Good News into all areas of humanity, and through its impact to transform that humanity from within, making it new' (18); sometimes it means more specifically 'the clear and unambiguous proclamation of the Lord Jesus' (22). The first includes within it the various forms of dialogue, the second is more limited to traditional forms of proclaiming the Gospel message.

The document was prepared by two Vatican dicasteries, the Pontifical Council and the Congregation for the Evangelisation of Peoples. It is a fair reflection of the debate going on at various levels about the place of interfaith dialogue in the mission of the Church. To analyse the document would take too long; nor would it be a particularly satisfactory process since the two elements, coming from very different experiences, are simply juxtaposed with little comment. It might be more useful to sketch a context and to suggest how the tensions need to be understood – if not resolved.

3. 'Dialogue and Proclamation: Reflections and Orientations on Inter-religious Dialogue and Proclamation', published by the PCID, *Bulletin* 77, (1991).

The difference between the two Vatican Councils in this regard is quite striking. Vatican I mentions *evangelium* once; evangelisation not at all. Vatican II uses Gospel one hundred and fifty seven times, evangelisation thirty one times. Why the change? Between the two, of course, came the massively influential kerygmatic theology of Karl Barth with its emphasis on the proclamation of the Word to those ignorant of Christ. For the most part the Council uses the term 'evangelise' in the Barthian sense. The opening sentences of *Lumen Gentium*, for instance, speak of the Church's eagerness to 'proclaim the Gospel to every creature', while *Ad Gentes* deliberates at length on the missionary's vocation to 'announce the Gospel among the nations'.[4]

Ten years later, Paul VI's *Evangelii Nuntiandi*, despite the ambiguity noted already, developed a much broader concept than that of the kerygmatic theologians. Proclamation and catechesis are only one aspect of evangelisation, which is to be directed not just at individuals but also at cultures (20); evangelisation includes the call to human liberation, even though it may not be reduced to it (30-4). The present Pope's *Redemptoris Missio*, which came out just before the joint Dialogue and Proclamation document, continues the same line of reflection. Evangelisation is to be identified with the total mission of the Church: a 'service' which the Church can render to the world (2). A distinction is made between primary evangelisation where the Church is not yet known – and 'new evangelisation' or the re-evangelising of formerly Christian areas. But the distinction is not rigid, and the emphasis throughout is on evangelisation not so much as the work of the Church but as the work of Christ *in* the Church. There is no evangelisation without conversion of heart, that interior change based in a deep experience of the God of Jesus Christ as disclosed in the Gospel (20).

---

4. LG 1, cp 16-7; AG 24, cp 35, 39.

Seeds of the Word must be sought and acknowledged in other faiths (18). Interfaith dialogue is seen as a particular component of the total mission of the Church (655). It is part of the mission to evangelise culture. The Church as a whole is called to understand the mentality of the modern world and to seek to illuminate and purify it with the light of Christian revelation (14-15).

Between Vatican II and the present day there is a remarkable shift. The concept of dialogue entered the theological vocabulary in the early sixties – born, no doubt, from the experience of the end of the colonial age. In very general terms, it is possible to detect two tendencies. The first tries to hold together traditional missiology with the 'new' way of dialogue; either the two are separate activities, appropriate for different situations and groups of people, or the one prepares directly for the other. The second is more radical, shifting attention to the Church and to its life and self-definition in the world.

Of course, it is difficult to make too strong a distinction between the two. I find it more helpful to draw attention to the values held by different theological approaches. Thus the traditional kerygmatic approach reminds us of the prophetic nature of Christianity, while the dialogue approach raises the question of how prophecy should be practised. Proclamation is not the only way of making the Good News known.

It is, however, difficult to see how, taken in the narrow sense of proclamation, evangelisation can be made compatible with dialogue. Either they are kept in such totally separate mental compartments as to lead to a theological schizophrenia or they are 'related' with the sort of subtlety that can only cast doubt on the intellectual integrity of the participants – and thus destroy that personal trust which is the *sine qua non* of any dialogue. On the one hand, we have different strategies for different occasions; on the other, dialogue is a preparation for the 'real thing' – no more than a pre-evangelisation.

Let us turn to the second, more radical, tendency – that

which seeks to place missiology more firmly within the theology of the Church. Amongst Catholics (but not just amongst Catholics) experience of interfaith dialogue, especially over the last twenty years and especially in less formal contacts, has quite profoundly altered the way the Church as a whole comes to terms with its missionary identity.

To broaden the meaning of evangelisation so that it means, in Paul VI's words, to 'bring the Good News into all areas of humanity' is not to dissolve the problem, but it does at least create the space in which we can learn to live with it, in which a theology of interfaith encounter can emerge. In India, for example, Protestant theologians such as Devanandan, Samartha and M. M. Thomas, and Catholics like Amaladoss and Amalorpavadass have drawn attention to a wider and more inclusive understanding of mission as God's mission in which different peoples participate, giving and receiving from God in and through each other. Evangelisation includes all activities which are undertaken under the inspiration of the values of the Gospel for the building of the Kingdom. In this latter sense of evangelisation, dialogue becomes a means of mutual enrichment and co-operation in a pluralist world one way of sharing the values of the Gospel.

What has caused this shift in our understanding of evangelisation? The Church's experience of dialogue is no longer based on what I would call the 'conference' model, which emphasises aims and ends, but on a 'threshold' model, which is concerned with beginnings. In the former there is a particular topic or issue to be debated; in the latter the object of the exercise is to make a move into uncharted territory, actually to experience the difference and strangeness of being 'other'. The value of the former is in clarifying issues rationally. The latter seeks to establish the context of discussion by building personal relationships. Logically it is prior. If there is to be any inter-faith understanding possible it is through the almost religious experience of physically *moving* across the divide – not just speaking across it.

These distinctions can be traced much further back than the early sixties. Kerygmatic missiology, which in its most radical neo-Kraemerian form gives a formal justification to the conference model, feeds off a post-Enlightenment approach to the other. Here, I would suggest, alterity is defined in terms of ignorance; the non-Christian has not yet heard the Word which alone can impart saving truth. In the modern (and, more particularly, the eclectic post-modern) age, otherness is explained through distinctions inherent in culture. However much different communities share a common humanity, it is local particularity which imparts a sense of identity. 'Non-Christians' are not defined by what they are not, but by their own definitions. Similarly with the Church existing in the midst of a pluralist culture: for the most part the Church in the Third World has failed to come to terms with culture, being associated with the religion of a western, colonialist power. As theologians like Aloysius Pieris constantly remind us, the first priority for the Church in Asia is that it becomes the Church of Asia.[5] Dialogue with other faiths springs from that demand: to become part of the local culture.

Thus, within Catholic teaching over the last thirty years can be detected a shift from the language of proclamation to that of inculturation. At the same time one detects an uneasy effort to hold them both together. Any sort of resolution means adopting the broadest possible view of the scope of evangelisation, to include inculturation as the necessary preliminary to, and accompaniment of, any form of mission.

In a discussion of various models of inculturation George Soares Prabhu says it should be seen 'as a process of conversion, that is, as the passage of a religious tradition from one cultural situation to another, in a movement that resembles the conversion of a person from a situation of sin to a situation of

---

5. Aloysius Pieris, *An Asian Theology of Liberation*, (Edinburgh, 1988), especially pp. 35ff.

salvation'.[6] Conversion is not to be understood simply as a passive response to a particular experience but as an active commitment, an on-going response. In the same way inculturation involves a continuity of growth, the progressive embodying of a religious tradition within a particular culture, but also a discontinuity, which leads to a new perception of the world and a style of life which may be very different from the old. Both are necessary if the Church is to be faithful to its prophetic mission.

Whether evangelisation is identified with proclamation in the narrow sense suggested by the term evangelism, or accommodated within the broader realms of inculturation, there is a continuing tension between the two. In the former case I have suggested that there are enormous difficulties in maintaining the tension in any creative and responsible way. What of the latter?

Missiology cannot be separated from ecclesiology. The Church is a 'community for mission'; its identity lies in its being sent with Good News of the Risen Lord. But where does that identity come from? A strictly evangelical approach to mission grounds itself in the Great Commission of Matthew 28:19. A Catholic – in the best sense – approach would want to draw attention to the nature of the Church as a 'worshipping community for mission', with its identity found within the liturgical and devotional life of the community – particularly in the Eucharist. To be faithful to that identity means striking a balance between the learning or 'pilgrim' dimension and the realised eschatological dimension of the Church.

Do the two activities we are dealing with, the two sides of the missionary tension, not correspond to these two aspects of the Church's existence? The interfaith encounter, as I have described it, derives from the Church's pilgrim nature with which it shares a common concern to search for the fullness of truth. At the

---

6. George Soares Prabhu, 'From Alienation to Inculturation' in *Bread and Breath,* ed. T. K. John (Anand: Gujurat Sahitya Prakash, 1991), p. 81.

same time, the Church's nature as the eschatological community means that it must bear witness to the Kingdom of which it understands itself to be the sign and first fruits. On the one hand, an engagement with the other who is yet a neighbour; on the other, the bearing of a message which challenges, questions and enlightens all people, both inside and outside the Church.

Beginning with a reflection on the experience of dialogue we begin to open up a 'space' in which it is possible for the Christian to explore his or her relationship with the other. The now familiar traditional strategies – exclusivism, inclusivism and pluralism totally fail to do this. They develop what I have called elsewhere a theology *for* dialogue rather than a theology *of* dialogue.[7] If they have anything in common it is that they all represent 'ego-centred' theologies of self-sufficiency. The imperialism which marked old-fashioned Protestant – and Catholic – exclusivism is still to be noted in some versions of what is often unhelpfully called 'inclusivism'. Here the 'other' is reduced to a 'cut-down' version of the established and defined Christian subject. Pluralism, in a more subtle way, subverts dialogue by reducing difference and thereby imposing a premature closure on the process. Each of these paradigms operates with stereotyped models of religion and, more particularly, with predetermined ideas of the boundaries between religions.

The alternative is an analysis of the 'threshold' model of dialogue. What happens to the subject when he or she crosses over the boundaries into another world, confronting the stranger and being forced out of the accustomed attitude of self-reference? Can this relationship not be understood by analogy with any liminal experience, most obviously the confrontation with death? In this final section let me sketch a brief outline of such an approach to the other.

A liminal event, crossing the threshold, is an entry into mystery – in the obvious sense that its meaning cannot be

---

7. Michael Barnes, *Religions in Conversation* (London: 1989), p. 89ff.

grasped. But it can also be an exercise in self-assertion. Such is the point made by Emmanuel Levinas in his reflections on the nature of the relationship with the Other. In a reflection in *Time and the Other*, Levinas attempts to distinguish his analysis of 'being-towards-death' from that of Heidegger.[8] The latter's portrait of 'authentic existence', he says, is 'a supreme lucidity and hence a supreme virility. It is *Dasein*'s assumption of the uttermost possibility of existence, which precisely makes possible all other possibilities, and consequently makes possible the very feat of grasping a possibility – that is, it makes possible activity and freedom'. He then goes on: 'Death in Heidegger is an event of freedom, whereas for me the subject seems to reach the limit of the possible in suffering. It finds itself enchained, overwhelmed, and in some sense passive. Death is in this sense the limit of idealism'. The analysis, he says, begins not with the 'nothingness of death', about which we can know precisely nothing, but with the *appearance* of that which is 'absolutely unknowable'. This absolutely unknowable is the experience of 'otherness' – where every assumption of possibility is rendered impossible, but 'where we ourselves are seized'.

Although explicitly directed towards an analysis of the encounter with the alterity of death, Levinas's argument sees death as the prime analogue of the social encounter with the total mystery of another person. His immediate point is the paradox that death is a reality yet never a 'now'. It is future and therefore *ungraspable*. 'Now' is the suffering which endures the nearness of death and which marks the reversal of the subject's activity into passivity. Death is important not because it brings the final test of our heroic capacity but because it marks the onset of that moment when we are no longer '*able to be able*'. The true hero is the one who accepts the 'end of virility' and the paradox that with the destruction of hope there is yet hope.

---

8. Emmanuel Levinas, *Time and the Other*, trans. Richard Cohen (Pittsburgh: Duquesne University Press, 1987). Reproduced in *A Levinas Reader*, ed. Sean Hand (Oxford: Blackwell, 1989), p. 37ff.

Levinas's analysis raises the whole question of what it means to be in relationship with another. We tend to assume that the human situation is one which the 'I' may dominate, as if 'I' am in control of, and able to dictate to, the other; in fact, taken seriously, the 'other' which is presented *to* me is always greater than that otherness which I may acknowledge within me. The face of the other makes moral demands which imply transcendence. The mystery of God lies in the face of the other. There is, in fact, for Levinas, something of the summons of the Infinite Other in every face-to-face encounter. The other that is announced is 'not unknown but unknowable... resembling us, but exterior to us; the relationship with the other is a relationship with a Mystery. The other's entire being is constituted by its exteriority, or rather its alterity'. If this is correct, then otherness must be taken with full seriousness and not reduced to an extension of what is known.

Levinas wants to emphasise that there is more to the experience of relationship with the other than the acknowledgement of the existence of 'another freedom next to mine'. The Heideggerian analysis leaves us with a collective 'we', formed around something common but which 'feels the other at its side and not in front of itself'. As long as we exist, individually or collectively, in positions of power or domination the sheer strangeness or difference of the other goes unremarked – and, therefore, the moral demand of the other goes unheeded. There are, however, those experiences of human relationship – whether through death, sex or birth – which introduce a sense of plurality into existence and which bring with them a radical reorientation: away from the mere juxtaposition of 'self' and 'other' towards the revelation of the mystery of Being in the other who is yet the face of the Totally Other.

It is not, I feel, ending on too portentous a note to suggest that the experience of dialogue is also liminal in the sense described. To seek to evangelise the other is to risk meeting with the Other, the One who is already there. It means leaving the position of control and power and facing the frightening otherness of the stranger, in the faithful conviction that here is God.

To that extent the missionary task of the Church is not that of putting something new where it is completely lacking, but of making an existent reality more explicit, of co-operating with what is essentially the work of the Spirit. To say that before evangelising others we must first evangelise ourselves is not a cop-out. Catholic spirituality is based on an experience of the Good News – the action of God in Christ – and that Good News must first be encountered before it can be proclaimed. Evangelisation in a world of many faiths necessarily involves the other in that process of conversion which begins with ourselves. This means taking responsibility for being Church – that community which is empowered to witness to the Good News of what it knows of God through its experience of Christ – but it also means taking responsibility for the other and for the demands which the other, as a person of faith, makes upon us.

CHAPTER NINE

Evangelisation and the Ghost of Lessing

GEOFFREY TURNER

Why is it that I feel a shiver down my spine when I hear the word 'evangelisation'? Is it because I dread the knock at the front door? Is it because I fear the manipulative rhetoric of a certain kind of sermon? For someone who teaches theology, evangelisation does not have a good feel to it. But why is this? Why do I try to steer clear of evangelists? It may be that I confuse evangelisation with evangelism. Is there a significant difference between the two? Is evangelisation good and evangelism bad? I leave that to the reader.

Certainly there is a difference between theology and evangelisation. That there is a difference does not worry me but the nature of the difference is worrying. Evangelisation has at its centre the *evangelium* and while this is not to be identified *tout court* with the canonical Gospels, evangelisation must at some point – and really rather frequently – make an appeal to the story the New Testament tells about Jesus. Those who evangelise must be deeply informed by our understanding of the Gospels and must represent the life, teaching, death and resurrection of Jesus of Nazareth that we find narrated there. Why then do we find in popular evangelism/evangelisation scarcely a trace of the critical-historical understanding of the Gospels that has become the stock in trade of academic work on the New Testament? That is the problem I want to draw to your attention: the naive, innocent, uncritical and often unhistorical outlook of popular evangelisation that remains untouched by two hundred years of academic research.

In the same way, why is it that there is such a gulf between bible study groups and biblical studies seminars? Is it inevitable that bible study groups find students of the New Testament threatening and negative, while theology students often find such groups pietistic and naive? I might also add that quite a number of the students I get who are religious, particularly those from Catholic schools, at first find working on the Bible with me quite threatening, though I try to be gentle with them.

The prime aim of New Testament study, I take it, is to develop an understanding of the text which involves, so far as this is possible, among other things, establishing what is historically and religiously true. This aim can be and often is vitiated in two ways. Firstly, the possible religious truth claims of the text can be ignored and the text reduced to a piece of archaeology. The text is perceived as a museum piece kept in a glass case; occasionally it is removed from the glass case, dusted down, examined under the microscope and then returned to its display case. We find this approach among those teachers who are concerned exclusively with textual matters, etymology, historical minutiae and the fine details of exegesis. That is New Testament study as 'archaeology'.

Secondly, some exponents of New Testament study are so concerned to establish their reputations in the academic world as exciting innovators that they develop daring but implausible theories that with luck might be taken up by the quality Sunday papers. These theories should preferably involve sex and drugs: for example Allegro's phallic mushrooms or Morton Smith's homosexual initiation rites associated with Mithras; or they should question the integrity of the rise of Christianity: for example Elaine Pagels on the Gnostic Gospels of the second and third centuries or Hugh Schonfield's *Passover Plot* or the hidden secrets of the Dead Sea Scrolls.

Despite these two very serious reservations the bulk of biblical study is altogether more temperate. It is not self-seeking and has theological integrity. However, one major problem that remains in academic study of the Gospels is that there is not a clear consensus about the historical authenticity of passages in the text, particularly the sayings of Jesus. This is a problem that Ed Sanders faced in *Jesus and Judaism* and which led him in that book to begin his historical survey with the actions of Jesus. There is broad consensus, however, outside fundamentalist circles, that a historical and critical understanding of the Gospels is inescapable but that the historical scepticism of Bultmann, for example, is not justified. Yet it is indisputable that the advent of the critical-historical method has not made faith any easier. On the contrary that approach demands a lot of hard thinking and will involve leaving behind the naive reading of the text that issues from far too many pulpits and which is found in far too many pamphlets.

I am talking here about a univocal reading of the text; a reading which is univocally literal and which sees no problems about the literal truth of the text. An approach which assumes both versions of the birth of Jesus in Matthew and Luke are historically accurate; which assumes that Jesus performed all the miracles; which assumes that Jesus said all that he is said to have said about himself not only in the Synoptic Gospels but in the Fourth Gospel too; that he claimed to be the divine Son of God, that he would be killed and rise after three days, and so on.

Of course, this is associated with a fundamentalist reading of the text, but evangelisation in Catholic circles is not knowingly and determinedly fundamentalist, it simply adopts far too often an innocent uncritical reading of the Gospels. Is this because evangelists know no better, because they are half-educated or intellectually flat-footed and unimaginative in their reading of the text? Or do they choose to ignore the outcome of academic study because their aim is to provoke faith in Christ and a critical reading of the Gospels complicates this? And it does.

Evangelists have indeed hit on a problem here, perhaps without realising the nature of it. Behind this divide between evangelisation and academic study lies the ghost of Gotthold

Ephraim Lessing (1729-1781) a true son of the Enlightenment who announced that 'the accidental truths of history can never become the proof of necessary truths of reason'. And within 'reason' he included the truths of faith, so we can for our purposes read his dictum as 'accidental truths of history can never become the proof of necessary truths of faith'. This is Lessing's 'ugly ditch' as he called it.

There is a historical context for Lessing's remark. At the end of the eighteenth century it was common even in theological circles to appeal to the miracles of Jesus and his resurrection to 'prove' that he was the Son of God. It is not that Lessing doubted the miracles or the resurrection; he thought the evidence for them was as strong as historical evidence can be. The problem was that statements of faith are a different class of proposition from those of history and the truth of the one cannot be used to demonstrate the truth of the other. The historical cannot bear the weight of the eternal. And more than that, historical truths can never be 'demonstrated' in Lessing's strong use of the term. In Lessing's own words, 'If no historical truth can be demonstrated, then nothing can be demonstrated by means of historical truths. That is: accidental truths of history can never become the proof of necessary truths of reason.' Or faith.

Lessing's claim is that we are dealing with two different logical classes: historical statements which cannot be demonstrated conclusively and necessary statements of reason or faith. In Kantian terms: historical, accidental, contingent, *a posteriori* statements, the truth of which can never have more than some degree of probability; and necessary, absolute, *a priori* statements whose truth carries complete certitude. In these terms Lessing is right: we cannot use *a posteriori* premises to arrive at *a priori* conclusions. The problem is similar to G. E. Moore's 'naturalistic fallacy' in ethics where, he claims, you cannot argue from descriptions of the everyday world to conclusions about value and moral obligation, from *is* to *ought*.

In Lessing's case crossing the ditch might be called the 'historicising fallacy'.

Lessing's ugly ditch has bedevilled Protestant theology ever since and, I suggest, may be the reason why evangelists choose to steer clear of critical-historical study of the New Testament, for the assumption of a majority of theologians since the eighteenth century has been that Lessing was right and the Christian faith is not derived logically from historical events, though it obviously makes reference to historical events. There are, for example, many statements to this effect in Karl Barth, a very traditional theologian you will admit, and this sentence from 1927 will serve as an illustration, 'As far as the eye can see, there is nothing in history as such on which faith could ground itself'. Barth's answer to Lessing, at least early in his career, was to root faith in a special kind of history, *Urgeschichte*, primal history.

Other theologians, Catholic and Protestant, have tried the same move by referring to 'meta-history' or 'salvation history', *Heilsgeschichte*. In this realm the foundation events of Christianity are seen as historical because they happened, it is assumed, but the cutting edge of historical criticism must be suspended, we are told; the meaning of this special kind of history is accessible only to the eye of faith.

The fear, of course, is that the secular historian will falsify, or at any rate cast doubt upon, the historical reliability of those events, of which the paradigm must be the resurrection of Jesus, but much else besides. In this view there are two worlds of history, one embedded in the other, the history of salvation in the history of the world (*Weltgeschichte*), but the historian is free to ply his trade with full freedom in only one of them. On what, then, is faith *based* if not history? Well, for Barth it is not based on anything; it comes as Revelation to be obeyed and believed.

It is much the same for Bultmann. The Jesus of history is 'Christ after the flesh' and to seek to confirm the veracity of one's faith by historical research would be a form of justification

by works. In fact Lutheran theologians generally take a perverse
pleasure in making their faith seem intellectually insecure to
illustrate the virtue of justification by faith, where faith is seen
as an intellectually undirected leap into the dark. We see this in
Ebeling and Fuchs and Käsemann, but the influence is that of
Kierkegaard of course.

Kierkegaard was certainly influenced by Lessing, but
Lessing's own appeal was to experience. The historical evidence
for the miracles of Jesus was sound enough but it would not
convince him because the evidence came from a remote time
and he, Gotthold Ephraim, did not experience any miracles in
his time. He thought that theologians and evangelists should
give up their appeals to history; he needed miracles now and
they were not evident. What Lessing required was proof of the
spirit and power and he found this in his heart: he wrote 'For
the Christian it is simply there, the Christianity he feels to be so
true, in which he feels himself so blessed'.

Note the emphasis on religious feeling. Just like
Schleiermacher who based the truth of Christianity on 'feeling
and strong emotion'. Barth's life-long opposition to
Schleiermacher, however, drove him to find an alternative to
'feeling' in his Theology of Revelation but he never doubted the
reality of Lessing's ditch.

The best known products of nineteenth century biblical
study were the lives of Jesus but many of these either resorted to
fantasy and piety – the golden haired hero by the banks of the
Jordan – or to irresponsibly destructive criticism, some of which
we find in D. F. Strauss. Albrecht Ritschl found salvation in
Jesus's ethics – love your neighbour as a good Prussian should –
and Harnack in a very small number of eternal truths that
transcend history. When nineteenth century writers really
looked at the history of Jesus and found, as they inevitably
would, Jewishness and eschatology, or 'apocalyptic' as Weiss and
Schweitzer called it, they found they could not shape their
beliefs on those lines. No, the path of twentieth century

Protestant theology was set by Martin Kähler in his formative book of 1896 which involved separating secular history from the history which is significant for faith, which is the history of the Bible and which is *kerygmatic*.

Catholic theology, so far as I am aware, did not get to grips with the problem for some decades because of the reaction to Alfred Loisy by Pius X's Biblical Commission which severely restricted Catholic biblical scholarship for years to come.

It seems to me there are four possible ways of responding to Lessing and his ugly ditch.

(i) We can accept it and agree that, if the Christian faith is true, we will find the source of its truth somewhere other than history.

(ii) We can reject Lessing's understanding of history.

(iii) We can reject Lessing's understanding of faith, or

(iv) We can supply a plank which will take us over the ditch from history to faith.

As we have seen, most of the leading figures of Protestant theology have accepted the reality of the ditch and have turned our attention away from history to other areas for the foundation of faith, or to nowhere in the case of those who think, like Tertullian that faith is without rational foundation. Other alternatives, which alike assume the correctness of Lessing, include David Pailin who in discussing this problem takes it that as Christianity believes, as it were, eternal nonworldly things about the nature of God, it is a metaphysical faith which can only be based on metaphysical assumptions, not historical judgements.

A sort-of-Catholic position might argue that our faith is not determined by history but by the Magisterium, the teaching authorities of the Church. But where do they get their beliefs from?

One wonders what Wittgenstein might have said about this problem, because one of his major concerns was to stop science imposing its methods on all other areas of discourse. He wanted religion to be religion and not some form of science in the modern sense of the word 'science'. One suspects that he would not have looked for the foundation of Christian belief in historical evidence; in fact one suspects that he would have been suspicious of any kind of evidence produced for religious belief.

That might be alright for religion as some generalised form of mysticism but we cannot escape the historical particularity of Christianity. Christians do not base their convictions on some feeling about their own unworthiness or dependency or on the goodness of the world (though they may all be true), they base their convictions on Jesus Christ as he appeared in the course of Jewish religious history. It seems to me that if Christian theologians turn away from history, we are sunk. The plug will have been pulled on our beliefs and the history of theology since Lessing does nothing to convince me that I am wrong.

I suggest that we take all of the three alternatives to accepting Lessing's position and combine the three of them. With the second on the list we can, like Alan Richardson for example, challenge Lessing's understanding of history as being positivist. While all the history that lies behind Christianity must be open to critical historical method, we are not looking for an atomistic listing of facts, objective history as it were. Nor on the other hand should we accept uncritically all manifestations of the critical historical method. There has been enough discussion among theologians in recent years, particularly in the area of hermeneutics, for me not to have to rehearse how history might be understood. Suffice it to say that above all we must overcome the division of history into objective factual history (*Historie*) and significant interpreted history (*Geschichte*) that German theology inherited from Martin Kähler. All history is interpreted history, but it must be factually based, and there is only one category of history.

Our main criticism of Lessing, I suggest, should be directed at his view of faith as a collection of necessary truths. If we accept like Lessing and, after him, Kant that faith in its noetic sense contains *a priori* statements, then we are in trouble. In Kant's logical categories there certainly are *analytic a priori* propositions which when true give total certainty, but these are the propositions of mathematics and logic, they are tautological and tell us nothing about the world.

Kant realised that Christian faith would be irrelevant if it was made up of those, so he spent some effort in trying to show that there are some few *synthetic a priori* propositions which give absolute certainty when true, but which also give information about the world, and while Kant gave examples of what he thought would count as such propositions it is far from clear that there are any *synthetic a priori* statements. Certainly you could never prove the supposed *synthetic a priori* statements of faith by means of the *synthetic a posteriori* evidence of history – on that Lessing was right.

So if there are no historical reasons for accepting the statements of faith you have to adopt the strategy of Kierkegaard and take a blind leap of faith and pretend that blindness is a virtue, like many Lutherans, or you have to appeal to feelings as Lessing did and, more famously, Schleiermacher. And in my experience, feelings are what evangelists and evangelicals appeal to as a last resort when they are outmanoeuvred on their understanding of biblical texts.

But this is what needs to be broken: the Lessing-Kant-Kierkegaard axis and their understanding of faith as containing necessary truths, truths of which we may be absolutely certain.

Catholic theology has traditionally ascribed different levels of certainty to various statements of faith, but there was always a category of faith-statements of which we could be quite certain: doctrines which are *de fide definita*. Where do these doctrines get their status from? From Church authority, the Magisterium, rather than argumentation. Forms of argument are produced to support the doctrines but, if that fails, the magisterium guarantee their certainty. But again, how do those who make up the Magisterium, come by their knowledge?

We have to accept that the content of faith about which we can construct doctrinal statements is made up of *synthetic a posteriori* statements which give us information about the world, that can be argued for in various ways including the support of historical evidence, but the truth of which amounts to no more than some degree of probability. If that is the case it would mean that statements of faith would have a provisional character and could be changed if new evidence or argument was powerful enough. Though I am not sure that the Magisterium would take kindly to this!

Of course, what is provisional here is not the objective reality at the heart of Christianity but our knowledge of it. We are dealing with an epistemological problem. But it does mean that, in principle at least, the content of our faith could be shown to be false in part or in whole. Now many theologians in the Kantian tradition have been fearful of this, as would be many Catholics, I think, and most of our evangelists. We must distinguish, however, as theologians for centuries have, between the objective content of faith and our knowledge of it (*fides quae creditur*) and faith as a subjective act, as commitment to a way of life and trust in the promises of God (*fides qua creditur*).

What has to be bridged here is the gap between the probability of our knowledge of the content of faith and the unreservedness of the commitment we make in faith – faith as trust. That is where the risk of faith is, in deciding to trust unreservedly on the basis of less than certain knowledge. The analogy is with taking vows, with which many of us will be familiar in marriage, in religious orders or for the diocesan priesthood. Our knowledge of ourselves and the person or the community with whom we make the vow is limited but our commitment must be total – at the time of taking the vow at least. The difference with Christian belief is not the status of our knowledge but the assumption that the God to whom we commit ourselves will prove to be reliable. Faith has that kind of certainty at its heart, but it requires a strong assumption on our part.

Allowing faith to be falsifiable by new evidence or argument exposes it in a dangerous way which is bound to make us feel uncomfortable. But on the other hand if there are *no* circumstances in which Christianity could be false then it cannot be offering any interesting information about the world and would be devoid of significance. It would die Anthony Flew's death of a thousand qualifications.

I said that we should criticise Lessing's use of history and that we should reject his view of faith and that we should supply a plank for moving between the two over the ditch. There is still a ditch. On the one side we now have a non-positivist understanding of history as interpreted history; on the other side we have a provisional, non-certain content of faith, both sides *a posteriori*. Yet they are not the same. There is still a ditch but not now so ugly. History is factually based but interpretative; faith represents an interpretation of our knowledge of the world; and the plank which mediates between the two could be, I suggest, the concept of 'interpretation'.

This needs clarification that there is not time for now but 'interpretation' could be the means of stepping between history and faith. This would make theology, in the context of this discussion, what Habermas has called a historical-hermeneutic science, though I realise there are in addition other practical and speculative tasks for theology. Theology has to be an arbitrator between conflicting interpretations. There is clearly a role in this arbitration for a Magisterium as representative of the whole believing community but only if it works closely with theologians and believers in that community.

Let me return for a moment to the difference between

history and faith. Critical historical study engages with the particularity of Christian history and the concreteness of Jesus in his historical context which was first century Judaism. Now to be a Christian is not the same as being a student of history, or all kinds of drunkards and lechers and atheists who do history would be called Christians. You can, of course, be a drunkard and a lecher and a historian and be a Christian, but you need something else as well. So if the discourse of historical study deals with the particularity of Christian origins, what does faith deal with? It is, I suggest, the *universal meaning* which can be derived from historical particularly. This is what evangelism sets itself to communicate. Its mission is to communicate the general meaning of Christianity which is grounded in historical particularity; and evangelical mission in this sense should be the motivation for the historical study of Christian origins.

I started with a problem about the practice of evangelisation and it would be appropriate if I returned to evangelisation after this journey through various theological problems. If we succeed in exorcising the ghost of Lessing will there be any consequences for evangelists? I can think of two.

Firstly, I would like to loosen the grip of evangelists on religious experience and piety and get them to look again at history and the critical work of New Testament scholars. Too often evangelists appeal to pious feelings beyond the text, and too often their accounts of the history of Jesus devolve into pious generalisations of a Jesus myth rather than a narrative tightly rooted in the text of the New Testament. At the same time I would like to repeat my criticism of the archaeological study of the New Testament which holds back from looking at the religious or theological significance of the text; and to that approach to the New Testament which seems more interested in contracts with the Sunday Times supplement than the truth about Christian origins.

Secondly, I would like to loosen the grip of evangelists on the Lessing/Kantian view of faith offering intellectual certainty. Our trust in God must be complete but there is still room to question and raise doubts about the symbolic content of faith without it being regarded as a weakness or, God forbid, a sin. This would take the intellectual hubris out of evangelisation in its presentation of the Christian faith.

CHAPTER TEN

Ministry of the Word or Comedy and Philology

NICHOLAS LASH

Topicality

Early in December 1986, I was siting in Charlottesville, Virginia, minding my own business (which is to say that I was on sabbatical leave) when a letter arrived from John Coventry, asking me to address this year's conference of the Association on the topic of 'ministry of the word'.

I agreed, and almost at once began to regret having done so. The topic seemed so vast, so comprehensive, so obviously central to every aspect of Christian speech and action, that I did not know where to begin. So I turned to the dictionaries, and got a bit of a shock. The *Dictionnaire de Théologie Catholique* has only one entry under 'ministry', and that is '*ministre des sacrements*'. Ah well, that was back in 1929, in the dark ages before Vatican II. Things would be better in the bright new postconciliar world, a world which had witnessed the proclamation of a dogmatic constitution entitled '*Dei Verbum*'. Well, perhaps, but not *much* better. *Sacramentum Mundi* (1969) has *no* entries under 'ministry', and the *New Catholic Encyclopaedia*, published in 1967, has *one*, which reads 'ministry, Protestant'.

Perhaps we should not make too much of this. It is, after all, perfectly possible that, gathered under other heads and quite compatible descriptions, our Catholic self-understanding has still been permeated by a sense of all our discipleship, all our prayer and compassion, all our disciplined distinctiveness, being set at the service of the word, the *diaconia tou logou*. Possible, but I somehow doubt it, because it was not simply the *ministry* of the word which had largely ceased to figure in our Catholic vocabulary. As Karl Rahner pointed out, in 1960, commenting on the absence from Denzinger of a section on 'the Word of God', the very doctrine of God's Word had almost disappeared from view.[1] All that we were left with in its place, as shadow or caricature, was an obsessive insistence on the authority of those who saw it as their duty to protect some valuable information which God had once provided for the human race. It was as if the guide-book to some great library had been replaced by a pamphlet giving details of the burglar-alarm system.

Be that as it may, what I want to do in this paper is to try so to reflect on what 'ministry of the word' might mean as to focus our discussion on two topics of absolutely central significance for the mission and ministry of the Church in what I am most reluctant to call 'Mrs Thatcher's Britain'. Although it will take us some little time to get there, these two topics will be: firstly, the cultural and political responsibilities of a community which seriously supposed its identity to be that of a ministry of the word; and, secondly, arising from this, some reflections on the plight of preaching and adult catechesis in contemporary British Catholicism.

Yes Minister

Let me begin at the beginning, with that phrase in the sixth chapter of Acts, '*diaconia tou logou*' (6, 4), which Miles Coverdale translated as 'the ministracion of the worde of God'. To what manner of ministration, 'diaconate', or service, does the text refer? My impression is that, by the beginning of the Christian era, a word which originally had meant simply 'waiting at table' had broadened to cover all kinds of personal service and supervision; from footman to chairman, perhaps.

---

1. See Karl Rahner, 'The Word and the Eucharist', in *Theological Investigations IV: More Recent Writings*, trans. Kevin Smyth (London: 1966), p. 255.

According to some authorities, the phrase in Acts echoes or reflects the original meaning, thus suggesting that 'word-service' is a kind of 'food-service'; that those who supervise the 'conversation' that is Christianity are administrators of God's nourishment of his people.[2]

We cannot, of course, discover from the Acts of the Apostles how *we* might most appropriately arrange and institutionalise, today, the various tasks which it is our duty, as Christians, to perform. Nevertheless, that original context, in Acts, of the notion of 'ministry of the word' may serve to remind us of how important it is not to *dissociate* meaning from feeding, conversing from caring, announcing from enacting. Here, as elsewhere, the slogan might be: distinctions are usually necessary, dichotomies are invariably disastrous. 'Ministry of the word', I shall shortly be arguing, is primarily to be understood not as the name of one of the things that some of us are supposed to be doing, but rather as one way of understanding who it is, as Christians, that we are, and what, in everything we do and undergo, we are required continually to become.

The analogy drawn, in Acts, between table-ministry and word-ministry, is not, however, without its inconvenience. 'Ministry of tables' (see 6, 2) suggests supervision or governance of the community's feeding arrangements, in somewhat the same way as 'ministry of transport' suggests supervision or governance of docks and railways. But it would surely be blasphemous to suppose that the Word of God could be subject to human governance or control?

Blasphemous, or just plain arrogant. Modern liberalism (whether Catholic or Protestant), sensitive to the damage done by inquisitors and ayatollahs (especially Christian ayatollahs!),

---

2. See A. M. Farrer, 'The Ministry in the New Testament', in *The Apostolic Ministry: Essays on the Doctrine of the Episcopacy*, ed. Kenneth E. Kirk, (London: 1946), p. 138; Gerhard Kittel & Geoffrey W. Bromiley, eds., *Theological Dictionary of the New Testament*, vol. 2 (Michigan: Grand Rapids, 1964), p. 87; Edward Schillebeeckx, *The Church with a Human Face*, (London: 1985), p. 72f.

tends to be quite properly suspicious of those who confidently thunder 'Thus saith the Lord'. And yet, simply to surrender the ground to liberal modesty would be to admit that we have only opinions to offer. And I do not see why other people should find hope in my opinions.

The problem might not be so intractable if 'word of God' referred to some message which God had given to us or to some information about him which we had somehow managed to acquire. On a classical Christian account of these matters, however, God's Word is neither message from nor information concerning him. It is, quite simply, the incomprehensible mystery of God himself as he has met us and as we, in the light of that meeting, understand him to be. The Word of God is that still wisdom of which all worlds and spaces, all storms and cities, all friendships and families, are particular, transient expressions; that wisdom which found definitive flesh and voice in Nazareth and Gethsemane. The more one thinks about it, the more obvious it *seems* to be that no human being could be *theotokos*, could produce or give utterance to *this* Word.

No twentieth-century theologian, I suppose, has sought more strenuously to get the priorities right, in these matters, than did Karl Barth. He insisted that human beings could not possibly *will*, or *decide*, or *claim*, to proclaim the Word of God. And in this he was surely correct.

And yet it seems, in God's providence, *necessary* (and therefore possible) that God's Word should be proclaimed; that there should be words and deeds which appropriately declare: 'Thus saith the Lord'. The clue (according to Barth) lies in the fact that what it *means* to be 'Church' is to have been given the commission, and permission, to do the impossible thing: to proclaim God's Word. There is a decision that we have to take. It is not, however, a decision as to whether or not to proclaim the Word of God, but a decision as to whether or not to acknowledge, to accept, the commission that has been given to us.[3]

3. See Karl Barth, *Church Dogmatics I/1*, trans. G. T. Thompson (Edinburgh:

In other words, the possibility of exercising a 'ministry of the word' is a function of our grace-given obedience, our acknowledgement that we have been enabled, commissioned, thus to serve. That is why I earlier made indirect mention of Mary, the *theotokos*, of whom it was said '*concepit prius in fide quam in carne*', that she bore the Word in faith 'before' bearing it in flesh. And I entitled this section 'Yes Minister' partly because our ministry (which simply is our human and Christian existence) *consists* in our obedience to the Word by which we are borne and partly because what, as Christians, we are thereby established to be are people who embody or bear witness to God's 'Yes' to his world. Through the 'Yes' of our obedience we are made ministers of God's life-giving, reconciling, liberating, 'Yes' to his creation.

Christianity as Philology

But is this true of all of us, or is it only true of some, of a minority set apart for just such ministry? We still have not, I think, quite exorcised the clericalist suspicion that recognising *all* Christian existence to be ministry somehow deprives those whom we call 'ministers' of their *raison d'être*. Yet no-one infers, from the fact that we call some people 'civil servants', that *only* these people perform a service, or serve the *civitas*. And only the most career-crazed bureaucrat would suppose belonging to the civil service to be the real or fundamental form of ministry in our society, in relation to which all other kinds of service were only indirectly or metaphorically so called.

In the Church, as in the wider society, there are all sorts of special tasks that need to be performed, and sometimes it is sensible to allocate these tasks to particular groups of people. Such tasks require description, and the names we choose to summarise the description may *also* refer (and hence more

---

1936), pp. 56-58. This passage is, somewhat surprisingly, one of only two places in all twelve volumes of the Church Dogmatics in which Acts 6:4 is discussed.

fundamentally refer) to some general feature or function of the Church. This is the case, for example, with such notions as 'priesthood' and 'teachership' and these, in turn, derive their Christian sense from our understanding of their applicability to the Church's Lord.[4]

In other words, the proper order of interpretative derivation is *always* Christ – Church – office. Let us, by all means, describe some officers or functionaries in the Church as 'ministers of word and sacrament' but, if this description is not most dangerously to mislead both them and us, it is important that their function be performed and understood in proper subordination to that more fundamental ministry of the word which is the very *existence* of a people set apart to minister to God's promise for all mankind. And it is with 'ministry of the word' in this latter, more basic, sense that I am principally concerned in this paper.

We are, by God's grace, made ministers of his Word, ministers of his *one* Word, ministers of the Word that he is, of the Word whose 'ecstatic' utterance makes and heals all worlds.

It follows that the image of the library (which I briefly used earlier) is doubly misleading. It is misleading, firstly, because God's Word is always utterance, happening, act. It is (to borrow a distinction from neighbouring territory) discourse, not just language. Language can be locked in libraries, whereas discourse – language-in-act, language-in-use – can only be uttered or attended to.

The second reason why the image of a library is misleading is because libraries are repositories of many objects, lots of words. But God has not many things to say, just one: himself. 'God', said Karl Rahner, 'does not say all sorts of things to men, and his words are not a miscellany of disconnected subjects. In

---

4. Anyone wishing to discover why that formulation is somewhat unwieldy should consult Robert Murray's illuminating study of 'Christianity's "Yes" to Priesthood', in *The Christian Priesthood*, eds. Nicholas Lash and Joseph Rhymer, (London: 1970), pp. 18-43.

the last resort he utters only one thing, which is himself as eternal salvation in the Spirit of the incarnate Logos'.[5]

God's oneness or simpleness is not, of course, without distinction: distinctions indicated in the threefold pattern of the creed and given formal expression in the doctrine of God's Trinity. Our faith is in one God whom we triply know and in relation to whom we say three things. On this vast subject, the only point I wish to make at present is that, in our attempts to think things through, to make some Christian sense of all our circumstance, we do better to take the three articles of the creed as three ways in which one single story may be told rather than as three chapters or stages in that story.

Creation, redemption, sanctification: my suggestion is that, instead of thinking of God as doing three things – first making a world, then sorting out the mess that we made of it, then bringing the newly ordered world into his presence – we should think of three aspects of God's one work, one deed. But, of course, whichever the aspect with which, on any particular occasion, we decide to work, *under* that aspect it is the *whole* story that requires to be considered.

Thus, for example, my present topic is 'ministry of the word'. But, in order to speak of God as word, as utterance, it is also necessary at the same time to speak of God as utterer and as enactment of the utterance that he is. To *think* as a Christian is to try to understand the stellar spaces, the arrangements of micro-organisms and DNA molecules, the history of Tibet, the operation of economic markets, toothache, King Lear, the CIA, and grandma's cooking – or, as Aquinas put it, 'all things' – in relation to that uttering, utterance and enactment of God which they express and represent. To *act* as a Christian is to work with, to alter or, if need be, to endure all things in conformity with that understanding.

God's utterance is, to use a fashionable philosophical idiom, performative. The story of the world, as Christianly told under

---

5. Rahner, 'The Word and the Eucharist', p. 278.

the aspect of word or logos, is the story of God's utterance of a world as a place for his indwelling. This is the story of the world as told in relation to God the promiser, God the promise, and God the achievement of the promise.

To tell the story of the world this way, and to try to act in conformity with this narrative and its implications, is to set a very high value indeed on the proper use of words. Even after so brief a sketch of what is at issue in the claim that all Christian existence and activity is required to be *diaconia tou logou*, *ministerium verbi*, service of the word, it should therefore come as no surprise to find Père Chenu insisting that the theologian is first of all a 'philologist'.[6]

This is a marvellously provocative claim because, for most of us, 'philology' conjures up images of elderly gentlemen, innocent of ordinary human intercourse, lovingly dusting down volumes of no possible use or interest to anyone except themselves. But, of course, the point of the suggestion is to turn the prejudice of pedantry on its head. Commissioned as ministers of God's redemptive Word, we are required, in politics and in private life, in work and play, in commerce and scholarship, to practise and foster that philology, that word-caring, that meticulous and conscientious concern for the quality of conversation and the truthfulness of memory, which is the first casualty of sin. The Church, accordingly, is or should be a school of philology, an academy of word-care.

A Comprehensive Grammar School

It is, unfortunately often supposed that the Church is a 'religious' institution. Consider the disadvantage of this view. When bishops talk about religion, they rarely have anything

---

6. 'Le théologien est d'abord un philogue; les techniques auxquelles il se livre sont l'invention de son "amour des mots", le moyen de sa fidelité à leur mystère', M. D. Chenu, 'Vocabulaire Biblique et Vocabulaire Théologique', in *La Parole de Dieu, I: La Foi dans l'Intelligence* (Paris: 1964), p. 186; this essay was first published in 1952.

interesting to say. And when they say something interesting, they get rapped over the knuckles for not talking about religion. We might call this the Hailsham predicament.

Religion, it seems generally to be supposed, refreshes the parts that Mrs. Thatcher cannot reach. But it is not easy to specify what these parts, these 'spiritual' parts, might be. If I were to make my own list of serious spiritual problems confronting this country, it would include: regional disparity of housing costs, insider dealing, the collapse of manufacturing industry, the banking system's influence on the Third World, private schools, AIDS, child-abuse, and Rupert Murdoch. But this is hardly a menu of 'religious' difficulties!

Most of the things that we do and say and undergo have little or nothing to do with 'religion' or, at least, with what nearly everyone now takes the term 'religion' to mean. Whereas there is *no* area of life that lies outside the scope of a good education, a genuinely comprehensive education. Therefore, it may be helpful to think of the Church as a school, a comprehensive school. And because it is a school of philology, an academy of word-care, it therefore is or needs to be a comprehensive *grammar* school!

It is, I hope, already clear that this view of the matter has political as well as theological presuppositions and implications. To be a little more precise, it expresses a view of the relationship between Christianity and the social order which will be strenuously resisted by those in whose political interest it is to insist that Christianity confine itself to 'religious' issues. But the ministry of the word admits of no such demarcatory stipulation.

Let me go back, for a moment, to the beginning. In the beginning was the Word. It is clear from the book of Genesis that God makes by speaking: 'God said "Let there be light" and there was light'. It therefore follows that God's world makes sense.

To say that God's world makes sense is to say two things. Firstly, it is to insist, against the darker and more anarchic 'constructivisms' of modern thought, that such sense as there is to things, such plot or order or intelligibility, is not simply placed there by the impudence of our imagination but is, more deeply, given and bestowed in the very fabric of things. It follows that the ministry of the word is a service of discernment, of attending to and learning from the meanings that there are.

But, secondly, to say that the world *makes* sense is also to acknowledge (this time, *with* the grain of the modern mind) that sense and meaning have a history, that they are products and processes, and that human beings (as the world's word-bearers) contribute enormously both to the making and enrichment of sense and also to its impoverishment and destruction. Dante and Einstein deepen the meaning of the world, whereas war destroys not only matter but meaning. It follows that the ministry of the word is a service, not only of discernment and discovery, but also of sustenance, construction, and repair.

God's Word makes and heals, not some things, or some kinds of thing ('spiritual' things, for example), but all things. God's Word makes and heals the world. It therefore follows that *all* words, all areas of discourse and discovery, of debate and design, are matter for our ministry. But, if *everything* is grist to the Christian mill, what then becomes of the distinctiveness of Christianity?

Christianity, I have suggested, is a school, an academy of word-care. The distinctiveness of Christianity arises from the fact that our schooling occurs at a particular place: namely, on the road to Emmaus. It is on that road and in that company that the pedagogy of Christian discipleship takes place. It is what we learn on the road to Emmaus, and the manner in which we learn it, which furnish us with criteria of speech and action appropriate for the exercise of our ministry on all *other* roads – from Fleet Street to Wall Street. Or, to put it another way, learning to be a Christian is a matter of discovering every road to be the way to Emmaus.

It is, of course, also necessary to insist that, as the recent report *Changing Britain*, prepared for the Church of England's Board of Social Responsibility, puts it: 'There is no such thing as a pure undiluted witness to the Gospel, uninfluenced by the context in which it is made'. From which it follows, according to this report, that 'it is foolish to imagine that the churches in Britain could in some sense stand over against the rest of British society, and address it as if they did not share its problems. This study has been written from within the problems'.[7]

It is good to have this reassurance. Without it, one might have thought that only people quite *outside* the pain and degradation, the slow rotting of dignity and energy in the long-term unemployed, the spreading stranglehold of centralised control in the name of individual liberty, the structured gratification of the crudest forms of financial self-interest, the dangerous demoralisation of nurses and teachers, the attempts made to reduce health and education, so far as possible, to the status of commodities, the tribal reassurance which the well-healed receive through the systematic misdescription of the causes of poverty, the energy expended in sustaining the illusion that somebody could win a nuclear war – one might have thought that only people writing 'outside' these problems could have produced, in the summer of 1987, such impeccably well-mannered and dispassionate observations concerning the recovery of 'balance' and the nurturing of common values in 'changing Britain'. If British Christians cannot see that this is a time in which word-care requires the risks of anger and the accents of Amos, then I fear that there is never likely to be such a time – not, at least, until it is much too late.

Anger, of course, can only serve the redemptive purposes of the Word when tempered and purified of self-indulgence. But then *all* appropriate uses of language call for discipline and precision. It is sheer philistinism to suppose that only academics and intellectuals care or need to care about the uses of language.

---

7. *Changing Britain: Social Diversity and Moral Unity* (London: 1987), p. 64.

Where the private realm is concerned, we have not yet lost sight of this. We know how difficult it is to 'say the right thing' in forgiveness or apology, in affection or anger, in description or enumeration, and we *work* at our discourse accordingly. It is, perhaps, one test of civilisation that the quality of *public* discourse is just as carefully nurtured. But, by this test, we are increasingly relapsing into barbarism. Nor, of course, does the decadence of public discourse leave the private realm long unaffected.

Consider, for example, 'our great British press', as recently described in *The Tablet* by a former assistant editor of *The Daily Mirror*. He spoke of the 'squalid, one-sided, often ludicrously and crudely unbalanced reporting and coverage of national life', of the 'overall cultural dishonesty' of the national press, and of the dangers to democracy in increasing 'sameness of content' and 'lack of editorial courage'. Nor, as he made quite clear, was it only the tabloids that he had in mind.[8]

The problem of the press has far-reaching economic, political, ethical, legal, and educational ramifications. And although it has, for the most part, little or nothing directly to do with 'religion', it is, quite certainly, among the graver spiritual problems of our time. It can therefore serve as a convenient illustration of the *kind* of issue to which, as a community commissioned to the ministry of God's creative and redemptive Word, we might be expected to devote much time, energy, study and organisation. My guess, however, is that it was *not* the kind of issue which came immediately to mind when you noticed that the programme included a paper on the ministry of the word.

5. The Catechist as Comedian

Christian existence, construed as ministry of the word, is laborious – because word-care requires unremittingly

---

8. Geoffrey Goodman, 'Our Great British Press', *The Tablet*, 13 June 1987, p. 629f.

painstaking attention to detail. Word-care (in Christian hands, *all* word-care) is reverence or prayerfulness, and prayer, as Enda McDonagh has said, 'is undoubtedly one of the fine things which "since Adam's fall needs much labouring"'.[9]

But where will such labour be *learnt*, if not in the day-to-day life of that school of philology which is, or should be, the Christian church? And yet, for all the lip-service paid to the importance of adult catechetics, very little seems actually to be going on (in terms of either ideas or organisation) which might facilitate the continuing theological education, in every parish in this country, of ordinary Catholic men and women.

By theological education, here, I mean education in that 'primary theology' which is each person's wrestling with the attentiveness to the Word of God in all the circumstances of their daily living. As Enda McDonagh brings out excellently, in the essay to which I referred just now, theological education in this sense (what I have been calling education in word-care) occurs in the interplay between prayer, and poetry, and politics. It is a quite practical matter, the pattern of whose pedagogy, as Joseph Cardijn knew and as 'basic Christian communities' throughout the world have recently been rediscovering, is 'See – – judge – act'.

Who is going to train the kinds of guides and teachers which such pedagogy requires? Not, or at least not directly, the universities, because 'secondary' or academic theology meets different requirements and operates with different criteria of what would constitute a job well done. Let me risk a parable of the differences I have in mind.

As a general rule, to which the exceptions are probably fewer than we might think, jokes are always arguments. But telling a joke is by no means the same thing as telling the argument of

---

9. Enda McDonagh, 'Prayer, Poetry and Politics' in *Language, Meaning and God: Essays in Honour of Herbert McCabe OP*, ed. Brian Davies (London: 1987), p. 234. The quotation is from W. B. Yeats' poem 'Adam's Curse'.

the joke. In fact, if you resort to spelling out the *argument*, you've killed the joke.[10]

Jesus taught in parables. Catechetics, like preaching, is a matter of telling jokes, though we must not forget that jesters are tragic figures, and that the centrepoint of divine comedy is the Cross of Christ. Some academic theologians, trained in the indispensable but subordinate business of working out, historically or philosophically, the argument of the joke, are also competent as Christian comedians, but the majority, I rather think, are not.

I mentioned preaching. There can be few more conclusive proofs of the extent to which Catholic Christianity is currently *not* understood to be 'ministry of the word' (in spite, incidentally, of the admirable sixth chapter of *Dei Verbum*) than the poor quality of most preaching. (In my experience, Catholics who deeply disagree about almost everything else nearly always agree, with some passion, about the poverty of preaching.)

On this sad fact, two comments. In the first place, much Sunday preaching is infected with untruthfulness. I do not mean that preachers lie to, or deliberately mislead, their congregations. By and large, this is not, I think, the case. I mean that they simply do not much care what they say. How do I know this? Because good speech, apt and accurate and truthful speech about things that really matter to the speaker, calls for the labour of craftsmanship. And with word-caring, as with woodcarving, the lack of such labour is not difficult to detect.

In the second place, the language of too many sermons hovers in some no-man's-land – far from particular fact, event, and need – born of collusion between, on the one hand, an indolent biblical fundamentalism and, on the other, abstract evocation of feeling or equally abstract exhortation to virtue. What is missing is, firstly, the particular *facts*, both ugly and beautiful, which surround us on every side and, secondly, the

---

10. Cf. Thomas F. Green, 'Learning Without Metaphor', in *Metaphor and Thought*, ed. Andrew Ortony (Cambridge: 1979), pp. 464-466.

words that might enable us to interpret these facts in the light of the Gospel. It is amazing how seldom one feels, at the end of the sermon, that anything has actually been *said*. This is a plea, not for 'relevance', but for honesty and hard work.

As Catholics, we hear much talk of 'magisterium' but receive very little teaching. My plea to the bishops would be that they take their responsibility for teachership much more seriously, and this in two directions. Where the world behind them, or over their shoulder, is concerned, it is surely their duty to correct the widespread, erroneous, and dangerous impression that whatever is said by the Pope, or by a Roman congregation, thereby constitutes the teaching of the Catholic Church. And, in front of them, if the plight of preaching and primary theological education is anything like as serious as I believe it to be, then it is surely a function of episcopal 'magisterium' to stimulate and coordinate the necessary transformations of structure, education, imagination and understanding.

The Rest is Silence

I must, at this point, apologise to those of you who have been irritated by my decision to touch lightly on a wide range of topics related to my theme rather than develop any one of them in depth and detail. I did so in the belief that, since mine was to be the opening paper at our conference, I would probably serve discussion better by casting my net fairly widely.

I have sketched an account of what 'ministry of the word' might mean which has (in my opinion) two rather important things going for it. First, it is an account of Christian existence, as ministry of the word, which operates at a much more basic level than that at which distinctions are (quite properly) drawn between being a Christian and being a Christian commissioned by the community to perform a particular kind of service *within* the community.

Secondly, it is an account of Christian existence, as ministry of the word, which owes nothing to those dualisms of matter and spirit, secular and sacred, culture and religion, which – however useful they may be to some of the friends and some of the enemies of some of the things that count as 'religion' – render it quite impossible to give a coherent account of what it might mean for human beings to serve God's word incarnate.

To construe Christian existence as ministry of the word is not, of course, to see it as something that is likely to be of particular interest to what *The Guardian* calls 'the chattering classes'. It may, in fact, be just as well that those of the chattering classes who take an interest in these things at all seem much more interested in religion than in Christianity.

Incidentally, with human beings, as with other apes, chattering is often an indication of fearfulness (as a talkative person, I should know!) It is, however, not *many* words, but words well used, words *cared* for, that we need, in order to be able, with *such* use of words, to hear beyond them, into silence.

Whether or not, as Christian philologists, we do our work well, faithfully execute our commission, is to be judged by the extent to which we help ourselves and other people to cope with the silence, to *bear* the silence, the sometimes empty-seeming, sometimes awe-inspiring, sometimes torturing darkness of God's utterance.

Let me try to unpack that remark a little, with reference to the last scene of Hamlet.

'The rest is silence', Hamlet says. And dies. There is nothing more to be said or done. Not, at any rate, by him. He is now dead. The action has ceased. The soliloquies are stopped. The rest is *silence.*

For Hamlet, perhaps, but not for Denmark, or for us. Immediately (though first heard off-stage a moment before) on comes Fortinbras with his army, flags flying, drums beating, pipes playing. And, as if this were not noise enough, Fortinbras gives an order: 'Go, bid the soldiers shoot'. Bang. Curtain. End of play.

But, of course, I have omitted something. Between Hamlet's death and Fortinbras' arrival, Horatio mourns his friend. 'Now cracks a noble heart; – good night, sweet prince; And flights of angels sing thee to thy rest'. Thy *rest?* Is *that* what Hamlet meant? Did his words, 'the rest is silence', echo the irony or tension in the word from the Cross: '*tetelestai*', '*consummatum est*', 'it is finished'? And, if so, what are we then to make of Fortinbras' instruction, which ends the play? Is 'bid the soldiers shoot', giving the *last* word to destructive clamour, some kind of blasphemous contradiction, or despairing denial, of that '*consummatum est*', the *rest* is silence?

Perhaps, and that is certainly one of the options open to us – especially if we set, behind Shakespeare's text and the image of Calvary, the further filter of the silence of nuclear winter. It is, I think, quite *possible* to read the logic of this last scene as, a logic of despair.

But we should remember that, in contrast to Hamlet's torturing uncertainties, his chaos-pregnant introspection, Fortinbras's stands for stability, continuity, and order. 'Bid the soldiers shoot'. Perhaps, with Hamlet's dying words in mind, we can read this last line as setting a question, a protest, a *plea*: can continuity, stability and order, making sense of things, *really* only be sustained in this way, through gunfire? Or are there, however fragile, other possibilities, possibilities which would (as it were) leave *Hamlet* with the last word? This does, at least, seem also to be an *option*, a way of taking the world. And it is, surely, the fostering and sustaining of this arduous but undespairing option which it is the duty of God's philologists to serve.

The purpose of word-care, I said, is to help people to bear the silence, both to body and to *hear* the silence. For we are, in fact, already surrounded by, borne by, breathed by, uttered by, that silence to which Karl Rahner once said: 'Then will begin the great silence in which you alone resound, you who are Word from eternity to eternity'.[11] And *this* silence *is* rest.

---

11. Quoted by Herbert Vorgrimler in *Understanding Karl Rahner: An Introduction to His Life and Thought*, trans. John Bowden (London: 1986), p. 139.

CHAPTER ELEVEN

Subsidiarity in the Church

JACK MAHONEY

In recent years the debate about the exercise and distribution of power within the Roman Catholic Church has settled increasingly around the notion of the principle of subsidiarity, which was given its classical formulation by Pius XI in 1931 in his social encyclical *Quadragesimo anno*. While acknowledging the growing need for collective state activity in many areas of life, the Pope added the important qualification of a 'principle of social philosophy', that just as one may not take from individuals and transfer to the community what those individuals are able to do on their own and with their own resources, it would be unjust to withdraw from groups at a lower level the functions which they can perform themselves, and hand those activities over to a larger body on a higher level. For the natural purpose of every intervention in social matters, he pointed out, is to help the members of the social body, and not to destroy or to absorb them.[1]

The word subsidiarity can be misleading in English, for in our normal usage 'subsidiary' tends to mean subordinate or secondary in importance, as when we refer to minor subsidiary companies serving a major parent company. What the principle refers to, however, is the idea of subsidising, and the function of larger social bodies with more powerful resources to help, or to offer subsidy to, smaller and less powerful bodies. Various

---

1. *AAS* 23, 1931, 203.

commentators explain it as based on a view of the human person and of society according to which the human person is the basis and purpose of society. For its part, the function of society is to help persons, either positively by providing whatever facilities they need in order to attain their individual and collective goals; or negatively by intervening only when necessary, and thus leaving individuals and groups the freedom to act as they judge appropriate.[2]

It would be misleading to view the principle of subsidiarity as simply one of non-intervention in social matters, for pursuing that element unilaterally could lead to an abandonment of weaker elements in society, in a manner similar to the 'enterprise culture' which some commentators today castigate as an uncaring abdication of social responsibility towards society's less powerful individuals. The principle is also seen as justifying intervention when necessary, for the good of less powerful individuals or groups, or for the common good.[3] This, of course, raises crucial political questions of who is to decide when intervention, or subsidy, is required, on what criteria, and what form such help should take. In general, however, what the principle of subsidiarity aims to achieve is a social balance between lesser and greater bodies within a society, but with a built-in preference for the identity and integrity of the lesser so far as this is possible.

As so expounded by Pope Pius XI, the principle of subsidiarity came to be applied regularly in Church and papal teaching as an essential element of any just social order. It was not surprising, then, that after the Second World War Pope Pius XII should invoke it in an address to new Cardinals on the subject of social reconstruction. What was surprising, however,

2. Cf. Joseph A. Komonchak, 'La subsidiarité dans l'Église', *Bulletin du secrétariat de la conférence épiscopale française* (January 1988).
3. Cf. R. E. Mulcahy, 'Subsidiarity', in *New Catholic Encyclopedia*, vol. 13, 762-3. M. Müller, 'Freedom, II Philosophical', in *Sacramentum Mundi*, vol. 2, 356b-357a.

and has proved uncomfortable in some quarters today, was the fact that so powerful a figure as Pius XII then went on to describe the principle as valid for life in society at every stage, including the life of the Church, while respecting, of course, its hierarchical structure.[4]

With such a papal seal of approval, the principle of subsidiarity within the church figured in numerous discussions in the Council, mainly with reference to decentralisation, and to finding a proper balance between the powers of the papacy and the Roman Curia on the one hand, and the powers of diocesan bishops and of regional or national conferences of bishops on the other. That is the context in which it largely occurs today, especially since the Extraordinary Synod of 1983 called for a study of two topics which it saw significantly connected, the applicability of the principle of subsidiarity within the Church, and the status and competence of episcopal conferences. A draft document on the status of episcopal conferences has recently been circulated to them arguing the Curia's position and inviting comment; and if the American reactions, both from bishops and theologians, are anything to go by, it is in for a very rough passage indeed.[5]

For in all the debates about power-sharing within the Church there is regularly considerable support from some quarters in the interests of decentralisation, but also powerful opposition and strong reservations from others, mostly expressed in terms of concern for unity in the Church and for papal primacy. So much so that I begin to think that the debate in the Church on the principle of subsidiarity is reaching an impasse, and this for two reasons: partly because of the hidden agenda underlying the debate, and partly because of the restricted theological context in which the debate is being conducted.

---

4. *AAS* 38 (1946), 144-6.
5. cf. *America* (19 March 1988).

The hidden agenda really concerns the need or otherwise for organisational changes within the Church. Accordingly as one sees or does not see the need for such structural reforms, then one will appeal to the principle of subsidiarity or reject it. The American ecclesiologist Joseph A. Komonchak, in a paper delivered earlier this year to a conference in Salamanca on episcopal conferences, observed perceptively that it was not so much that theories about subsidiarity suggested the need for reforms in the Church, as that the desire for reforms suggested recourse to the principle of subsidiarity as a convenient rationale to justify them.[6] And, of course, underlying the differences about the need and possibilities for organisational change and reform are to be discerned the fundamental differences in ecclesiology which emerged to light in the Council and have tended to become stronger and polarised in the years since then. It is these differing theological views of the Church which on the one hand lead some to stress its human dimension and therefore the light which can be thrown on it by human realities and the human sciences, and on the other hand lead to a reaction which has come recently to stress the mysterious character of the Church. It may be noted that such reaction does not stress the divine aspect of the Church to the detriment of the human, for this would be a form of docetist ecclesiology. More subtly it stresses that the Church must not be conceived in *too* human terms. And so the debate on subsidiarity in the Church is in danger of exhausting itself in an endless interchange of 'yes buts'.

Thus, if the Catholic Church has claimed for so many centuries that it constitutes a visible, and indeed, perfect, society, on the analogy with secular society, then should not the principles of any just human society apply also to the Church? And if such principles are resisted, then are not those who otherwise claim that the Church is a genuine society in danger

---

6. French text in Mononchak cited above.

of being selective, if not evasive, in applying the analogy? On the other hand, however, if every comparison limps, then the same must be said *a fortiori* of every theological analogy, which is by definition partly true but also partly false. And if the social analogy of the Church is true in some respects but false in others, then in which of these areas, truth or falsehood, is the principle of subsidiarity to be located? The canon lawyer, Jean Beyer, in a recent survey of the debate, concludes that subsidiarity cannot be applied without qualification to the life of the Church without ignoring the element of mystery in the Church and seriously deforming the nature of the Church. For the sovereign power of a nation resides in its people, and adopting this political philosophy within the Church would call in question the primacy of Peter and the collegiality of the body of bishops, both of which are of divine institution.[7]

There are, no doubt, various ways in which one could counter such claims that subsidiarity has no place in the Church. One could argue that subsidiarity is essential to the very nature of any just society, as Pius XII did, and that if the analogy of the Church as a society is to possess any truth at all, it must include this basic of any just society. One could claim that only the recognition of the principle of subsidiarity can safeguard human rights and human dignity within the Church, and that it does not call in question the Church's hierarchical structure, but on the contrary clarifies it. For, as Pope Pius XI observed in first articulating the principle, governments ought to realise that not only will this principle assure a happier and more prosperous state of affairs, it will also enhance social authority and power, and give more perfect expression to the hierarchical order of the various groups within society. One could therefore argue that subsidiarity is not a levelling up or levelling down principle in Church life, but a simple expression of common sense and administrative efficiency that higher and

---

7. Jean Beter SJ, 'Le principe de subsidiarité: son application en église', *Gregorianum* 69:3, (1988), 435-459.

more extensive powers should not waste and dissipate their time and energy in meddling in matters which can equally well be settled at a more local level.

One could also argue, as I have done elsewhere, that what is basically in question is the difference between subsidiarity and delegation.[8] Delegation is the granting of power by a higher authority to a lower in terms of a carefully prescribed function and limited sphere of activity. The superior might do it better, and might prefer to do it in person. But we cannot all do everything, and so *faute de mieux* one recruits assistants and delegates them, while keeping a careful eye on them and requiring of them a regular account of their stewardship. Subsidiarity, by contrast, is almost entirely different in principle from delegation. It is not a trickle-down theory of power, but an acknowledgement of particular stratified competences at each level of society. It does not impart power; it recognises it wherever it already exists. It is an honest acknowledgement of the inherent tension in any society between particularity and universality. This element of recognising power, rather than imparting power, is evident in the idea which Pius XI and Pius XII explained as basic to subsidiarity, that 'a social undertaking of any sort, by its very nature, ought to aid the members of the body social, but never to destroy and absorb them'. It would in fact be more accurate to the present debate to take up this papal idea and to restate the principle as basically one of non-absorption. Such a restatement in terms of non-absorption recognises that there is something already there in possession which should not be subsumed or taken over except when absolutely necessary.

Ultimately, however, the debate over subsidiarity in the Church is a confrontation of mentalities indicating differing priorities in where one starts from in considering the idea of the Church. Does one start from the universal Church, with a stress

8. J. Mahoney, *The Making of Moral Theology* (Oxford: 1987), pp. 168-72.

on its worldwide unity, and then ask how much diversity and how much initiative is permissible consonant with that unity? Such a universalist perspective is probably more congenial to Roman curial personnel with a tradition of exercising power on a world-scale and suspicious of anything which appears to erode their power. Or does one start from the ecclesial and collegial reality of local or regional churches and their particular cultural and pastoral characteristics, and then ask how much restriction or self-denying ordinance is required of them in order to maintain communion with others in the universal Church? In the nature of the case, such a perspective will flourish more outside Rome and engender a climate of resistance to any encroachments on local powers of initiative. Nor will appeal to the principle of subsidiarity automatically resolve this difference in basic mentalities. It will only at best express it in different terms, while also contributing its own problems of whether or not social categories and the principles of social justice can apply across the board to a body of divine institution.

That is my first reason for suggesting that the debate on the principle of subsidiarity within the Church is reaching an impasse. My other reason is the restricted theological context in which the debate is being conducted. The focus of the current debate is on the nature and status of episcopal conferences; but there is an element of theological weakness in that attempt to identify the comparative powers of Rome on the one hand and regional episcopal conferences on the other. For it is in danger of being conducted in an ecclesial vacuum and is to that extent a debate not about ecclesiology but about episcopology. Before it can be adequately identified, not to mention resolved, there is need for further theological work on the role and rationale of episcopacy within the Church. For instance, current thinking on the episcopate seems to view it as first and foremost the historically continuous apostolic body into which individuals are coopted in order collectively to exercise a care for the universal Church. Only secondarily are individual bishops assigned by the head of the college to local communities of believers. Apart from the universalist perspective on the Church which such a theology of the episcopate safeguards, it also has the advantage of making sense of auxiliary bishops, preventing them from being theological anomalies, and also of preventing curial bishops from being theological monstrosities. What it cannot account for, however, or only with great difficulty, is the ecclesial reality and the territorial uniqueness of actual local Churches, which tend to be seen more as administrative units reminiscent of the late Roman Empire than as the communities of Christians and instances of Christ's eucharistic initiatives which they primarily are.

Even if the theology of episcopacy is given a fuller ecclesial perspective, however, the debate over the recognition and exercise of power can still degenerate into conflict expressed in political terms over either democratisation and federalism on the one hand or absolutism and collectivism on the other. What still appears to be lacking in the discussion is the christological dimension, and that can be uncovered by asking what sort of power it is which is in debate within the Church. In this connection it is revealing to recall the anxieties which Pope Paul VI expressed about the possible abuses of subsidiarity when he observed that it should not be confused with a claim for pluralism which would affect the faith, the moral law, and the fundamentals of the sacraments, liturgy and canonical discipline.[9] In other words, he viewed the debate about subsidiarity as globally one about the exercise by the hierarchy in the Church of its triple traditional powers of governing, teaching and sanctifying.

This, of course, is where my suggestion of the idea of non-absorption as preferable to that of subsidiarity takes on significance. For, as one looks back on the history of the Church, it is clear that the development of the episcopal office as characteristically one of ruling, teaching and sanctifying the

---

9. *AAS* 61 (1969), pp. 10-11.

faithful has been to a notable extent a development in absorption, and of the gradual concentration within the clergy of the prerogatives given to his whole Church by Christ of sharing in his triple mission as priest, prophet and king. The connection between the two threefold activities was noted by the Council when it observed in its decree on *The Apostolate of the Laity* (no. 2) that 'Christ conferred on the apostles and their successors the duty of teaching, sanctifying and ruling in his name and power. But the laity share in the priestly, prophetic and royal office of Christ and therefore have their own role to play in the mission of the whole People of God in the Church and in the world'. Christ's priestly, prophetic and kingly activity is therefore something in which his whole Church shares, and the Constitution on the Church devotes considerable attention to spelling out how each of these prerogatives is shared in varying degrees throughout the Church.

One liberating result, which has not yet been fully appreciated, is that what we have come historically to term *magisterium*, or official power to teach on faith and morals in the Church, was identified more biblically by the Council as the expression of Christ's prophetic office, and that such prophetic activity, both in the church and in society, is not intended to be absorbed by, or be the monopoly of, any one group within the Church.[10]

Another significant conclusion from locating the functions of bishops within the christological endowments of the whole Church can be seen in the area of worship and liturgy, which shows perhaps the most obvious historical example of absorption, in the concentration in the hands of the clergy of the priestly birthright of all the baptised. It is particularly interesting to note in this context the reform in the Council's decree on the liturgy (no. 28) which expresses the principle of non-absorption in microcosm: 'in liturgical celebrations each

---

10. Cf. J. Mahoney, 'Magisterium and Moral Theology', *The Month* (March 1987), pp. 90-94.

person, whether minister or faithful, performing their function, should do only what relates to them, and all that relates to them, from the nature of the rite and the liturgical norms'.

If recovering the prophetic role of all in the Church provides a richer context in which to enquire why teaching power concerning faith and morals should be concentrated in the hierarchical and papal *magisterium*; and if recovering the priestly role of all the baptised offers a theological context to consider why some exercises of sanctifying power should be the prerogative only of some within the assembly of the faithful; then consideration of the royal role of all the faithful may be expected to cast a searching christological light on the exercise of administrative power, or jurisdiction, within the church. It does not seem enough, important though it obviously is, to enjoin on those who possess such power the evangelical qualities of humility and service, nor even to preach the qualities of humility and obedience to those who do not. The question surely is, how does the Christian body as a whole exercise its christly royal power?

One stock response has been to invoke the principle of the division of labour, so that the laity are to exercise Christ's kingship in secular society, while the clergy exercise it through jurisdiction by governing the laity. Among the several difficulties, however, which arise from such a distinction of lay and clerical spheres of activity, the most important one here is the systematic exclusion which it perpetuates of all who are not clerics from any share in the Church's internal governance. By contrast, what the Christian kingship of the baptised seems to make theologically incontrovertible, and what the Council recognised, if only in theory and in embryo, is that each individual does and should have a contribution to make in such matters within the Church as a consequence of their baptismal birthright of freedom and sovereignty in Christ.

And this quite apart from any appeal to subsidiarity or to social philosophy, or even to the recognition of human rights within the Church, which, as I have suggested, are too debatable, or contentions, to yield agreed conclusions or practical improvements in the organisational life of the Church. There remain, evidently, even in this richer and more stimulating christological context, further questions of how such Christian baptismal power in organisational and structural matters is to be deployed in local and regional communities, as also at the level of the universal Church. At the very least, however, what the kingship of all Christ's baptised entails is that deliberations and decisions in such areas should be matter not for dictating, far less for despotism, but for dialogue as between royal equals.

As a practical application of what I have been exploring on the principle of nonabsorption I should like to reflect now on a matter which will in the not too distant future, please God, be a matter of major ecclesial import in Britain. I refer to the remit given by the Pope and the Archbishop of Canterbury to ARCIC II to consider the practical steps to be taken when unity is achieved between our two Communions. Inevitably the major items on the ARCIC agenda are concerned with matters of faith more than with detailed matters of Church order. And while it is cause for Christian satisfaction that the recent Lambeth Conference gave a positive reception to the Final Report of ARCIC I, there can be little doubt that its own internal divisions on the admission of women to the fullness of the ordained ministry in the Church is viewed by some as a major ecumenical setback in securing unity in belief; although others may be more influenced on this divisive topic by the view, to adapt Aristotle, *Amicus Petrus, sed magis amica veritas.*

Nevertheless, the pursuit continues for the mind and will of Christ for his Church, as it must, and it is not too early to attempt to discern the visible features which it might in the future possess. I should, however, point out two very important qualifications on what I am about to suggest. One is that, since one of the partners involved will be the Church of England, I am limiting my consideration to its Roman Catholic parallel in England, rather than to the Catholic community in Britain as a whole. The other qualification I must stress is that it would be insulting, and indeed offensive, to other Christian churches and ecclesial bodies in England to view the future or the future structure of Christian unity in England as simply one worked out as between Anglicans and Roman Catholics. I believe, however, that even such a selective perspective as I have chosen may be hoped to provide some practical pointers towards one possible major step into our ecumenical future, especially given the already close affinities between Roman Catholics and Anglicans, which Pope Paul described as a sisterly relationship between their Churches.

On the previous occasion when formal conversations about unity were held between Roman Catholics and Anglicans, at Malines in 1921-26, the Roman Catholic participants, Cardinal Mercier and the Abbé Beauduin, coined what was to become the classic phrase used to describe the future of the Church of England in any union with Rome as 'united, not absorbed'. What this envisaged was a type of uniate Anglican Church in communion with the Church of Rome and existing in parallel alongside the Roman Catholic community in England, at least initially, since there were also suggestions of gradually phasing out the Roman Catholic dioceses which dated from the restoration of the hierarchy. The conversations were discontinued after the death of Mercier in 1926 and were followed two years later by the repressive encyclical _Mortalium animos_ of Pius XI, which was warmly supported in England by a Cardinal Bourne aggrieved at having been bypassed by Malines.

When ecumenical relations were resumed the concern of the Anglican Communion to maintain its corporate identity by retaining its own cherished traditions of worship and order was acknowledged by Pope Paul VI in his comment in 1977 that 'the pace of this movement has quickened marvellously in recent years, so that these words of hope "The Anglican Church united not absorbed" are no longer merely a dream'.[11] The subject was pursued further on the eve of the papal visit to England, when the Archbishop of Canterbury began a public address on 'Rome and Canterbury' by referring to the Malines principle as a fruitful approach which respected the autonomous traditions within the Churches of the Anglican Communion.[12] Dr Runcie then asked what this would mean in practice, given what he apologetically referred to as 'the Roman tendency towards an authoritarian centralization and uniformity'. He saw this as presenting difficulties for both parties which perhaps I might not unreasonably sum up as how much diversity could Rome tolerate and how much unity could Canterbury manage.

In the light of this the Archbishop went on to suggest 'some questions Anglicans should now be asking Roman Catholics in order to elucidate what unity not absorption would mean'. He referred again to Vatican centralisation, and then added:

> To bring the matter nearer home, how much freedom does the Roman Catholic Episcopal Conference of England and Wales have to pursue moral and pastoral initiatives culturally relevant to the mission of Christ in this country'? The question is acute when we consider moral issues relating to particular interpretations of Natural Law and the anglo-saxon tradition of the informed Christian conscience.

From the Roman Catholic viewpoint the subject was taken further in 1986 by Dr Edward Yarnold, a member of ARCIC since its inception, who described in an article in *The Times* (8 March) how 'Many people in each of the churches are afraid of

11. Cf. *One in Christ*, XX. 2 (1984), p. 103.
12. Archbishop of Canterbury's Lenten Address, 11 March 1981, Church Information Office.

having to sacrifice their identity, the Anglicans of becoming absorbed into the larger church, the Roman Catholics of diluting their faith for the sake of the others'. Yarnold himself seemed to favour the Malines principle when he envisaged 'a unity of sister churches', 'united but not absorbed', which, within the full 'communion of life, worship and mission... would retain their individuality'.

What I wish to suggest is that applying such a principle of non-absorption to relations in England between the Roman Catholic community and the Church of England is not only in practice impossible, but also theologically undesirable. On the other hand, applying the principle to a united Anglican and Roman Catholic Church in England in its relation with the universal Church, and with the See of Rome in particular, would be a most creative and fruitful line of development. To explore this suggestion it first seems necessary to distinguish between unity between our two communions at the universal or international level, and unity at the regional or national level. It is, of course, with universal unity that ARCIC is concerned, in considering what degree of shared faith and mutual recognition of ministries is requisite and possible for full communion between us. This is a matter for ecumenical summit meetings to negotiate and agree upon; and it is at this level that the issues raised by Archbishop Runcie about Roman centralisation and uniformity and more generally about the legitimacy of differing expressions of faith, will fall to be settled in principle.

When it comes, however, to working out the practical expressions of such agreements at the local level of Anglican provinces and Roman Catholic regional churches, then three questions need to be asked: At what level of competence and of jurisdictional power will this be done? And by whom? And what account will be taken of particular local and cultural conditions? It would be entirely in the spirit of unity-in-diversity that a variety of local applications would be found desirable, rather than a uniform pattern be proposed, or even imposed, throughout the two world-communions. It is a matter of history that the Malines conversations took place without the participation of the (admittedly hostile) Roman Catholic hierarchy of the time in England. But it would be a theological scandal if anything approaching such disregard for the voice of the local churches in the land were again adopted in any future ecclesial planning for England.

If the future scenario of unity, then, is recognised as a matter of theological competence for the two representative Christian bodies in England to work out between themselves, how would the agreed principle of 'united, not absorbed' apply in practice? In my view, the idea of a separate uniate Anglican church, or of our two churches proceeding in full mutual recognition on parallel lines of beliefs and practices, simply could not be sustained. I surmise that the ironic consequence of maintaining here a universal principle that Anglicanism should not be absorbed by Roman Catholicism would be that in England the Anglican Church would itself absorb a sizeable proportion of the Roman Catholic community, and be itself changed in the process.

For the Anglican questions which Dr Runcie put to Rome are also questions which very many Roman Catholics in England have been, and are, themselves raising with increasing persistency. And consider what might happen once union was achieved in a faith which included not only an Anglican recognition of the petrine office in a united Church, but also (to use the traditional terminology) the recognition by Rome of the validity of Anglican orders. In that happy eventuality Anglican liturgy and worship, Anglican moral positions on contraception and other topics which are not matters of faith, Anglican positive respect for conscience, and Anglican church order and discipline in such areas as the remarriage of the divorced and the celibacy of the clergy, would constitute an overwhelming attraction to innumerable Roman Catholics, with the resulting disintegration of Roman Catholicism in England. The only check to such a process of reverse-absorption could be at the level of Roman Catholic discipline, a tactic which would not only be of questionable effectiveness but also be the subject of continual questioning and controversy, as indeed is the discipline even at present on intercommunion.

There could also be a corresponding phenomenon among some members of the Church of England, that of resting satisfied, perhaps even self-satisfied, with full Roman recognition of its ecclesial reality. An influx, however, of Roman Catholics could not but affect the internal life of the Church of England, much more so than the Oxford Movement affected the Roman Catholic Church last century. There would probably also be a departure of those Anglicans unable to accept any agreed terms of union (as there would also be from the Roman Catholic Church). And in any case, an Anglican Church content to continue much as before, though now confirmed in Roman Catholic esteem, would be in danger of ignoring the challenge of Christ implied in such an English ecclesial revolution. Quite apart from such material, but not unimportant, considerations as the efficient use of church buildings and schools, that challenge is not only one of pastoral concern for all of Christ's faithful in England, but also one of mission to the society of which they all form a part. One of Cardinal Mercier's successors, Cardinal Suenens, writing in 1969, commented that 'the unity we are aiming at is not a human affair, not a diplomatic compromise' nor, I would add, one of at best peaceful co-existence. 'We need', he continued, 'to discover the will and commandment of the Lord'.[13]

The Archbishop of York on the same theme viewed the idea of 'parallel Churches, united in faith and in common allegiance, yet preserving their own identity' as only a halfway house, an intermediate stage on the road to full and complete unity, which should not be allowed to continue indefinitely, for he acknowledged that it could be 'criticised as administratively

13. Cf. *One in Christ*, p. 104.

untidy and theologically anomalous'. Yet he considered it essential precisely as an intermediate stage providing time to permit the development of trust and mutual understanding of each other and each other's traditions. As he concluded, 'with too much commitment demanded too quickly, the problems of identity loom too large'.[14]

I find myself, then, in agreement in principle with Archbishop Habgood on the ultimate goal of full Roman Catholic-Anglican Christian union in England, but I question whether the impetus of events, including a mounting ecumenical impatience, will in fact permit of the gradualism which he considers necessary, and which others consider sufficient. It is a question of identity, I admit, but I suggest that it is more one of discovering our joint identity in Christ for the future than a question of retaining our separate, even nostalgic, past or present self-identities.

If that is so, what might be the key to discovering that future joint identity of a new Church in England which would be united with the universal church but not absorbed by it? And what might be the most practical means of negotiating such an identity, both within England and with Rome? I suggest that an answer must be sought based on the eccelesial foundations of *episcope*, collegiality and conciliarity. The key lies in *episcope*, for the most significant immediate consequence of any mutual recognition of orders would be a notable increase in the number of bishops in England. This would not necessarily be the Gilbertian situation where 'Bishops in their shovel-hats Were plentiful as tabby cats, In point of fact, too many!' It could, and should, mean at a stroke a single and enlarged English episcopal conference. It would then fall to such a body to exercise its collegial power, and its ecclesial leadership, in determining the shared future of their hitherto separate Churches, by agreeing a genuinely native liturgy, by recognising the natural features of local communities and redrawing the lines of parishes,

---

14. Ibid., pp. 154-5.

deaneries, and dioceses accordingly, and by disposing ministerial resources and personnel, all in preparation for a fresh mission of Christ's Church to the England of the twenty-first century.

You will recall, of course, that I have already remarked on the danger of pursuing episcopology in an ecclesial and christological vacuum. For such an exercise as I propose of English episcope and of English episcopal jurisdiction to be theologically authentic, it must take place within the ecclesial and christological contexts of Christ's kingship as imparted in baptism and dispersed throughout our joint churches. This in practical terms means the utmost in open consultation, in unguarded discussion, and in coresponsibility and shared decision-making. In brief, it seems to me that any joint acceptance of an agreed formula of union, or any ceremonial uniting of our two Communions at an international level, and of our two communities at a national level, must be prepared for in England and by English Anglicans and Roman Catholics. And this by a national assembly of our two churches led by a joint episcopal conference and planning to integrate the resources, the traditions, and the Christian prophecy, priesthood and kingship of our two communities in this land. Nothing less can do justice to the full ecumenical challenge facing us.

This, I think exemplifies for us more than any other eventuality the importance of the current debates within our Church, both on the subject of subsidiarity or, as I have preferred to call it, of non-absorption, and on the significance within such a general debate of the nature and status of episcopal conferences in the Church. In the more theological terms in which I have been exploring the realities underlying the debate, I suggest that only such a national initiative could adequately stimulate and express the recognition and the exercise of the royal power which has been imparted throughout his Church by Christ, and in so doing respond to the unique national challenge in joint mission with which, in my view, we are being confronted by Christ.

CHAPTER TWELVE

Necessary Fictions, Real Presences

PETER PHILLIPS

George Steiner in his subtle and richly suggestive essay, *Real Presences*, sees in the origins of modernism a breaking of the covenant between word and world which he regards as the significant characteristic of the decades following 1870. For Steiner, this sundering of continuities constitutes 'one of the very few genuine revolutions of spirit in Western history'.[1] Mallarme and Rimbaud represent the beginnings of a genuinely new aesthetic, 'a parting of the semantic ways'. Before this time, he argues, we could have presumed upon a logocentric order, a Logos-aesthetic, which included the assumption of correspondence, understood as something 'strictly inseparable from the postulate of theological-metaphysical transcendence'.[2] Such a world presupposes 'real presence'.

While there is much to appeal in this argument, I wonder whether the Christian tradition has always had a more healthy suspicion of the innocent collusion of word and world than Steiner allows. The monist ontology at which Steiner hints does not allow for the rich sense of mystery that confronts us in the world of which we are a part: things as things stand over against us, ultimately unfathomable. There are aspects of the Nominalist agenda deeply rooted in the Christian tradition and rightly so. We come to what is real by way of the particular.

---

1. George Steiner, *Real Presences* (London: 1989), p. 93.
2. Ibid., p. 119.

Steiner, of course, is far from unmindful of this and comments
with some force:

> The arts are most wonderfully rooted in substance, in the
> human body, in stone, in pigment, in the twanging of gut
> or weight of wind on reeds. All good art and literature
> begin in immanence. But they do not stop there. Which
> is to say, very plainly, that it is the enterprise and privilege
> of the aesthetic to quicken into lit presence the
> continuum between temporality and eternity, between
> matter and spirit, between man and 'the other'. It is in
> this common and exact sense that *poiesis* opens on to, is
> underwritten by, the religious and the metaphysical.[3]

However we might talk of transcendence, we must argue that
we are afforded no direct access to that which transcends; our
language cannot be other than indirect. We humans are beings
embodied in an unfolding, physical and material universe and
that materiality forms the conceptual matrix of our thinking.

This was something worked out once and for all in the fires
of the great Trinitarian and Christological debates which shaped
the thinking of the first centuries of the Christian era. The
concept 'Logos', with its strong roots in Hebrew as well as Greek
thought and its pre-eminent role in the Prologue to John's
Gospel, might have seemed to be the most appropriate way of
articulating a doctrine of Christ but it was soon to be replaced
in the language of the creeds by the much more recondite and
elusive notion of substance. Logos allows for transparency. It
provides a way of expressing that great chain of being which
unites creator and creation. But there is no place here for that
important sense of the opaque, that necessary otherness which
must remain between God and creation, and between things
themselves. Although we cannot overlook the difficulties raised

---

3. Ibid., p. 227.

by the term, and undoubtedly there are many, substance remains inescapably a category in our talk about the divine.

This is as true in a discussion of the nature of sacraments, which provides the theme for this paper, as it is in the more comprehensive discussion of the mystery of the Trinity and the nature of Christ. In the course of a subtle and probing exploration of the implications of asserting a union between the humanity and divinity of Christ at the level of *hypostasis*, Donald MacKinnon insists:

> ...what is intended is that that altogether unique relation to the Eternal that we name hypostatic union is *malgré tout* internal to the term assumed in such a way that it is constituted by an openness to the divine so uniquely thoroughgoing ... that it is rendered in itself impersonal. Any corresponding reciprocity between godhead and manhood is denied as ultimately imperilling the sovereign freedom of the Divine, expressed in the redemption of the human race, and its very changelessness .[4]

Here MacKinnon is invoking the logical distinction between material implication and entailment, established in G. E. Moore's influential paper 'External and Internal Relations', to make an important point about the Incarnation. This is a distinction central to the classical tradition of ontological discussion. Aquinas' position is similar, though maybe here at least lacking Moore's elegance of logical form: 'Substance is a thing, whose essence it is, not to have its being in another thing; accident is a thing, whose nature it is to be in another'.[5] Of course, the language finds its origin in Aristotle's discussion of being. This is a distinction MacKinnon uses with considerable

---

4. Donald MacKinnon, 'Prolegomena to Christology', *Journal of Theological Studies* 33, (1982), p. 153.
5. Aquinas, *Questiones Quodlibetales*, IX, a. 5 ad 2.

force on a number of occasions.[6] Rowan Williams brings out the significance of this:

> what is being claimed is that the substantiality, the 'subjecthood', the continuous identity of this individual is so related to the substantiality of God that it cannot be grasped in its full reality without allusion to God as *constitutively* significant for it: this human individual's relation to God is 'internal to the term assumed', so that the humanity of Jesus as independent of its assumption by God is abstract or 'impersonal' (*anhypostatic*) ...If we say less than this, the identity of Jesus becomes external to God and so 'parabolic' in its significance: it is one determinate thing pointing to another.[7]

I am suggesting that this language clarifies what is being asserted when we use the concept 'substance' in relation to sacraments. The classical language of Eucharistic presence uses substance to claim that the Eucharist ceases to be merely 'parabolic', 'one determinate thing pointing to another'. Christ's presence is '*constitutively* significant', it is 'internal to the term assumed', there is no 'corresponding reciprocity... imperilling the sovereign freedom of the Divine'. It is this central insight

6. G. E. Moore, 'External and Internal Relations' was published in his *Philosophical Studies* (Routledge & Kegan Paul, 1922), pp. 276-309. Apart from the articles by Rowan Williams, we must refer to three pieces by MacKinnon himself: 'Aristotle's Conception of Substance', in *New Essays on Plato and Aristotle*, ed. Renford Bambrough (Routledge & Kegan Paul, 1965), pp. 97-119; '"Substance" in Christology – a Crossbench View', in *Christ, Faith and History*, eds. S. Sykes & J. P. Clayton (Cambridge: 1972), pp. 279-300; 'The Problem of the "System of Projection" appropriate to Christian Theological Statements', in *Explorations in Theology* 5 (SCM Press, 1979), pp. 70-89, esp. pp. 85-88. Here he refers the reader to the important paper by Professor Jonathan Bennett, 'Entailment', *Philosophical Review* 78, (1969), pp. 197-236.
7. Rowan Williams, 'Trinity and Ontology', in *Christ, Ethics and Tragedy*, ed. Kenneth Surin, (Cambridge: 1989), p. 80.

that the concept 'substance', problematic though it inevitably remains, is invoked to preserve. We talk of a *communicatio idiomatum* between the divine and human in Christ just as we might wish to talk of a *communicatio idiomatum* between the *sacramentum* and *res* of the sacrament Of course, Aquinas does not do this, insisting that after the Eucharistic consecration 'the accidents do not inhere in any subject'.[8] Substance is in no sense part of what something is: it is simply what it is. Sacramental presence is not a physical presence: in other words the accidents make Christ present sacramentally (they *contain*, or *hold*, him) but do not have Christ as their subject. The underlying thrust of Aquinas' language at this point seems to rest in the combating of a crude and simplistic realism. It would be inappropriate to dwell on this for it is something which has been explored at length on many occasions. This is, however, a significant indication that the terminology of substance is invoked for many different reasons and it functions in many different ways.

MacKinnon's careful reflection on Aristotle's account of substance is a reminder of just how elusive the notion of substance remains. All too often, and particularly in language relating to the Eucharist, people claim to know what is meant by substance. We do not. Our approach to substance hovers between a sneaking feeling that we can define its meaning and a sneaking feeling that it always escapes us. Aristotle appears to be arguing for the making of a logical distinction between primary and secondary substances,[9] primary substance being what is individual and concrete, secondary substance being the general and common. This is certainly how G. L. Prestige saw it in his discussion of the nature of the Godhead, linking *hypostasis* with the former and ousia with the latter,[10] and many have followed in his footsteps.

---

8. *Summa Theologiae*, 3a, 77, 1.
9. See *Categories*, 5, 2a. 11-16; *Metaphysics*, VII. 11. 1037a5.
10. G. L. Prestige, *God in Patristic Thought* (SPCK, 1964), pp. 168-178.

Dr P. J. FitzPatrick's study, *In Breaking of Bread*, offers a telling illustration of this theme as it is related specifically to discussion of the Eucharist. With an insight marked by inimitable humour, FitzPatrick points to the absurdities that emerge in the language of what we might refer to as neo-scholasticism: here we have talk of substance concealed by accidents, of reality somehow disguised by appearance, of an underlying meaning safely insulated from ordinary usage.[11] FitzPatrick is surely right in regarding much of the discourse of substance as an 'apparent camouflaging of Christ in the Eucharist' which uses 'the terminology of substance and accidents... to offer a way of fencing off Christ from the indignities bound up with the fate of food'.[12] FitzPatrick draws the conclusion that substance is a concept so irretrievably flawed that it can only be abandoned. He goes on to suggest that the more recent phenomenological approach represented by theories of transfinalisation and transsignification fail equally to offer a coherent way of talking of the Eucharistic presence. He points to the sometimes acrimonious debate regarding the rite of celebrating the sacraments that has petered on in the Church for the thirty years following Vatican II as something representing a 'tragic failure' insofar as it 'ignores the irreducible particularity of what concerns the humanities'.[13] There is much here of which we should take note. FitzPatrick suggests that we turn from the language of substance and embrace what he refers to as the 'Way of Ritual':

> It is because ritual and sign are essential that we need to do justice to the reality of what we see and touch, the reality which is ritually used as a means towards the far deeper reality to which we can only gesture. Aquinas,

---

11. P. J. FitzPatrick, *In Breaking of Bread* (Cambridge: 1993), p. 138; see also pp. 206 and 264.
12. Ibid., p. 231.
13. Ibid., p. 354.

following Augustine, uses the rich and multiple associations of human eating to point towards a transforming union with Christ which is far closer. It is the reality and associations of the starting-point in eating that give content to what follows, and provide the means for suggesting what lies beyond our conceiving. Once more, the humbler creation is not all the story; but there would be no story at all without it.[14]

While we might wish to give a qualified approval to this position, we would do well to hesitate before abandoning the language of substance. It has become clear that, although we cannot do without the notion, we cannot do with it as apparently it is. The absurdities of neo-scholasticism, however, should not entice us from what is valuable. I am suggesting that it might be of value to follow Moore and MacKinnon in retrieving the logical and linguistic implications inherent in the conceptual apparatus of the notion of substance and use these as a way of mapping something of the possibilities of sacramental discourse.

To develop this point a little further, we might appropriately return to a discussion of the work of Donald MacKinnon and take our cue from the fine paper on 'Aristotle's Conception of Substance', to which we have already referred. Like FitzPatrick, MacKinnon is concerned with 'irreducible particularity', that elusive thinginess of things. So, too, was Aristotle. MacKinnon argues forcefully that to regard primary substance as a sort of 'bare substratum, a clothes horse on which qualities are draped' (the image, MacKinnon acknowledges, he owes to Columba Ryan OP) fails to do adequate justice to Aristotle's regard for 'the concrete selfsubsistent thing'.[15] There is in Aristotle a recognition of the subtle interplay, at times almost impossible

---

14. Ibid., p. 206.
15. MacKinnon, 'Aristotle's Conception of Substance', p. 103.

fully to tease out, between general and particular. MacKinnon
comments:

> Yet even while (Aristotle) is drawn to exalt the formal, he
> is at the same time reminded that where the efficient,
> transeunt causality of form is concerned... the finished
> article whether statue or building demands for its
> achievement the active participation of an agent who
> cannot be regarded as form *tout simple*, but is the
> necessary instrument without which form is powerless to
> initiate or sustain its realisation. If the stress still falls on
> form, it is on *embodied* form that it is laid.[16]

We are, in other words, failing to do full justice to the notion of
sacramental presence if we regard it as to do with merely
underlying reality. Why is it, we might ask, that though there
are many types of bread – bread made from rye, bread made
from maize, bread made from wheat, and many different types
of wheat grain at that – we are encouraged to use wheaten bread
for our celebration of the Eucharist? Is it perhaps because the
substance of that wheaten bread is thought to have been
kneaded into shape by a long history, a history of which we
cannot be unmindful?

It is instructive to turn to St Augustine. In his sermons on
chapter 6 of John's Gospel, Augustine teases out the
resemblances between the manna of the old dispensation and
the Eucharist of the new, the water struck from the rock in the
desert and the cup of salvation. The discussion in the Tractates
might be less precise than we might wish, yet it is in many ways
more fruitful than much later discussion of the sacraments in so
far as Augustine never overlooks the fact that the sacraments
remain signs. Although he certainly distinguishes between the
sacrament and what is signified, Augustine emphasises that
sacraments are always signs, and that we cannot dispense with

---

16. Ibid., p. 105.

the significative character of the sacrament. It is perhaps worthy of note that Portalie, in his great dictionary article on Augustine, saw it necessary to defend Augustine at some length against what he felt to be a 'protestant' appropriation of Augustine's doctrine of the real presence.[17] Augustine does indeed bring into the foreground of his discussion an important emphasis on the 'significative nature of the Eucharist as signifying the reality of the immanent union of Christ with the believer and the believer with Christ and the union of all the believers in the body of Christ, as well as the spiritual effect of the sign, the attainment of eternal life'.[18] For St Augustine, it is the sacramental symbol, the mysterium, which truly signifies the reality:[19] the reality is not some thing underlying the appearances but it is truly expressed and made present by the sacramental sign.

The reality expressed by sacramental substance can, I suggest, only be properly expressed by invoking the full range of meanings with which a sign resonates. Here we must draw on the rich resources of imagination, not merely as a way of adding illustration upon illustration, but of teasing out and enriching the very notion of sacramental substance itself. Metaphors

17. E. Portalié, *A Guide to the Thought of St Augustine*, trans. R. Bastian (Burns & Oates: 1960), pp. 247-260.

18. St Augustine, *Tractates on the Gospel of John*, 11-27, trans. J. W. Rettig, *Fathers of the Church*, vol. 79, (Washington: Catholic University of America Press, 1988), p. 268, n. 34. Rettig refers the reader to an important series of studies. M. F. Berrouard, 'Pour une refléxion sur le "sacramentum" augustinien. La Manne et l'Eucharistie dans le Tractatus XXVI, 11-12 in Iohannis Evangelium', in *Forma Futuri: Studi in onori del Cardinale Michele Pellegrino* (Turin: 1975), pp. 830-844; M. F. Berrouard, 'L'être sacramental de l'eucharistie selon saint Augustin: Commentaire de Io 6, 60-63 dans le Tractatus XXVII 1-6 et 11-12 in Iohannis Evangelium', *Nouvelle Revue Théologique* 99 (1977), pp. 702-721; E. Siedlecki, *A Patristic Synthesis of John VI*, 54-55, Mundelein, III (1956).

19. See P. Th. Camelot, 'Réalisme et symbolisme dans la doctrine eucharistique de S. Augustin', *Revue de Sciences Philosophiques et Théologique* 31 (1947), pp. 394-410.

change the way we see things (substances). We are dealing, as
Paul Ricoeur has pointed out, with 'metaphorical utterance':
this is not merely a 'deviation in denomination' but a 'deviant
use of predicates... in which the logical distance between far-
flung semantic fields suddenly falls away, creating a semantic
shock which, in turn, sparks off the meaning of the metaphor'.[20]
Such symbols provide us with models, with inhabitable fictions,
which, in the way of the physicist perhaps, allow us not only to
interpret our world but to transform it. This complex pattern of
signification works in two spheres of meaning, the one
reinforcing the other. On the one hand the great sacramental
symbols, bread, water, oil, fire, and the like, because of their
deep roots in the human subconscious, reverberate in many
contexts, they represent a play of meanings which lead us
towards an intuitive grasp of our nature as a human family. On
the other hand, invoking the rich resources of this symbolism,
the sacraments re-enact and make present the Christian's
conformity with Christ. They are experienced as the 'first fruits'
of the Age to Come. Within the narrative of the Christian life,
sacraments provide us with 'models', which, possessing a
heuristic force, allow us to remake reality.[21] We see something of
this in Augustine's sermons to the newly baptised:

> If you have received worthily, you are what you have
> received, for the Apostle says: 'The bread is one, we
> though many, are one body.' Thus he explained the
> Sacrament of the Lord's table: 'The bread is one; we,
> though many, are one body'. So, by bread you are
> instructed as to how you ought to cherish unity. Was the
> bread made of one grain of wheat? Were there not, rather,
> many grains? However, before they became bread, these
> grains were separate; they were joined together in water

20. Paul Ricoeur, 'Imagination in Discourse and in Action', in *Analecta
Husserliana*, vol. 8, ed. Anna-Teresa Tymienieka (London: 1978), p. 7.
21. Ibid., pp. 9-10.

after a certain amount of crushing. For, unless the grain is ground and moistened with water, it cannot arrive at that form which is called bread. So, too, you were previously ground, as it were, by the humiliation of your fasting and by the sacrament of exorcism. Then came the baptism of water; you were moistened, as it were, so as to arrive at the form of bread. But without fire, bread does not yet exist. What, then, does the fire signify? The chrism. For the sacrament of the Holy Spirit is the oil of our fire.[22]

The central significance of the language of substance is to be found in its various attempts to express the idea of identity with Christ: the identity of Christ with the Father, the identity of the Christian with Christ. This is a theme preserved most evidently in Eastern thought but it is certainly not without its representatives in the West. St Hilary of Poitiers in the *De Trinitate* reminds us that Christ dwells in us by the mystery of the sacraments: 'He Himself, therefore, is in us through His flesh, and we are in Him, while that which we are with Him is in God.'[23] This is a theme taken up also in the early Middle Ages by Isaac the English Cistercian, who was abbot of Étoile, in fact not very far from Poitiers, from 1147 to 1169 and who, as Étienne Gilson reminds us at least once felt sorry that he had not stayed comfortably at home.[24] Isaac's writings represent a style of 'speculation oriented towards mysticism'.[25] There are

---

22. Easter Sunday, Sermon 227, *Fathers of the Church*, vol. 38, trans. Sister Mary Sarah Muldowney RSM (New York: 1959), pp. 195-198. See also the very similar sermon on the Holy Eucharist, Sermon 6 in *The Fathers of the Church*, vol. 11, trans. Denis J. Kavanagh OSA (New York: 1951), pp. 321-326.
23. St Hilary, *The Trinity*, trans. Stephen McKenna, *Fathers of the Church*, vol. 25 (New York: 1954), Bk 8, 14, p. 286.
24. PL 194, 1896 A B. See Étienne Gilson, *History of Christian Philosophy in the Middle Ages* (London: 1978), pp. 168f, 632.
25. Gilson, op. cit., p. 168.26. Isaac of Stella, *Sermons*, 42. See also 2 (man and woman capable of deification).

significant echoes here of the thought of the fourth century
bishop of Poitiers:

> Everything then which is with God makes one God. The
> Son of God is with God by nature, the Son of Man is
> with him by person, and Christ's body is with Christ by
> the sacrament. Consequently the faithful and spiritual
> members of Christ can truly say that they are what he is,
> even the Son of God, even God. But he is so by nature.
> they by sharing; he of his fullness, they by participation.
> In short, what the Son of God is by birth, his members
> are by adoption, according to the words of scripture: 'You
> have received the Spirit of adoption as sons, enabling us
> to cry, "Abba! Father!"'[26]

Much of the earlier part of this discussion has focused on
talk of substance in relation to the Eucharist. This has been
perhaps inevitable, but it is unfortunate. It would be contrary to
the tenor of this paper to treat the Eucharist in isolation from
the other sacraments. The sacraments are not discrete events. As
the Orthodox theologian John Zizioulas has it:

> Our Lord, before He left His disciples, offered them a
> sort of 'diagram' of the Kingdom when He gathered them
> together in the Upper Room. It was not one 'sacrament'
> out of 'two' or 'seven' that he offered them, nor simply a
> memorial of Himself, but a real image of the Kingdom...
> In the Eucharist, therefore, the Church found *the
> structure of the Kingdom*, and it was this structure that she
> transferred to her own structure.[27]

26. Isaac of Stella, *Sermons*, 42. See also 2 (man and woman capable of deification).
27. John D. Zizioulas, 'Apostolic Continuity and Succession', in *Being as Communion* (Crestwood, New York: St Vladimir's Seminary Press, 1985), p. 206.

This 'diagram' is given flesh and blood in a life-style shaped by our communion together and allows an intimate and rich pattern of interrelationships, which the sacramental system calls into being.

It is of the nature of sacraments that God reveals himself through what he is not. In a way, we can claim for a sacrament what Wallace Stevens claims for a poem in saying that the poet speaks 'of things that do not exist without the words':[28] sacraments speak of things that do not exist, things that have no presence, without the sacramental sign. The reality of sacramental presence works as 'a kind of constant flickering of presence and absence together'.[29] Levi-Strauss was wont to remind his students of things that are not only *bonnes à manger* (good to eat) but also *bonnes à penser* (good to think with). In what are necessary forms of communication, grounded in our finite nature as human beings, we are offered a way of understanding our relationships and our world anew. Having established the logical function of substance in sacramental language, our understanding of the sacraments becomes more and more enriched as we tease out the notion of substance, of what something is, by way of the contribution made by the poet, and as we allow the subtleties of imagination to illuminate and add depth to our experience. We must come to the sacraments, having gained from insights that the Old Testament might offer, and the New, adding to this the witness of the anthropologist and historian. The things with which we are involved not only point our way to Christ, but allow us to experience and relish his presence.

---

28. Wallace Stevens, *The Necessary Angel* (London: 1984), p. 32.
29. This phrase from an unattributed work by Terry Eagleton in which, in a completely different context, Professor Eagleton talks of meaning, is cited in Steiner, *Real Presences*, p. 123.

CHAPTER THIRTEEN

Lay Appropriation of the Sacraments in the Later Middle Ages

EAMON DUFFY

Perhaps the most crucial single utterance of the Second Vatican Council, at least in terms of impact on our shared experience as Catholics, occurs at paragraph 14 of the Council's constitution on the liturgy, *Sacrosanctum Concilium*. This was the first of the conciliar documents to be promulgated, and in many ways its most bloodily contested production. The paragraph in question runs like this:

> Mother Church earnestly desires that all the faithful should be led to that full, conscious and active participation in liturgical celebrations which is demanded by the very nature of the liturgy, and to which the Christian people, 'a chosen race, a royal priesthood, a holy nation, a redeemed people' (1 Pt 2:4, 9) have a right and obligation by reason of their baptism.

> In the restoration and promotion of the sacred liturgy the full and active participation by all the people is the aim to be considered before all else, for it is the primary and indispensable source from which the faithful are to derive the true Christian spirit. Therefore, in all their apostolic activity, pastors of souls should energetically set about achieving it through the required pedagogy.[1]

---

1. *Sacrasanctum Concilium* 14.

'Full, conscious and active participation', pastoral energy and liturgical pedagogy: these were momentous notions, laden with an agenda whose implications were sketched out in the rest of the document, and which were embodied in the reforms which followed. The summons to 'active participation', indeed, a phrase which occurs sixteen times in all, was singled out subsequently as the main refrain of the document.[2] As anyone who has lived through the generation of change which flowed from this paragraph knows, those words were to have revolutionary implications for the character and celebration of Catholic liturgy and sacraments, as both rites and texts were revised and simplified so that the people 'should be able to understand them with ease and take part in them fully, actively, and as a community'.[3]

Only a fool or a Lefévrist would deny the flood of benefit which the post-conciliar liturgical reforms have brought, but only a fool or an ICEL groupie would maintain that the process has been an unmitigated blessing. We are only now, I think, beginning to be in a position to draw up a balance sheet of loss and gain from changes which were based on the assumption that the mysteries celebrated in the sacraments could or should be 'understood with ease', that the liturgy was an activity concerned primarily with pedagogy, that liturgical rites should be 'short, clear and free from useless repetitions',[4] or that 'full, conscious and active participation' in worship and sacraments inevitably involved ritual regimentation, with everybody doing or saying or listening to the same things, at the same moment, all the time. Professor John Bossy has spoken of the 'polyphonic mysteries' of the pre-reformation Mass,[5] and a stronger sense that the sacraments speak not univocally, but polyphonically, might well have served to raise serious questions about some of

---

2. J. A. Jungmann, 'Constitution on the Sacred Liturgy', in *Commentary on the Documents of Vatican II*, ed. H. Vorgrimler (New York: 1967), p. 17.
3. *Sacrasanctum Concilium* 21.
4. *Sacrasanctum Concilium* 34.
5. J. Bossy, 'The Mass as a Social Institution', *Past and Present* 100, p. 61.

the principles and assumptions which underlay the transformations of our sacramental experience in the years since the Council, and to avert some of the more disastrous processes of simplification and 'rationalisation' which those transformations have involved.

In this paper I want to bring history to bear on sacramental and liturgical theory, or rather, I want to challenge the version of history on which some of the theorising which underlay the post-conciliar liturgical reforms was constructed. Behind those reforms was an account of the nature of lay experience of the sacraments in the Middle Ages which I believe to have been quite profoundly mistaken. In the writings of the fathers of the liturgical movement, including those, like Josef Jungmann, who played decisive roles in the shaping of Conciliar thinking about the liturgy, we find an account of medieval liturgy as a simple story of decline from the true liturgical participation of all the people during the patristic age, to subjective and incomprehending pietism in the later Middle Ages. The Middle Ages were seen as an era in which the liturgy and sacraments were overlayed with 'fanciful interpretations and developments' foreign to their nature, thus preparing the way, in Louis Bouyer's words, 'for the abandonment of the liturgy by Protestantism and its final disgrace and neglect in so much of post-tridentine catholicism'.[6]

This reading of late medieval sacramental and liturgical experience can be found at its clearest and most explicit in Josef Jungmann's important book *Pastoral Liturgy*, a collection of lectures and essays published as preparations for the Council were being put in train in 1960, and the English version of which appeared in 1962, as the schema which eventually became *Sacrosanctum Concilium* was being considered.[7] In an extended account of what he called a 'revolution in religious culture'

6. Louis Bouyer, *Life and Liturgy* (London: 1956), p. 15.
7. For the importance of Jungmann's views in determining the character of *Sacrasanctum Concilium*, see Annibale Bugnini, *The Reform of the Liturgy 1948-1975*, (Collegeville, Minnesota: 1990), p. 12.

Jungmann traced the decay of the 'close connection between altar and people' in the early Church 'in which the people's Amen resounded like a peal of heavenly thunder' round the Roman basilicas, and in which a constant interplay and dialogue within the celebration culminated in universal communion, through the distancing and silencing of the laity which he believed took place in Carolingian Europe. Lay communion dwindled to a rarity reserved for special feastdays, the priest 'consciously detached himself from the congregation', and the people 'only followed from a distance the external and visible action of the celebration in terms of its symbolic meaning', a process assisted and symbolised by the retention of Latin, so that the language of the liturgy became increasingly remote and incomprehensible. These ritual developments had their theological equivalents, as the cult of the crucified Jesus took over from that of the risen Christ, a sense of personal sinfulness and unworthiness overwhelmed the earlier consciousness of the baptismal dignity and sanctity of the Christian, with a consequent decline in frequency of communion, and there was an increasing emphasis 'on the individual and upon what is subjective': in a word, the Teutonic triumphed over the Latin. According to Jungmann this process climaxed in the later Middle Ages when, despite the lush elaboration of the cult of the Blessed Sacrament and the boom in church building and decoration, a 'broad gulf' separated clergy and laity, celebrations of the sacraments were no longer 'a people's service in the old sense', and at them 'the people were not much more than spectators'. Liturgy dwindled to pious theatre, and 'the fundamental mystery itself, the sacramental making present of the work of salvation, the Mysterium Christi which ought to enfold us, and into which we ought to enter deeper and deeper', ceased to be grasped. No longer, declared Jungmann, was 'the Christian mystery seen as something very much present, as the leaven which must constantly penetrate and transform Christianity'. Instead, it was perceived 'almost entirely as an event of the past upon which to meditate more and more deeply by means of such laudable devotions as the Way of the Cross or the Rosary'.[8]

Jungmann was a great scholar, and with the broad outlines of his picture of the transformation of liturgical and sacramental celebration I would not wish to quarrel. The key developments to which he points, here and elsewhere in his writings, are real enough – the failure to translate the Mass into the germanic and frankish vernaculars, the screening of the altar, the disastrous emergence of low Mass, and the appropriation of the chants in sung Masses to professionalised choirs, the promotion of allegorical interpretation of ritual gesture, the tendency to emphasise the objective work of the sacraments, at the cost of eclipsing their symbolic dimension, and hence to adopt as normative the minimum ritual requirements for their valid celebration. The classic case here is baptism, where the sign of total immersion in living, flowing water was ultimately reduced to the trickling of a spoonful or two of oily and not very clean standing water onto the child's head. All these certainly contributed to a profound transformation in lay experience of the sacraments and the liturgy in general, an experience which, in the senses intended by Jungmann, did indeed become less articulate and proactive.

Where Jungmann's analysis seems to me to fall down, and to fall down disastrously, is in his assumption that in this whole process the laity and their local clergy were passive and inert, progressively excluded from an understanding of the 'true' meaning of the sacraments and from participation in the 'right' sort of liturgical celebration, at the mercy of the reduced and impoverished sacramental and liturgical catechesis offered by the medieval church, so that they became, in Jungmann's phrase, 'not much more than spectators'. This assumption was to prove crucial for the character of *modern* liturgical revision, for it resulted in a conception of one of the principal tasks of liturgical reform as that of improved catechesis. Louis Bouyer declared in

---

8. J. A. Jungmann, *Pastoral Liturgy* (London: 1962), pp. 1-101.

his influential book *Life and Liturgy* that 'the liturgy is to be considered as the central treasury containing all doctrinal tradition, and is, as Pius XI once said in a golden sentence, the "principal organ of the ordinary magisterium of the Church"'.[9] That reference to the liturgy as the vehicle for the 'ordinary magisterium', which Bouyer characterises as a golden sentence, we may be forgiven for thinking a chilling one. There is of course an obvious sense in which it is true: the liturgy, in which the scripture is read, reflected on and preached, and the sacraments celebrated, is plainly the principal means of transmission of the tradition of the community. But 'magisterium' and 'tradition' are very different concepts, and equally obviously, the notion that the celebration of the liturgy and sacraments is designed to put across a *message*, which may be straight-forwardly right or wrong and which can be summarised in catechesis, bristles with problems. Yet I suspect that some such notion lies behind the Council's stipulation that, for educational reasons, a 'noble simplicity' was to be the keynote of all liturgical reform, and it has certainly underlain much of the relentless didacticism which characterises so many modern celebrations of the liturgy, in which we are *directed* to the meanings which we are to take away, either from the rite or from the readings.

But in fact liturgy rarely works by simplicity, as such. It works by symbolic word and gesture, and it is of the essence of a symbol, as opposed say to an allegory, that it is polyphonic, polysemous. Consider the water of baptism. Its Christian meaning is established and defined by use and context – by reference to scripture certainly, but by scripture as it is employed in the liturgy of baptism, supremely, for Catholics, in the liturgy of Easter night. Reflect on the words and actions of the liturgy for the Easter Vigil, especially the vigil in the form. it took at its first restoration by Pius XII in the early 1950s, and you will see from its contexts there that the water of baptism holds a bewildering range of meanings, all of them important for a

---

9. Bouyer, *Life and Liturgy*, p. 31.

grasp of what the sacrament itself is, yet many of them consorting awkwardly, and some of them apparently contradictory. The baptismal water is the water of washing, it is the stream for which the parched deer longs, it is the rivers of Eden in the beginning and the water of healing and life in the garden of Paradise at the end of the world, it is the salt water of chaos over which the Spirit hovers, it is pools of sweet water in the desert, it is the nurturing water protecting the unborn child, it is the destructive water of Noah's Flood on which the Ark of the church floats, it is the rain which drowns the sins of the earth, it is the rain which moistens the dryness of parched grass, it is the Red Sea which brings life to fleeing Israelites and death to pursuing Egyptians, it is the wine of Cana and the water of Jordan, it is semen, it is oil, it is milk and honey, it flows from the rock, it flows from the Temple, it flows from Christ's side, it is a cistern, it is a fountain, it is for drinking, for washing, for crossing, for drowning, for judgement, for mercy, for escaping from, for escaping into, it makes an end, it marks a beginning, it is a womb, it is a tomb.

Meaning in the sacraments, therefore, is rarely characterised by 'noble simplicity' (though of course complex networks of meaning can be and often are evoked by simple gestures) for liturgies don't work at a simple or a single level. That is why they can rarely simply be invented, and why we should attempt to rationalise or streamline them only with caution and always at our peril. Rituals are by their very nature traditional, inherited, for to make a symbolic gesture we must always harness and stretch existing and inherited patterns of meaning. Liturgies, therefore, are palimpsests which grow by accretion, by the overlaying and juxtaposition of layer upon layer of meaning and sign, which are often in tension with each other, and held together not by a single dominant explanation but by performance, by the complex of recitation, repetition, song, prayer and gesture through appropriate and enter into the web of realities symbolised rite, by which we live within the tradition.

None of this is arbitrary, of course, for the range of possible meanings in any rite is limited by the restraint of the tradition, and by the juxtapositions and patternings of meanings within its variety. We are never in the position of Humpty Dumpty:

> 'When I use a word', Humpty Dumpty said in rather a scornful tone, 'it means just what I choose it to mean – neither more nor less.'
> 'The question is', said Alice, 'whether you can make words mean so many different things.'
> 'The question is', said Humpty Dumpty, 'which is to be master – that's all.'[10]

We are never the masters of the meaning of the liturgy, and no one performance yields or exhausts all the meanings of a rite. That is why sacramental rites are probably better when they are at least a little complicated than when they are 'simple', because they are by their very nature complex repositories of, or better, vehicles for, a whole range of meanings, not all of which any individual, congregation or even generation will be able to appropriate or grasp. To attempt to eliminate from our liturgies what we do not understand or cannot presently appropriate is always fraught with danger, for it runs the risk of reducing the polyphony of the rite to a thin monotone. As Peter Cramer put it in a fascinating study of patristic and medieval baptismal rites, 'Liturgy is a job-lot. It is a structure only in a loose sense. Some bits of it may be ignored at some times, stressed at others. Sometimes it is barely a structure at all: it is just bits and pieces that come to hand, that happen to be there, and which can be put together in many ways'.[11]

And yet, as that last remark suggests, we are always not merely the inheritors or executants, but the makers of the

---

10. Lewis Carroll, *Through the Looking Glass*, ch. vi.
11. Peter Cramer, *Baptism and Change in the Early Middle Ages* (Cambridge: 1993), pp. 242-3. My thinking about this whole topic owes a good deal to this lively and stimulating book.

rituals, however traditional, however prescribed, which we use. The couple in love who dance a slow waltz are running through the prescribed steps of a dance – yet they are not merely *following* the waltz, but doing it, and it is part of their courtship, an expression of their feeling for each other. What is true of the dance is truer of liturgy: dances are often complicated, but liturgies are always complex. And even more than in the dance, we are the makers of the rites we employ. We *make* ritual, even inherited and prescribed ritual, because we bring to it a network of association and intention which shapes its meaning for us. Every rite is our own work of art, and in every celebration of the liturgy there is always more going on than the words, rubrics or intentions of the celebrant or the liturgists explicitly envisage.

Viewed in this light, the complex and elaborate liturgies of the Christian past, in particular of the Middle Ages, don't look so obviously decadent or impervious to lay appropriation, and the designer-crafted, carefully focussed liturgies of the post-conciliar Church look less like a restoration of primitive liturgical purity than an assault on the necessary polysemic character of liturgy. Carried to extremes, the rationale behind ritual simplification and redesign can amount to an act of profound schism of sensibility with and comprehension of the human and Christian past, which can amount to a real breakdown of Catholic communion. Readers of *The Tablet* may have been struck, as I was, by the complaint of the architect Austin Winkley about the unreformed state of the liturgical space in Westminster Cathedral. 'A Cathedral today', Mr Winkley is reported as saying, 'should be a didactic centre. It is the chair of the bishop and his teaching. Here we have a Cathedral, the most important in the land, that has not been permanently reordered, and is therefore setting a bad example. *How do we live out our faith through the liturgy and sacraments in that place?*'[12] These emphases, a million miles away from Eliot's

---

12. *The Tablet* (July 1995), pp. 867-8.

injunction to kneel, 'here, where prayer has been valid', are familiar, for they recur again and again in apparently well-meaning but ultimately crass attempts to rework and 'purify' the liturgy so that it becomes modern: not to wrestle with the inherited complexity, and so to tap the meaning and resource encoded in the rite, but to start with a clean slate. Note the concepts explicitly or implicitly present in Mr Winkley's reported remarks: didacticism, simplification, restructuring, and a sense of the necessary elimination of the mark of the past in the celebrations of the present, tradition envisaged as a prisonhouse rather than a powerhouse. It was Humpty Dumpty, you may recall, who told Alice when she could not remember the last remark but one, 'In that case we start fresh'. In liturgy, above all, we may indeed have forgotten, may even have laboured to forget, the last remark but one, but we never start fresh, for really to do so would be to be struck dumb.

By now you may be forgiven if you are asking what all this has to do with the lay appropriation of the sacraments in the Middle Ages. I think it goes like this. Jungmann marvelled that at the end of the Middle Ages there was a great deal of liturgical business, with the Christian people highly active in attending the rites on offer. Yet in a fundamental sense, he thought that beneath this hectic activity, nothing whatever was actually going on – the liturgy was a slot-machine from which people expected to derive material benefits: it was not, however, something in which, in any real sense, they were involved. For Jungmann there was no lay appropriation of the sacraments – they did not appropriate, make their own, the sacraments, they watched or consumed them. The liturgy, he wrote, was no longer understood in its sacramental depth, and 'lay unused'.[13]

Jungmann was measuring medieval appropriation of the liturgy and sacraments not in its own terms, as a manifestation of a particular moment of Christian culture, of equal value with every other moment of Christian culture, but by a paradigm, real

---

13. Jungmann, *Pastoral Liturgy*, p. 73.

or illusory I am not competent to judge, derived from an idealised account of the liturgy of the patristic era. For him, there was a right and a wrong way of using the liturgy, of celebrating the sacraments: by implication, and with whatever qualification, the reform of the liturgy meant a return to or recovery of this paradigm. Because medieval Christians were not participating in the liturgy as fourth century Romans had done, because they were not singing the chants and thundering out the responses, they were doing nothing at all, they were passive. But if instead of imposing such a paradigm onto the Middle Ages, and so finding it wanting, we attend to the particular quality, character and modes of lay experience of the sacraments in those centuries, a radically different and much more positive picture emerges, and one which, as I hope will become evident, has implications for our own understanding and performance of liturgy.

The first thing to be said about medieval experience of the sacraments was that far from being individualistic, as Jungmann thought, it was profoundly social: in a Christian society, the sacraments were understood as impinging directly on the life of the polis, providing both the cement which bound people together, and, on occasion, the solvents for undesirable forms of anti-social alliance against the polis. This theme has been much explored by social and religious historians in the context of the Corpus Christi processions and play-cycles which are such a feature of late medieval urban life.[14] On some accounts these processions expressed and assisted the harmony of society, as the carrying of the body of Christ around the boundaries of the town expressed its corporate identity and unity, and united rival gilds and other sub-groupings in a common allegiance. Here the Pauline injunction to endeavour to keep the unity of the Spirit in the bond of peace took concrete form. John Bossy has memorably characterised this use of the sacraments to heal the feuds and divisions of society 'the social miracle'.[15] A less benign reading of

14. For which see, for example, Miri Rubin, *Corpus Christi* (Cambridge: 1991)
15. J. Bossy, *Christianity in the West 1400-1700*, (Oxford: 1985), ch. 4.

these processions sees them as intrinsically contested and conflictual, events in which nearness or distance from the Host in the procession became the measure of social status, and in which rival individuals and groups jostled for position, and harnessed the sacrament to the quest for power or recognition. In fact both these readings of the nature of the medieval celebration of Corpus Christi seem to me to encapsulate important dimensions of the reality of the Eucharist, which is simultaneously the sacrament of our brokenness and of our unity, the enactment of the handing over to death of the Son of God by the rest of humanity, and the reconstitution of humanity in his death and resurrection. In that sense the sometimes ferocious rivalries which underlay the ritual unities of medieval Corpus Christi processions are a truer enactment of the eschatological hope of the eucharist for the healing of the sin of the world than the enforced and cloying friendliness of many modern celebrations of the eucharist, which dissolve the 'now but not yet' of the unity which the eucharist promises, into an illusion of present and achieved harmony – eucharistic unity as the togetherness of the like-minded, the Mass and therefore the Church reduced to a golf club or a Conservative Association supper.

The eucharist was by no means the only sacrament which was encountered and celebrated by medieval people as the maker or healer of society. The healing of social divisions and the creation of alliances through marriage, what one might call the Romeo and Juliet effect, is a case in point. Peter Cramer has drawn attention to the way in which the baptisteries of medieval Italian cities, and the liturgies celebrated in them, became the expression of overarching unity within the context of feuding clans. The existence of a single baptistery for a whole city was of course a consequence of its original status as an episcopal sacrament, and the celebration of all baptisms at Easter and Pentecost. But in the medieval town, where local churches were often in origin and use family chapels, private, clan or factional sanctuaries, the common baptistery enacted that unity over faction to which the human city aspired but which remained in practice an ideal imperfectly achieved. In the baptisteries, often modelled on the Holy Sepulchre or actually using mausoleum buildings, the strife of the human city was buried, and the future unity of the civita, heavenly Jerusalem, was born. The breaking down of the barriers of hatred, incomprehension and division, which the death of Christ effected and the sacrament of baptism celebrated, was here given a concrete reality within a society which recognised the heavenly city as the source and goal of human community.[16]

In a different way, John Bossy has traced the development of the institution of godparentage in medieval Europe, as lay people, despite the resistance of the clergy, pressed the institution of baptismal sponsorship into service as a means of transcending natural kinship alliances and creating wider relationships of protection, support and friendship in a feuding society: the sacrament of baptism established a network of relationship which disarmed hostility and brought unity and peace. The English believed that the Irish chose wolves as godparents, because the friendship so created would oblige the wolf to do them no harm, a belief, as Bossy remarks, which is as interesting if the English were mistaken as if they were right.[17]

Theologians and pastors, as might be expected, often viewed such lay transformations of sacramental experience as abuses, 'wrong' or inappropriate use of the sacraments, and social historians in modern times have been inclined to follow this lead. Lay use of the words, ceremonies and materials of sacramental worship, for example in rituals of healing, has often been seen as superstitious or magical, the distortion of the real Christian meaning of the sacraments to achieve some lesser and often misguided end, and a proof of the gulf between popular religion and that of the clergy and the elite. Jungmann himself,

---

16. P. Cramer, *Baptism and Change*, pp. 267-290.
17. J. Bossy, *Christianity in the West*, pp. 15-6.

as we have seen, subscribed to something like this view. I don't want to enter into the particularities of that debate now, though elsewhere I have argued that much that has been taken to be magical or superstitious in late medieval religion can in fact be shown to employ in a perfectly cogent way the ideas and ritual strategies found in the liturgy itself, and so should be viewed not as pagan survival or superstition, but as lay Christianity.[18] Modern historians of religion have been intrigued by the generation round the sacraments proper of a penumbra of sacrament-like blessings and sacred objects and actions, over which lay people had more control than over the clerically managed sacraments themselves. The multiplication of such sacramentals has been seen by historians and theologians, as it sometimes was by reform-minded contemporaries like Nicholas of Cusa, as a symptom of disorder and superstition, a departure from what was central to the peripheral.[19] The point I want to make here is that in fact this sort of medieval sacramental or para-liturgical activity, properly understood, often demonstrates not a disfunctional displacement within the liturgy, the exaltation of marginal elements over those which are central, but a profound sacramental wisdom and a vigorously Christian sacramental culture. I want to illustrate this from two examples, both derived from the same eucharistic para-liturgical institution or sacramental, the distribution of holy or blessed bread after Mass.

Jungmann thought that medieval perceptions of the eucharist were the crux and key of all that was wrong with their understanding of liturgy and sacraments. The 'eucharistic movement' which produced the great celebrations of Corpus Christi was not in his view 'an approach to the Blessed Sacrament' but rather a 'withdrawal from it', not the use of the

---

18. E. Duffy, *The Stripping of the Altars*, (New Haven & London: 1992), ch. 8.
19. See the discussion of the relation between 'official' liturgy and the sacramentals in R. W. Scribner, *Popular Culture and Popular Movements in Reformation Germany* (London: 1987), pp. 17-47.

sacrament but its cult, in which excessive concentration on the eucharistic presence eclipsed every other dimension of the sacrament.[20] The proof of this for him was the reduction of lay communion to an annual event. To compensate for this, a series of communion substitutes emerged. England's distinctive contribution to this process was the invention in the thirteenth century of the '*Instrumentum Pacis*' or Pax-Board – a book, plaque or painting of some sacred symbol, such as the lamb of God, which was kissed by the celebrant and then carried round the congregation to be kissed in their turn, at the *Agnus Dei*. The practice spread from England to the rest of Christendom. Even more evidently a communion substitute was the custom of distributing pieces of blessed but unconsecrated bread at to the people at the end of the main parish Mass on a Sunday. The baskets of bread used were blessed by the recitation of the first fourteen verses of St John's Gospel together with a prayer over them. They were then cut up and distributed. The blessed bread was believed to have healing and protective powers, and so was used in healing rites for human beings and animals, and it was supposed to be the first food one tasted on a Sunday morning. In many places strict order of seniority or social clout within the parish was observed in this distribution, householders going before servants or labourers, and in some places the pieces of bread were distributed in graded sizes. Congregations felt strongly about the social proprieties involved in this distribution, and the ritual was often the focus of conflict and litigation.[21] Here, if anywhere, one might think, was a clear example of disfunction within the liturgy, in which an unscriptural sacramental has displaced meanings and functions properly belonging to the Holy Eucharist itself, and has gathered round it in the process a cluster of superstitions and dubious social functions.

---

20. Jungmann, *Pastoral Liturgy*, p. 63.
21. For all this, *The Stripping of the Altars*, pp. 125-7.

The first example I want to examine in order to suggest that this is not so comes from the stormy events surrounding the Peasants Revolt of 1381 in England, the rebellion of Wat Tyler, Jack Straw and John Ball. That rebellion in itself had eucharistic resonances – it erupted decisively, surely by prearrangement, on the feast of Corpus Christi, June 13th 1381, and historians have recently become intrigued by the interplay between the social dimensions of that feast and the social breakdown expressed in the Rising.[22] Our fullest information about the revolt focusses on St Alban's, where a monk of the Abbey, Thomas de Walsingham, produced several exceptionally full and detailed accounts of the course of the rising.[23] The grievances of the Commons at St Albans were varied, but one important issue was the Abbey's much resented monopoly on the milling of flour. An earlier Abbot had succeeded in forcing the local tenantry to surrender the small domestic millstones used for grinding flour at home and, in token of this assertion of the Abbey's control over milling, had the confiscated millstones set in the floor of the monastery parlour. During the rebellion, therefore, a mob of the Commons, armed with the implements of their trades, burst into the monastery, marched to the parlour and dug the stones out of the floor. In an extraordinary ritual, they proceeded to break the millstones up, and distributed a piece to each of the men present to take home. The monastic chronicler was much struck by this action, and recognised in it a deliberate reference to the distribution of blessed bread at parish Mass on Sundays: the Commons took the particles of stone home, he declared 'that seeing the pieces, they might remember that they had once triumphed in this dispute with the Monastery': he went on to lament the damage to the monastery in a cluster of

22. For example Margaret Aston, 'Corpus Christi and Corpus Regni: Heresy and the Peasants' Revolt', *Past and Present* 143 (1994), pp. 3-47.
23. R. B. Dobson, ed., *The Peasants' Revolt of 1381* (London: 1983), p. 29ff.

phrases from the psalms which ring the changes on the eucharistic images of bread, corn and sheaves.[24]

I don't want to enter here into the complicated question of the rights and wrongs of the grievances of the commons of St Alban's against the Abbey in 1381. What I want to draw your attention to is the extraordinary and assured power of their deployment of para-eucharistic ritual to express their sense of injustice, and its setting to rights. The sensitivity to social order and decorum which generally characterised the distribution of Holy Bread is here revealed not as a sub-christian preoccupation with power and status, but as an attempt to reflect an ideal and just ordering of society, in which the fragment of stone becomes what in the Corpus Christi antiphon *O Sacrum Convivium* St Thomas calls the bread of the Eucharist itself, a 'pignus', a token, sign and downpayment of a hoped-for reality, at once a reminder of liberation achieved and a standing testimony to the power of that victory in the present and the future. For the commons of St Alban's in June 1381, the victory and freedom celebrated in the Mass was in some very concrete sense reflected in their protest against the oppression of the Abbey which put an unjust price on their daily bread. I do not think it entirely fanciful to see here something like a liberation theology derived from their eucharistic experience, and which they instinctively and eloquently expressed in eucharistic imagery.

My second example, which also centres on the Holy-Bread ritual, is one which I have used elsewhere.[25] It concerns the resolution of conflict in the small Bristol church of St Ewen's in the early 1460s. The Church derived much of its income from the rent of shops and tenements in the town centre, and the church wardens were locked in an expensive and long-drawn out dispute with one wealthy parishioner, the corn merchant John Sharp, over the rental of one of these properties. It was

---

24. H. T. Riley, ed., *Gesta Abbatum Monasterii Sancti Albani a Thoma Walsingham*, vol. 3, (London: 1869), pp. 308-9.
25. Duffy, *The Stripping of the Altars*, pp. 127-8.

finally resolved in January 1464, and in token of restored charity Sharp changed his will to include a handsome donation to parish funds, in return for which he, his wife Elizabeth, and deceased members of their family, were entered in the Church's bede-roll to be prayed for publicly as benefactors. On the following Sunday, as it happened, it was the turn of the Sharp household to provide the loaf which would be used for the Holy-Bread ritual. There was a prescribed ceremony for presenting this bread, which happened before Matins and Mass began. On the Sunday in question Elizabeth Sharp turned up in pomp, accompanied by a maid who carried the bread and the candle which was offered with it, and also a long embroidered linen towel. This was a 'houselling towel', the long cloth held under the chins of communicants at the annual parish reception of communion at Easter. Having duly presented the holy loaf, Mistress Sharp summoned the parson and the chief parishioners. She expressed her great joy at the restoration of unity and charity within the parish and between her family and the rest of the community, and she donated the towel as a sign of that restored unity. Up till then, the parish had not owned a cloth long enough for the purpose, and had pinned three short cloths together. The unity of the new towel symbolised that the peace which had been established in the community was no patched up affair, but a seamless whole, and it was to be used on the one day of the year in which the whole community celebrated and cemented its unity by the reception of the eucharist. Once again, what is striking here is the sophisticated harnessing by a lay person, in this case a woman, of a powerful cluster of eucharistic symbols – the moment of the presentation of the holy loaf, the replacement of a patched and pinned assortment of towels by a single communion cloth, the reception of Easter Communion – to express the restoration of unity, charity and justice in the community.

There are of course a great many subtexts here: in both incidents there is a lot more than theology going on, and one might want to say a good deal about the jostling for prestige and status in the community which is implicit in Elizabeth Sharp's swanky gesture. But whatever else is in evidence here, both incidents seem to me to display a practical eucharistic theology of a very high order, a eucharistic theology, moreover, which is by no means mesmerised, as Jungmann thought late medieval thinking about the eucharist was, by the single issue of the real presence, but which is alert to the sense in which the eucharist both symbolises and makes community. Jungmann complained that the late medieval laity had little sense of the way in which the sacramental mystery 'made present the work of salvation', yet that seems to me to be precisely what is so strongly in evidence in both these stories.

Of course, there is no denying that in both incidents there is evidence of one very uncomfortable displacement in the eucharistic practice of the late medieval Church. It could perfectly properly be argued that both these clusters of eucharistic symbolism have attached themselves to an element of the rite which was only present because the people had ceased to receive the true 'Holy Bread', the eucharistic Body of Christ itself; a sacramental has displaced the true sacrament. No doubt this is so, but if so we need to reflect on the extraordinary richness and social realism of their eucharistic theology despite this displacement, and its closeness to the concerns and preoccupations which Paul articulates in talking about celebrations of the eucharist at Corinth. We are recognisably in touch with New Testament themes, as well as the preoccupations of the English parishioners of the fourteenth and fifteenth centuries. At the very least we have proof here of the theological resourcefulness of the laity in a period when the liturgy might at first sight seem to have been wholly and exclusively appropriated by the clergy: Jungmann's perception of the late medieval scene was too elitist, too much mesmerised by what was going on at the altar and among the clergy.

I am very conscious of the partial nature of my discussion of the sacraments and the laity in the Middle Ages. Had I started this discussion, as at one stage I had planned to do, with the sacrament of matrimony, the whole dynamic of the paper would have been altered, for there it was not so much a question of the laity appropriating a sacrament offered to them by the Church, and directing it towards their own needs and preoccupations, as of the Church trying, often vainly, to tame and sacralise energies and institutions which predated it and could not easily be accommodated within its thinking. With the other sacraments, it was a question of moving out of the sanctuary ultimately carrying the Blessed Sacrament along with them – into the world beyond. With matrimony, the last of the sacraments – so far – to be recognised, the movement is the other way, from a rite celebrated in the home or at the threshold between Church and world, the Church porch, into the sanctuary – a comparatively recent movement into the Church, which the apparent collapse of marriage even among many who would describe themselves as Christian appears to be about to reverse. And yet, odd case out as it is, marriage has some claims to be the paradigmatic case of lay appropriation of the sacraments, at any rate in the dimension I have been considering, of the sacralising of the life of people together, of society. Once again, it is at least in part a story of the resourcefulness of the Christian people, for the clerical Church had difficulty in giving a positive value to sex, procreation and the structures of family life: there was no cult of the Holy Family in the early Church. Fascinatingly, when that cult came in the Middle Ages it was not at first as we now know it and as successive modern Popes have endorsed it, the nuclear family envisaged as a single boy-child, a virgin and an impotent old man. For the Middle Ages the Holy Family was the matriarchal, vastly-extended and largely female or pre-pubertic family constituted by the three daughters and the multiple grandchildren of that much married lady St Anne, the mother of Mary. The cult of St Anne in the

Middle Ages is part of the story of the determination of lay people, against clerical and theological resistance, to celebrate as holy, as sacrament, their experience of sexuality, childbearing, marriage, and even remarriage.

We don't live in the Middle Ages, and I am wary of drawing too many applications from what I have had to say here. But at least it seems clear to me that the assessment offered by Jungmann and others of the quality of the sacramental life of Christians in the medieval period was both far too negative and far too patronising. Ironically, given Jungmann's desire to give the Mass back to the people, it was rooted at least in part in clerical elitism, for he and the other founders of the liturgical movement saw the restoration of the liturgy as a task involving a return to the 'true' values to be uncovered in the fathers and the early liturgical texts by an elite corps of experts.[26] More seriously, that negative assessment of medieval liturgy helped nourish a programmatic and abstract sense of how liturgy 'worked'. Too much attention was paid to text and rubric in liturgical rites, too little to the concrete embedding of liturgy in social reality, and the complex uses to which the Christian people actually put the language of liturgy and sacrament. In the process, liturgical theorists underestimated the value of the para-liturgical proliferation of secondary rites, and what was thought of as the clutter of sacramentals which, if my reading of the evidence has any validity, were signs not of decadence but of vigorous lay appropriation of the meaning of the sacraments. As a result, liturgists failed to grasp the hospitality to such diverse and dynamic use and appropriation of the sacraments which was afforded by the very complexities and bagginess of the medieval rites which they deplored. For the lay appropriation of the sacraments, which I hope I have persuaded you was both resourceful and theologically profound, often fixed on those

---

26. See Annibale Bugnini's revealing remark that the liturgical movement was 'a fruit produced by the thought and prayer of elite minds and then gradually shared with ever wider circles of the faithful', *Reform of the Liturgy*, p. 3.

very elements within the liturgy which the liturgists judged to be marginal, and which modern reforms have planed away as accretions and corruptions, in the name of 'noble simplicity' and too narrow and fundamentalist an understanding of the return to sources.

At the very least, then, I am appealing for second thoughts about 'noble simplicity', and for a more reverential and receptive attitude to tradition in this area above all, a greater respect for the quality of the experience of the Christian mystery among our predecessors in the faith, and so a second look at and maybe a reappropriation of dimensions of their sacramental and liturgical experience which were set aside in the post-conciliar sense of new beginnings. We can't of course reinvent the Middle Ages, any more than we can or would want to re-invent the Counter-Reformation Church. But then, we can't re-invent the early Church either. It should be evident from what I have said that the Christian society in which the sacraments were celebrated by medieval Christians differed radically from ours in possessing an infinitely richer and more varied pool of shared symbolism than we do. They inhabited a symbolic culture, shaped by Christianity, and so sufficiently coherent, for all its fissures and variety, for the language of liturgy to resonate, even if to different notes, at every level of society. Our dilemma as a Church is the dilemma of our culture, the disintegration of a shared set of symbols. As a Church we must somehow find means of reforging a language which draws life, continuity and focus from the tradition, but which is also hospitable to the new meanings and new tasks which the evangelisation of our world – and ourselves – demands. What I am certain of is that as a religious culture the Church itself needs to become more hospitable, more receptive to symbol, not least to the symbols which it already possesses. The cultivated austerity of much modern liturgy springs less from theological roots than from a mixture of philistinism and puritanism which is as inimical to celebration as it is to lamentation, which mistakes individualistic intensity for sincere public utterance, and which is so often informed by a disturbing and baffling hostility to the cultural forms in which inherited Christian experience and wisdom has been transmitted. Yet the infinite resourcefulness of that tradition is at least one antidote to the bleak dilemma articulated in David Jones' devastating and fragmentary poem *A a a Domine Deus*:

> I said Ah! what shall I write?
> I enquired up and down.
>   (He's tricked me before
> with his manifold lurking-places.)
> I looked for his symbol at the door.
> I have looked for a long while
>   at the textures and contours.
> I have run a hand over the trivial intersections.
> I have journeyed among the dead forms
> causation projects from pillar to pylon.
> I have tired the eyes of the mind
>   regarding the colours and the lights.
> I have felt for his Wounds
>   in nozzles and containers.
> I have wondered for the automatic devices.
> I have tested the inane patterns
>   without prejudice.
> I have been on my guard
>   not to condemn the unfamiliar.
> For it is easy to miss Him
>   at the turn of a civilization.

I have watched the wheels go round in case I might see the living creatures like the appearance of lamps, in case I might see the Living God projected from the Machine. I have said to the perfected steel, be my sister and for the glassy towers I thought I felt some beginnings of His creature but *A a a Domine Deus* my hands found the glazed work unrefined and the terrible crystal a stage-paste...*Eia Domine Deus.*[27]

27. John Matthias, ed., *Introducing David Jones: A Selection of His Writings,* (London: 1980), p. 31.

CHAPTER FOURTEEN

Sacramental Language

BRUCE HARBERT

We use the word *figure* in many ways. We speak of figure-skating, of cutting a figure, of a fine figure of a man, the fuller figure, a figure of fun, figuring things out, figures of speech and being good with figures. These are all current senses. In the past, figure has had other meanings. When, in *The Merry Wives of Windsor* Mistress Ford encourages Mistress Page to 'scrape the figures out of your husband's brains', she does not mean that he has been worrying about the mortgage, but that his head is full of mistaken ideas or fantasies.

FIGURA

Figure comes from the Latin *figura*. In 1944 the German literary critic Erich Auerbach published an influential article entitled *Figura*.[1] He showed the wide range of meanings that *figura* has in classical Latin, and how these developed further in Christian usage. From the earliest records, *figura* could mean 'the shape of a thing', just as we now speak of a person's 'figure'. But it could also mean a shape representing something else. Sculptors, for instance, make *figurae* of human beings; in our dreams we see *figurae* of people who are dead.

---

1. Erich Auerbach, 'Figura', in *Scenes from the Drama of European Literature, Theory and History of Literature*, vol. 9, *Theory and History of Literature* (Manchester University Press, 1984), pp. 11-76.

Figura in Christian Latin

Christian writers developed this second sense in a new and important way. For them, figura could refer to an object or event belonging to a particular point in time that represented something in the future. For Tertullian, Isaac, Joseph, Moses are all figurae of Christ;[2] the marriage of Adam and Eve is a figura of Christ and the Church.[3] (Theologians are familiar with this way of looking at history, though we usually call it by a word of Greek origin, typology) A figura finds its counterpart in truth, *veritas*.[4] Ambrose says that reconciliation was achieved in figura through Isaac and in veritate through Christ.[5] This does not mean that a figura is a fiction. Moses really existed: in one sense he was 'true', in another he points to a greater truth.

Auerbach's chief concern was Dante. He emphasised that the personages of the Divine Comedy were not mere personifications, but had actual historical existence. Virgil might represent Reason, but he was also a historical figure who in some sense prepared the way for Christ. Above all, Beatrice is significant not merely by representing something else, theology, for instance, or divine illumination, but by her concrete existence as a living woman. Dante's love for her opened his eyes to the possibility of the divine love which is the theme of the Commedia and prepared him for it.

Figure and Allegory

Auerbach's essay was something of a reply to C. S. Lewis, who eight years earlier in *The Allegory of Love* had emphasised the importance of allegory to the medieval mind. Auerbach insisted that for most people the figural mode of understanding was the dominant one. As for allegory,

---

2. *Adversus Marcionem 3*, 18. 2-7.
3. *Adversus Marcionem 5*, 18, 10.
4. *Adversus Marcionem 5*, 19, 9.
5. *De Isaac vel Anima 4*, 22.

there is something scholarly, indirect, even abstruse about it... By its origin and nature it was limited to a relatively small circle of intellectuals and initiates.[6]

The roots of allegory were in Greek thought, particularly in Plato and Alexandrian neo-Platonism, while the figural mode, more friendly to Semitic patterns of thought, is found already in Scripture in the Pauline letters.[7]

In fact, both the figural and the allegorical approaches belong within a Christian view of reality, since in Christ the timeless intersects with time. He reveals to us the unchanging nature of the God who is and the mystery which that God unfolds through history.

Figura as a Eucharistic Term

I move now to the Eucharistic controversies of the ninth century, in which a central question was whether the Eucharist is a *figura* and, from now on, I shall use the word in its English form, figure. Ratramnus, a monk of Corbie, begins his treatise on the Body and Blood of the Lord with two definitions.[8] A figure is a veiled way of speaking about something, as when Christ says *I am the living bread*, or *I am the true vine*: figures say one thing and mean another. Truth, on the other hand, is the direct expression of a reality, as when we say that Christ was born of the Virgin, suffered, was crucified and so on.

The Eucharist is the body and blood of Christ in truth insofar as it feeds the faithful spiritually in a manner not apparent to the senses. The Eucharist is also a figure in at least three senses, since it represents to us at least three things: the body of Christ, glorified and present with the Father outside time; the historical event of Christ's suffering and death; and that body which is the people that believes in Christ and has

---

6. Auerbach, '*Figura*', p. 55f.
7. Rom 5:12ff.; 1 Cor 10:6, 11; 15:21; 2 Cor 3:14; Gal 4:21-31; Col 2:16f.
8. PL 121, 125-170.

been reborn in him. On the last page of his treatise Ratramnus moves towards a fourth sense in which the Eucharist is a figure, saying that it teaches us that when we see Christ we shall not need such helps, for we shall see him face to face: that is, the Eucharist is a figure of the beatific vision.

Some words that Ratramnus uses as equivalents of *figura* are *sacramentum*, *mysterium* and *memoria*. In his hands *figura* is a rich word, able to speak of how the Eucharist relates to past, to present and to future. Western theology lacks a word with this richness and has felt the lack. Only in recent years, the long and often sterile debate about how Christ's sacrifice is present has been given a new direction by the recovery of the Greek word, *anamnesis*. In the uses of *figura* that I have discussed, and in some of the uses of *sacramentum* that I shall be discussing soon, we find Western expressions of the understanding of history, of the idea that two separate moments can be simultaneously present, which is contained in the concept of *anamnesis*.

Ratramnus was by no means the first to use figure of the Eucharist. Tertullian says that Christ gave to bread the figure of his body,[9] and that he said at the Last Supper 'This is my body', that is, 'This is the figure of my body'.[10] A fourth-century version of the prayer that we now know as Eucharistic Prayer I (the 'Roman Canon'), attested in Saint Ambrose's work on the Sacraments, says: Make this offering for us approved, spiritual, pleasing, because it is the figure of the body and blood of Our Lord Jesus Christ. Gaudentius of Brescia (early 5th century) speaks of the Eucharist as the figure of Christ's passion. Paschasius, Ratramnus' confrater, calls the Eucharist a 'figure of flesh and blood'.[11] Two centuries later, Lanfranc was able to admit *figura* into discussion of the Eucharist, even when arguing against Berengar, whom he regarded as having too weak a

9. *Adversus Marcionem 3*, 19, 4.
10. *Adversus Marcionem 4*, 40, 3.
11. *De Corpore et Sanguine Domini 4*, 2 (PL 120, 1279).

concept of the Eucharistic change.[12] Writers were encouraged in their use of the word by the Vulgate text of Hebrews 1.3, which speaks of Christ as the figure of God's substance. But the traditional contrast of *figura* with *veritas* told against it when writers wanted to assert the full reality of Christ's Eucharistic presence.

Perhaps there is another reason for *figura*'s disappointing career. Auerbach was right, I think, to claim that the figural sense of reality was dominant throughout the Middle Ages among the bulk of the population. Such iconographical schemes as that of the stained glass at Fairford in Gloucestershire and the huge historical structures of the mystery plays are indications of this, that a figural perception of the relationship between the Old and New Testaments was as alive among the people of fifteenth century England as it was in sixth-century Ravenna, when San Vitale was built. But alongside the association of the Eucharist with salvation – history in the mystery-cycles, devotions arose which isolated the eucharist from any reminders of history. In this development we see the waning of the figural approach. Among the intelligentsia allegorism gained ground, so that C. S. Lewis was right to speak of Allegory as the dominant mode in late medieval literature.

The Council of Florence in its Decree for the Armenians (1439) said that the sacraments of the Old Law 'only figured (*solum figurabant*) the grace that was to be given through the passion of Christ'.

The Council of Trent insisted that Christ is contained in the Eucharist, and not only 'as in a sign or figure'.[13] Sacramental theologians today are preoccupied with recovering the sign-value of sacraments, and know that Trent's insistence on other aspects has given us a weak sense of sacraments as signs. We have lost something, too, by losing figure from our theological vocabulary. A word that can denote relationships between

---

12. *De Corpore et Sanguine Domini 6*, 14 (PL 150, 416c, 424b).
13. Canon 1 on the Eucharist, D-S 1651.

something we do today, things that happened in the past, things that will happen in the future, and realities that are present and independent of time could have served us well. The Eucharist is a figure of Christ's Paschal Mystery and of his Second Coming. It is a figure of his body, now glorified in the presence of the Father. It is a figure of the Church. But we are not accustomed to saying these things.

SACRAMENTUM

Having shown what can happen when a word drops out of theological vocabulary, I turn now to another word, *sacrament*. Familiar though it is, *sacrament* has lost many of the senses it had in earlier times. The history of its Latin root, *sacramentum*, is fairly well known, and I shall only sketch it briefly before dealing with the English word.

Sacramentum is derived from *sacer*, which meant 'holy' or, more precisely, 'consecrated to a deity'. Anyone who instituted legal proceedings had to leave a deposit with the court which he would forfeit if he lost his case. In early times this deposit could only be used for religious purposes: it was *sacer*, whence its name *sacramentum*. A person who took an oath, for instance on entering the army, was similarly in danger of religious penalties if he broke his commitment. He himself was *sacer*, and his oath was a *sacramentum*. Both senses refer to an action done at a particular time whose effects endure through a period of time.

Patristic Uses

In Tertullian we find both the classical senses developed. He compares baptismal promises to the military oath when he says 'we were called into the militia of the living God when we answered to the words of the sacramentum'.[14] He also uses the name *sacramentum* for persons, things and events in the Old Testament that point to the New, such as the wood laid on Isaac

---

14. *Ad Martyras* 3, 1.

(Gen 22.6), the wood with which Moses sweetened the water of Marah (Ex 15.25) and the stick used by Elisha to recover an axe-head (2 Kgs 6.6), all of which look forward to Christ's Cross.[15] It is as if they were God's deposits, put down before Christ to be taken up at his coming. *Sacramentum* in this sense is synonymous with *figura*, and Tertullian sometimes uses them as equivalents.[16]

Thirdly, the basic sense of 'holy thing' led to *sacramentum* being used for Baptism and Eucharist, and also for Christian doctrine.

Around the same time, *sacramentum* was developing an important new sense in the earliest Latin translations of the New Testament, where it was used to render Greek *musterion*. In the Pauline writings, *musterion* refers to God's hidden plan, the realisation of that plan in Christ, and the continuation of the plan in the Church. Nobody knows for sure why *sacramentum* was chosen to translate it, but its already established use to express links between different points in time will have been one recommending factor.

In the later patristic period, *sacramentum* was often used of an event in the life of Christ, as of Old Testament events. Had this sense continued in use, we should speak of 'the five glorious sacraments of the Rosary'. Leo the Great frequently uses *sacramentum* for a season of the liturgical year.

Augustine in particular develops the use of *sacramentum* as referring to a rite, the sense with which we are most familiar now. He was also responsible for a simple but important definition of a sacrament as 'a sacred sign',[17] which was adopted by Aquinas.

The Middle Ages and Trent

As the Middle Ages advanced, the practice grew of classifying rites as 'major' and 'minor' sacraments and making lists of them,

---

15. *Adversus Iudaeos* 13.
16. *Adversus Marcionem* 3, 16, 5.
17. *De Civitate Dei* 10, 5.

some as long as twelve. Peter Lombard's list of seven became classic, and was accepted by Aquinas and Trent. Thus the notion that there are seven rites called sacraments gained ground, and *sacrament* became a technical term. However, the word continued to be applied to other referents. Aquinas speaks much of the sacraments of the Old Law, and the Roman liturgy has preserved other senses of the word in its prayers. To give one example, the Prayer over the Gifts for the First Sunday of Lent, found already in the Gregorian Sacramentary (7th century), speaks of 'the beginning of this venerable sacrament',[18] where 'sacrament' means the season of Lent.

Also, the figural sense of *sacramentum* when applied to the seven rites was retained from the patristic period. Aquinas explains that the seven sacraments are signs that signify simultaneously the past passion of Christ, divine grace and virtues in the present life of the Christian, and eternal life in the future.[19] The same theme is taken up in the Catechism of the Council of Trent, and illustrated by the Magnificat Antiphon for Corpus Christi *O sacrum convivium*:

> O sacred banquet in which Christ is received,
> the memory of his passion is recalled,
> and a pledge of future glory is given to us.

However, controversy with Protestants who saw sacraments only as signs led Trent to play down the sign-character of the seven sacraments, and a desire to stress their efficacy led to emphasis on what they contain rather than what they point to or evoke. Thus, Catholic Christianity has in the period between Trent and Vatican II had a narrower concept of sacramentality than previously.

---

18. *ipsius venerabilis sacramenti ... exordium.*
19. ST 3a. 60 a3.

The Sixteenth Century: The Reims New Testament

In English, the word *sacrament* was used before the Reformation in several different senses drawn from the range of meanings of *sacramentum*, but in the sixteenth century it became controversial with the translation of the New Testament made from the Vulgate by Gregory Martin and published at Reims in 1582. Martin tried to keep his English as close to the Latin as possible. *Sacramentum* occurred eight times in the Vulgate, translating *musterion* and, on seven of these, Martin used *sacrament*.

Martin defended his translation in his *Discovery of the manifold corruptions of the holy Scriptures by the Heretikes of our daies, specially the English Sectaries, and of their foule dealing herein, by partiall and false translations to the advantage of their heresies, in their English Bibles used and authorized since the time of Schisme* (Reims, 1582). We might think, he says, that Protestants take a high view of matrimony, since they regard it as equal to virginity, yet the truth is that they flatly deny that it is a sacrament:

> And to this purpose they translate in the Epistle to the Ephesians 5, where the Apostle speaketh of Matrimonie, *this is a great secret*, Whereas the Latine Church and all the Doctours thereof have ever read *this is a great Sacrament*: the greeke Church and all the Fathers thereof. *This is a great Mysterie*, because that which is in Greeke, mysterie: is in Latin, Sacrament…

If the Protestants allow the word *mystery* elsewhere in their writings, but here translate *musterion* as 'secret',

> must we not needs thinke… that they doe it because of their hereticall opinion against the sacrament of Matrimonie, and for their base estimation thereof?

Martin is aware, however, that the mere name *sacrament* does not make marriage a sacrament:

> For… Sacrament is a generall name in Scripture to other things. Neither do we so translate it, as though it were forthwith one of the seven Sacraments, because of the name: but as in other places wheresoever we finde this word in the Latine, we translate it Sacrament… so finding it here, we do here also so translate it. and as for the divers taking of it here, and elsewhere, that we examine otherwise, by circumstance of the text, and by the Churches and Doctors interpretation: and wee finde that here it is taken for a Sacrament in that sense as we say, *seven Sacraments*, not so in the other places.

Baptism is nowhere in the Scriptures called a sacrament, and Martin grants that were it anywhere so called, the Protestants would not claim that that in itself proved Baptism to be a sacrament:

> Yet I trowe they would not avoid to translate it by the word Sacrament, if they found it so called. Even so, we finding Matrimonie so called, doe so translate it, neither concluding thereby that it is one of the Seven, nor yet suppressing the name, which no doubt gave occasion to the Church and the holy Doctors to esteeme it as one of the Seven.

Martin found an able opponent in William Fulke, whose *Defense of the sincere and true translation of the holy scriptures into the English tongue, against the manifold cavils, frivolous quarrels, and impudent slaunders of GREGORIE MARTIN, one of the Readers of Popish divinitie in the traiterous Seminarie of Rhemes*, published in 1583, reprints Martin's Discovery and replies to it paragraph by paragraph:

The English word secret signifieth fully as much as the Greeke word *musterion...* And it is very false that you say that the Latine word *Sacramentum* is equivalent to the Greeke: for both it signifieth an oath which the Greeke word doth not, and also it includeth holinesse, which the Greeke word doth not.

In 1589 Fulke published a complete New Testament, dedicated to Queen Elizabeth, answering Martin's notes with notes of his own. On Ephesians 5:32 he asks:

And what other argument hath Peter Lumbarde, the Maister of your divinitie, to prove that Matrimony is a Sacrament, but onely the name of Sacramentum, used in this place?

Fulke has a good point here: Lombard gives no justification for his enumeration of seven sacraments.

Fulke taunts Martin for failing in one place[20] to translate *sacramentum* as 'sacrament' and says that if he were true to his principles, he would use 'sacrament' in all the eight places where *sacramentum* occurs in the New Testament. This was in fact what was done in the Douai Old Testament.

Revisions of the Reims New Testament

However, the uses of *sacrament* in the Douai Bible were found puzzling by readers. The 1633 edition printed at Antwerp by John Cousturier contains an Appendix entitled *The explication of certaine words in this translation, not familiar to the vulgar Reader, which might not conveniently be uttered otherwise.* 'Sacrament' for 'mysterie' is one of these. In 1718 Dr Cornelius Nary, an Irish priest, published with the encouragement of the Archbishop of Dublin a new translation of the Vulgate New

---

20. Apoc. 17:7: *sacramentum mulieris.*

Testament. In the Preface he gives as one of his motives the defects of the Rhemish Testament,

> the Language whereof is so old, the Words in many places so obsolete, the Orthography so bad, and the Translation so very literal, that in a number of Places it is unintelligible, and all over so grating to the Ears of such as are accustomed to speak, in a manner, another Language, that most People will not be at pains of reading them.

In Nary's version, *sacramentum* is translated 'mystery', except at Ephesians 5:32. There, marriage being under discussion, *sacrament* is retained. The same practice was followed by Challoner when he came to revise the Douai Bible in the middle of the century and, so far as I have been able to ascertain, by all subsequent editions of that version.

Thus, through controversy, the breadth and richness of meaning that *sacramentum* has in Latin was lost from the English language and, as often happens, the vernacular, far from handing on tradition, served to conceal it.

SACRAMENTALITY IN THE MODERN LITURGY

The Wedding Service

I now turn to the liturgy of the Roman Rite as we currently celebrate it in English, to point out how we use and avoid the word *sacrament*. I hope thus to shed some light on the concept of sacramentality that is operative in our liturgy. I shall concentrate initially on the Wedding Service.

The Introduction. I suspect I may not be the only person who has winced at a Catholic wedding on hearing the words:

> He (i.e. Christ) has already consecrated you in baptism

and now he enriches and strengthens you by a special sacrament…[21]

This gives the impression of the sacrament as an injection of power from God delivered during the wedding ceremony. *Sacrament* is used here in its narrow, technical sense, not only in the English but also in the Latin original, which was composed in the 1960s for the liturgical reform. But the English goes further than the Latin. As so often, it is the little words that do most damage, in this case *now* in '*now* he enriches and strengthens' which focusses God's action too narrowly. A more faithful translation would be:

> he enriches and strengthens with a special sacrament those whom he has already consecrated in Baptism.

The Latin speaks of God's action throughout a couple's married life, and on married couples throughout Christian history. The English restricts the reference of the text to this couple and this ceremony: '*now* he enriches and strengthens *you*.'

'The Sacrament of Christ and the Church.' Other texts in the marriage rite contain older senses of *sacramentum*. Two prayers contain the phrase *Christi et Ecclesiae sacramentum*, literally 'the sacrament of Christ and his Church', which is drawn from a Nuptial Blessing in the Gregorian Sacramentary, and ultimately based on Ephesians 5:32. *Sacramentum* here is plainly used of the bond between Christ and the Church, not one of the Seven. I would offer as a faithful if not elegant translation:

> God, who consecrated the union of husband and wife to be so excellent a mystery that you made the marriage-

---

21. In Latin, *eos peculiari ditat et roborat Sacramento, quos ipse sancto iam Baptismate consecravit.*

bond prefigure the sacrament of Christ and the Church...[22]

I do not advocate Gregory Martin's policy of using *sacrament* on every occasion to translate *sacramentum*, but here it might be suitable. We are accustomed to thinking of Christ and the Church as sacraments, so to think of their union as a sacrament is an extension and deepening of those ideas: the patristic expression might well find a new home among us. The ICEL translators backed away from using sacrament here. Instead they say:

> Father, you have made the bond of marriage a holy mystery, a symbol of Christ's love for his Church.

I see several difficulties here. Firstly, the original does not say marriage is a mystery, but that it has been consecrated to be a mystery. That is, marriage, one of the blessings of creation, is transformed in God's plan of redemption: creation is distinguished from consecration, the natural sacrament from the Christian one. Secondly, the original says that marriage is not merely a symbol but a *prefiguration* of the sacrament of Christ and the Church. I think this means both that before Christ marriage was a sign of what was to begin when he came and that now it shows what will happen when he comes again. *Sacramentum* here expresses a figural view of marriage. All this historical richness is lost in the English. Furthermore, whereas the Latin speaks of the sacrament of Christ and the Church, the English says 'Christ's love for his Church', allowing no room for the Church's love of Christ, and turning the model into a male dominated one, implying a disparity of roles between husband and wife, which is exactly what the Council wished to avoid when it decreed that the Prayer over the Bride should be

---

22. *Deus, qui tam excellenti mysterio coniugalem copulam consecrasti,*
    ut Christi et Ecclesiae sacramentum
    praesignares in foedere nuptiarum...

revised![23] This version also implies a view of sacraments as something done by God to passive humans rather than by God and humans together.[24]

Nuptial Blessing II. The second alternative Nuptial Blessing was composed in the 1960s, and contains a bold use of *sacramentum*:

> O God, who to make known the plan of your love
> willed that the covenant you made with your people
> should be foreshadowed in the mutual love of husband
> and wife,
> and the meaning of that sacrament be fully revealed
> when the married life of your faithful people,
> makes known the nuptial mystery of Christ and the
> Church...[25]

Here, *sacramentum* seems to have the meaning 'sacred sign', a sign present in creation whose meaning is fully revealed in the life of the Church. Thus marriage is a 'sacrament in process', whose sacramentality is complete only insofar as its significance is recognised. The liturgical reformers were operating with a renewed and enriched concept of sacramentality which found its way into their texts. Translators are not always so theologically aware. Our version reads:

---

23. *Sacrosanctum Concilium* 78.
24. The Anglican translation from 1549 onwards was 'the spiritual marriage and unity betwixt Christ and his Church'; the Alternative Service Book translates 'the marriage of Christ with his Church'.
25. *Deus, qui ad amoris tui consilium reverandum,*
    in mutua dilectione sponsorum
    foedus illud adumbrari voluisti
    quod ipse cum populo tuo inire dignatus es,
    ut, sacramenti significatione completa,
    in fidelium tuorum coniugali consortio
    Christi et Ecclesiae nuptiale pateret mysterium...

> Father, to reveal the plan of your love,
> you made the union of husband and wife
> an image of the covenant between you and your people...

There is no sense of distance in time between the sign and what it signifies, between creation and covenant. The prayer continues:

> In the fulfillment of this sacrament,
> the marriage of Christian man and woman
> is a sign of the marriage between Christ and the Church.

I am not sure how to take this. 'Sacrament' has been retained as a translation of *sacramentum*, but its coupling with 'this' will, I think, suggest to the majority of worshippers that what is being referred to is Christian marriage, or perhaps the wedding currently being solemnised, rather than the institution of human marriage throughout history, already sacramental before Christ. This shows how we cannot enrich our sacramental theology simply by using the word *sacrament* more frequently. In fact, if we use it frequently but narrowly, we impoverish our understanding of sacramentality.

Marriage Preface I. Nonetheless, our present rites are very fond of the word *sacrament*, often introducing it where *sacramentum* does not occur in the Latin, for instance in the first Preface for Weddings, which comes from the Gelasian sacramentary. The original may be translated:

> you have united men and women in the covenant of marriage,
> an indissoluble bond of peace (cf. Eph 4:3)
> laying upon them your gentle yoke (cf. Matt 11:30)[26]

---

26. *Qui fodera nuptiarum blando concordiae iugo*
    et insolubili pacis vinculo nexuisti...

All this is about marriage as a human institution, part of creation. The Preface goes on to say that God has instituted marriage for the increase both of the human family and of the Church. The Latin does not use *sacramentum*, but our English version reads:

> By this sacrament your grace unites man and woman in an unbreakable bond of love and peace...

losing the echoes of Scripture. Furthermore, most people hearing the words 'this sacrament' will think they refer exclusively to Christian marriage and will consequently lose the figural dimension, the parallel between marriage in Creation and marriage in Redemption.

'This'

In that last example, the word *this* works together with *sacrament* to narrow the focus of the prayer. I said earlier that it is the little words that cause most trouble. Perhaps the most misused word in our English liturgy is *this*. Let me end with some examples of its use which help to give our liturgy its narrow concept of the sacramental. I begin with one from this week's Mass-texts.

Week 22: Prayer Over the Gifts. After the preparation of the Gifts in Week 22 of the Year we pray:

> Lord, may the sacred offering always bring upon us your saving blessing,[27]

but our current version runs:

> Lord, may this holy offering bring us Your blessing.

---

27. *Benedictionem nobis, Domine, conferat salutarem sacra semper oblatio...*

Whereas the original thinks of the effects of the eucharist
throughout our lives, the English narrows the focus of the prayer
to *this* celebration, pointing exclusively to the here and now.

Eucharistic Prayer 2. In the second Eucharistic Prayer we say:

> we offer you, Father. this life-giving bread,
> this saving cup,[28]

where the original could more accurately be translated

> we offer you, Lord, the bread of life
> and the cup of salvation.

The echoes of Scripture here (Jn 6:35, 48 and Ps 116:13) invite
our imaginations beyond the immediate ritual context towards
Christ's discourse after feeding the Five Thousand in John 6 and
his sacrificial death which Christian tradition sees prefigured in
Psalm 116:

> I will lift up the cup of salvation
> and call on the name of the Lord,
> Precious in the sight of the Lord
> is the death of his saints. (Ps 116:13,15)

Eucharistic Prayer 3. In Eucharistic Prayer III we speak of:

> our Lord Jesus Christ
> at whose command we celebrate this eucharist...[29]

---

28. *tibi, Domine, panem vitae
et calicem salutis offerimus...*
29. *Domini nostri Iesu Christi, cuius
mandato haec mysteria celebramus.*

but what the original says is:

at whose command we celebrate these mysteries.

That is, whenever we celebrate the eucharist we do so at Christ's command: the focus is not on 'this Mass', but on the whole eucharistic activity of the whole Church.

'This is the Word of the Lord'. 'This is the Word of the Lord', we say at the end of a reading from Scripture, and some embellish the words by picking up the Lectionary and waving it about. But that is to localise the Word of God excessively. The form proposed for the revised Missal currently in preparation is simply 'The word of the Lord'. ICEL has given as one reason for this change a desire 'to counter the tendency evoked by 'This is...' to make the acclamation the equivalent of a narrow "pointing gesture" rather than a faith acclamation to God who speaks when the Scriptures are read'. In this case, ICEL has seen the pernicious force of the word 'this'.

'This is the Lamb of God'. The words before Communion 'This is the Lamb of God'[30] are taken from John 1:35, where the Baptist points to Jesus from a certain distance and says 'there is the Lamb of God'. This would not be an appropriate translation in the liturgical context, since the priest is actually holding the Host. But his words invite us to do more than look at the Eucharistic Bread and affirm its identity with the Lamb of God. They prepare for the words that follow: 'Blessed are they who are called to the Supper of the Lamb'. Perhaps no moment in the liturgy is more patient of a figural understanding. The words invite us to see at once Jesus beside the Jordan at the beginning of his ministry, the Host in the hands of the priest, and the Lamb to whose wedding-banquet we look forward. The

---

30. NJB and RNEB have 'there is the Lamb...'; NRSV has 'here is...'; New American Bible has 'Behold...'.

traditional translation 'Behold the Lamb of God', adopted for the revision, will allow room for these broader connotations.

CONCLUSION

I have tried to show how theological controversy led to a narrowing of the meaning of two words, *figure* and *sacrament*. As a result, the number of things called 'sacraments' was gradually reduced to seven. Also, understanding of the meaning of these seven was impoverished. They were seen as windows onto the transcendent, channels of grace, but not as events which make powerful for us other events, both past and future. The figural sense of sacramentality was lost.

The twentieth century has seen a recovery of this richer concept, largely under the influence of the Mystery Theology of Odo Casel and his successors. This movement has passed by our vernacular liturgy, the production of which has been one further stage in the impoverishment of sacramental awareness among English speakers. We theologians are, I think, too passive in our acceptance of vernacular liturgical texts. A revision of the Catholic liturgy in English is now in progress. If the Catholic Theological Association of Great Britain does not turn a critical eye on its results, then who will?

CONTRIBUTORS

Michael Barnes SJ teaches Theology and Religious Studies at Heythrop College, University of London.

Sarah Jane Boss is Director of the Marian Study Centre, Ushaw College, Durham.

Gavin D'Costa is Senior Lecturer in Theology and Religious Studies at the University of Bristol.

Eamon Duffy is a Fellow of Magdalene College and Reader of Divinity who lectures in ecclesiastical history at the University of Cambridge.

Bruce Harbert is a former tutor in English at Mansfield College, University of Oxford and is now a parish priest in Sutton Coldfield and Lecturer in Theology at Oscott College.

Nicholas Peter Harvey is a former lecturer in theology at the Queen's College, Birmingham and now a freelance theologian and writer in Birmingham.

Nicholas Lash has been Norris-Hulse Professor of Divinity at the University of Cambridge from 1978 until 1999.

Jack Mahoney SJ is Emeritus Professor of Moral and Social Theology at the University of London.

Herbert McCabe OP lectures in theology at Blackfriars, Oxford.

John McDade SJ has been Head of Systematic Theology and is now Principal of Heythrop College, University of London.

Peter Phillips is a priest of the Shrewsbury diocese who teaches systematic theology at Ushaw College, Durham.

Timothy Radcliffe OP used to teach theology at Blackfriars, Oxford and is now Master General of the Order of Preachers.

Janet Martin Soskice is a Fellow of Jesus College and lecturer in theology at the University of Cambridge.

John Sullivan is Research Fellow at Trinity and All Saints College, University of Leeds.

Geoffrey Turner is Head of Theology at Trinity and All Saints College, University of Leeds.

Edward Yarnold SJ is University Research Lecturer at the University of Oxford.